BLOOD AND BONES

BLOOD AND BONES 2

Copyright © Yang Seok-il 2022
Translation copyright © Adhy Kim 2022

Published in 2022 by Seoul Selection U.S.A., Inc.
4199 Campus Drive, Suite 550, Irvine, CA 92612
Phone: 949-509-6584 / Seoul office: 82-2-734-9567
Fax: 949-509-6599 / Seoul office: 82-2-734-9562
Email: hankinseoul@gmail.com
Website: www.seoulselection.com

ISBN: 978-1-62412-150-0
Printed in the Republic of Korea
The Work is published under the support of Literature Translation
Institute of Korea (LTI Korea).

BLOOD AND BONES

2

Yang Seok-il

Translated by

Adhy Kim

Seoul Selection

Contents

Chapter 14	7
Chapter 15	39
Chapter 16	78
Chapter 17	113
Chapter 18	147
Chapter 19	183
Chapter 20	218
Chapter 21	252
Chapter 22	292
Chapter 23	328
Chapter 24	359
Chapter 25	393
Chapter 26	425

Chapter 14

In September of that year, Lee Young-hee moved from Gojo to Taisei Street in Osaka. She lived in a two-story tenement house on the corner. Other Koreans lived in the tenement houses that ran parallel to hers. The Takamuras across from them were a six-person family crowded into a hut with only a two-*jo* and four-and-a-half-*jo* room. The two houses beside them were empty. Benten Market stood at the end of Taisei Street, next to which the elderly Kangs and their five children lived in another small hut, rearing two pigs on the dirt floor of their two-*jo* room. That meant seven people all slept in a single four-and-a-half-*jo* room.

In comparison, the tenement house where Lee Young-hee lived was more spacious. Mrs. Ishihara lived next door with her four sons and worked as a seamstress.

7

Her husband was a professor at a university in Korea—something Mrs. Ishihara was quite proud of. She had a bright, chatty, eccentric personality. But if anyone were to mention the rumors about how her husband was living with another woman in Seoul, she would get offended and start a big fight.

The Sakamotos lived next to the Ishiharas. They were the only Japanese family living on that block. Their youngest child could be seen playing outside by himself every now and then. Mr. Sakamoto and his second son were furniture workers who came and went at irregular hours. They were an uncommunicative family, perhaps all the more so since they lived in an indecent neighborhood dominated by Koreans. The Takadas and Kunimotos lived next to them. The Kunimotos kept a cast-metal workshop on their first floor. Behind them, the Yanagimotos, Kinkais, Kuremotos, Kanemuras, and Tomimuras all ran iron foundries next to each other. The pumps for the pit latrines stood in a row in the back alleyway, and the stench of urine and shit filled the air at all hours. Almost everyone had Japanese names, but these were simply the names they'd kept after the 1939 name-change policy.

Harumi and Han Masahito lived in a single-story

tenement house two hundred meters away from Lee Young-hee, nestled within a complicated web of alleyways. It was hard to find them on a map.

During the air raids, Morimachi, Nakamichi, Tsuruhashi, and Fuse had turned into fields of fire, but this area was somehow spared. Nakamichi Citizen's School also remained standing: it was an impressive three-story building with iron reinforcements, and the schoolyard was furnished with a gym and pool. At that time, schools with pools were rare.

The other children in the neighborhood attended Taisei Citizen's School, but Hanako and Sung-han went back to Nakamichi Citizen's School. Hanako was of age to begin secondary school courses, and Sung-han his fourth year of primary school, but they were both held back a year due to the evacuations.

After they came home from school, Hanako cooked, cleaned, and did laundry, while Sung-han rode his bike to the black market in Tsuruhashi. The black market started at the Tsuruhashi area of the government loop line and extended along the former evacuation route, crammed with stalls and clamoring with all manner of returning soldiers, vagrants, prostitutes, gang members, mothers, and children. This black market was mostly occupied by Koreans, and the recently defeated Japanese were in no position to shut it down. Lee Young-hee sold *sake* and pork in a corner of the crowded market. The tariffs were still in effect, and *sake* and pork were forbidden. After leaving his bike with his mother, Sung-han went around hawking Lucky Strikes and Camel cigarettes, keeping his eyes peeled for the police. The never-ending stream of people resembled a deluge of muddy rainwater. Sung-han pulled on the sleeves of potential customers and showed them the cigarettes. Smokers coveted the brightly colored, cellophane-wrapped cigarette packs, which were American-made. At first Sung-han hawked his items indiscriminately, but he soon got a handle of his target customers and managed to sell thirty packs a day.

Sung-han's cigarette supplier worked with about seven other kids and ten women, and the turf wars between them never ended. A single step into someone else's territory sparked a fight. Sometimes alliances formed, realigning the boundaries between territories. One couldn't afford to be inattentive. A Korean smuggler habitually came up to Sung-han with four children and a teenage prostitute in tow. One of his arms was wrapped in a bandage, where he hid a razor blade. His eyes looked like inverted triangles as they glared down at Sung-han, who always resolutely refused to join the man's ring.

"You think you can defend your territory by yourself, motherfucker?" said one of the boys, who looked only about nine or ten years old but spoke like a full-fledged punk.

"Hey, kid, you know what a pussy feels like? You don't, huh. Come with me and you'll find out. We're friends here." The smuggler rolled up the girl's skirt and showed her thigh. The girl smirked strangely and bent down to bring her chest closer to Sung-han's face. Sung-han inhaled the scent of her breasts and felt like he couldn't breathe. Feeling humiliated and frustrated, he resolved to someday parade a lover of his own around.

The police raids came with and without warning. Lee Young-hee was prepared at all times to stash her goods at a nearby store owned by an acquaintance of hers. Some kind of disturbance arose in the black market every day. It was common to see men with bloodshot eyes walking around with clubs, bats, and knives. New gangs formed and drew territorial boundaries, and the fights between them never seemed to end.

One day a seller of dried fruits named Oh Dae-sik got into a heated argument with a new gang that demanded payment for letting him keep his stall on their turf. Oh Dae-sik was sick and tired of these gangs, and he lashed out at them:

"You think you're gonna fleece your fellow Koreans like this? You're gonna squeeze your fellow Koreans of the money we made with our own blood and sweat? You're the same as those Japanese imperialists. Korea is independent now. We should take Koreans like you to the people's court for being traitors to your country. The Japanese war criminals are facing trial right now, you know. You're the same as them. Beware!"

In response, a young gang member drew out a knife and stabbed Oh Dae-sik in the stomach. Oh Dae-sik luckily survived, but the incident sparked collective anger among the Zainichi Koreans in Osaka. An informal organization for Zainichi Korean interests, formed through the work of the popular front and the labor unions, rallied behind Oh Dae-sik. Hundreds of Koreans surrounded the gang's headquarters, trapping the twenty or so members inside. Brandishing clubs, the throng of Koreans shouted "Traitors! Sellouts! Murderers!" and threw rocks and burning wood at the building. As the gang members tried to escape, the crowd piled on them and beat them up. Their rage didn't stop there. They ran amok at the black market, going around attacking various gang hideouts. The Japanese police didn't intervene. Instead, they chose to stand by and watch.

The chaos and confusion after the war continued. Japanese soldiers and civilians returned en masse from the former colonies, while Zainichi Koreans left Japan for Korea. Lee Young-hee wondered if she should go back to the motherland as so many of the others were. But ever since she'd absconded from her village in disgrace, Lee Young-hee had no "home" to go back to. And it wasn't like her husband Kim Shunpei would go with her.

Han Masahito was depressed about Japan's loss in the war, but he later joined a Korean organization and, thanks to his eloquence and adaptable disposition, soon became part of its leadership. He was one of the people who instigated the actions against the new gangs. Meanwhile, he threw himself into commerce. He lacked capital, though, and a group of brokers pulled him into a string of get-rich-quick schemes, all of which failed. Cho Myung-jin converted the first floor of his house into an office space, where Han Masahito and other men strategized all day and indulged in pipe dreams. They were a bunch of useless men megalomaniacal enough to think they would be rolling in money the next day. They opened one bank account after another under false names and issued promissory notes willy-nilly. And they drank themselves to oblivion at the bar run by Cho Myung-jin's Japanese wife.

Lee Young-hee supported the struggling Han Masahito and Harumi, who had given birth to a third child and was busy with her children. The scraps of money she made from her sewing went to buying powdered milk. Every three days, Lee Young-hee sent Sung-han to Harumi's house with rice, vegetables, and various leftovers. Han Masahito came by to pester Lee Young-hee for money in his own way, and sometimes he brought his friends with him to take advantage of Lee Young-hee's *sake*. Their conversations were a jumbled mess regarding Korea's liberation and new opportunities for making profits. Of course, shortly after liberation the Korean Peninsula was divided along the thirty-eighth parallel, but not many knew how that had come about. Regardless, everyone agreed to support the anti-imperialist Kim Il-sung.

One day in December, Sung-han returned home from the black market to see Hanako waiting for him by the front door. As soon as she saw him approaching on his bike, she waved him to the side of the house. She looked nervous.

"What's wrong?" asked Sung-han suspiciously.

"Dad came back," said Hanako in a low voice.

"What . . ." Sung-han stiffened.

After their house in Nakamichi burnt down nine months ago, Kim Shunpei had disappeared. This wasn't the first time he'd gone off somewhere for months at a time, but it was true that he made an appearance whenever December came around.

"He's sleeping in the inner room," said Hanako.

Sung-han tiptoed into the house. The four-*jo genkan* led straight into a two-*jo* living room and then a four-and-a-half-*jo* room. Further in was the bathroom, which could also be accessed through the long kitchen.

The glass-paned door to the four-and-a-half-*jo* room was closed, and Sung-han couldn't see if Kim Shunpei was inside. But an oppressive feeling rippled through his whole body like an electrical current. He went back outside and saw Mrs. Takamura looking at him from across the street as she cleaned mud from the ditch.

"Go tell Mom," said Hanako.

Sung-han nodded and got back on his bicycle glumly. It was hard to pedal with the wind blowing against him. He threaded his way through the crowds of people to get to his mother's stall. Two men were standing and drinking *sake.*

"What's the matter?" said Lee Young-hee.

"Dad's back," Sung-han told her in a low voice.

Lee Young-hee's face clouded over.

"Gimme a refill," said one of the men, thrusting out his cup. Lee Young-hee smiled courteously and filled his cup to the brim with *shochu.* The war veteran said with his mouth full, "Never eaten pig organs before, but damn, they're good." Organ meat was full of nutrients these men had lacked when they were soldiers in the war.

Lee Young-hee knew Kim Shunpei would show up at her doorstep eventually, but she was shocked when it actually happened. She didn't want to sleep with him. Having lost three of her children, she didn't want to bring any more children into the world. She was too old in any case. But she didn't have the power to refuse Kim Shunpei's advances.

She closed shop when the two men left. She put the *sake* in a crate and entrusted it to her acquaintance. She brought the meat with her so that it wouldn't spoil. On the way back, she asked, "What's *abeoji* doing?"

"He's sleeping."

"In the inner room?"

"Yeah, on the futon."

Kim Shunpei had probably run out of money and had nowhere else to go. She was terrified at the thought that he would harangue her for losing her latest child. He would use that as an excuse to press his unreasonable demands on her, and he would ravage the house. When he'd hounded her for money at the Osaka Detention Center, she told him about the two hundred yen behind the picture frame, but she didn't tell him about the four hundred yen hidden elsewhere. Those four hundred yen had gotten her family through the evacuation. He surely held a grudge against her for that as well.

Hanako was in the kitchen cooking rice in the dark. When Lee Young-hee and Sung-han came home, she turned on the fluorescent light bulbs in relief. Lee Young-hee got out the pork chilling in the refrigerator and began preparing dinner without any delay. She set pork, fresh vegetables, boiled vegetables with kimchi, peppers, and miso soup on the low table. Hanako brought the table to the inner room where Kim Shunpei was sleeping.

"*Abeoji,* dinner's ready."

Kim Shunpei opened his eyes and looked at Hanako, who timidly set the table down in front of him and withdrew. Kim Shunpei ate his dinner on the futon with his legs crossed and then lay back down. Hanako took the table back to the kitchen. Then the three of them ate dinner in the two-*jo* room with the wooden floor. They chewed their food in silence, cleaned up quickly, and snuck up to the second floor. From then on, Kim Shunpei lived on the first floor, while Lee Young-hee, Hanako, and Sung-han lived on the second.

Kim Shunpei and Lee Young-hee barely spoke. She avoided him when she could, while he sent her hateful glares. He told Hanako to tell Lee Young-hee that he wanted to speak with her. Hanako became the messenger for her two parents and managed the affairs of the house that way. It was a burdensome responsibility for the twelve-year-old girl. She had a nervous, reserved personality and had to constantly monitor her parents' emotional states.

For a little while, they all managed to get by without anything bad happening. But one night, a drunk Kim Shunpei kicked down the door of the house and charged up to the second floor. When he opened the door to the inner room, he found it deserted. Lee Young-hee and the children, having accumulated years of experience with Kim Shunpei, had escaped through the back balcony and roof and were hiding at the neighbor's. Furious, Kim Shunpei went through the house screaming and breaking the furniture, kitchenware, and house fixtures. The neighbors were shocked. To see a man they hadn't been properly introduced to in such a frothing rage, they figured something serious must have happened, and the women on the block tried calming him down. But Kim Shunpei wasn't one to be pacified so easily. Ignoring the women's pleas, he broke into the Kanemura family's house. Forty-year-old Kanemura confronted him, puffing his chest out confidently.

"What time do you think it is? Behave yourself!" he scolded.

"What did you say, motherfucker?" Kim Shunpei grabbed Kanemura's collar, enraged at being addressed like that by a younger man.

Kanemura was dragged forward like a magnet, and Kim Shunpei rammed his head against his face. Kanemura collapsed, his head bleeding profusely. There was no way to oppose Kim Shunpei. The neighbors shrank back from his brutality.

"Come forward if you have a problem with me!" He seemed to bare tiger fangs, and a nauseating miasma emanated from his fearsome body.

The day after Japan surrendered, Kim Shunpei went by himself to Korea and traveled through Busan, Jeju Island, Daegu, and Seoul, observing what was happening there. He wanted to live in Korea, whether because it was his long-standing wish or because a lot of Zainichi Koreans were repatriating after liberation. From what he observed, it didn't seem like a good idea to live in this unstable country. Back in his home village on Jeju Island, he found that his mother had died long ago, and all the land in the village was already sold off. His relatives had scattered, and the village was in ruins. If Korea weren't reduced to such a state, Kim Shunpei probably would have started a new life there. It wasn't uncommon for Korean men to leave their families behind in Japan and live with another woman in Korea.

Giving up on the prospect of living in Korea, Kim Shunpei returned to Japan and visited Gojo for the first time. But his family was gone. He thought Lee Young-hee had disrespected him by not waiting for him to come back. For this, he nursed an unrelenting grudge against her.

It was easy to find out where Lee Young-hee was. There was no way she would leave Osaka to start anew somewhere else. When he arrived at the burnt ruins of Nakamichi, a Korean acquaintance living in a makeshift hovel told him where she'd gone.

When he reached Taisei Street, his eyes landed on a nameplate with "Kim Shunpei" written on it. He knew at least how to read his own name, and he entered the house. Hanako was in the kitchen and stared at Kim Shunpei as if she'd never seen him before. Then she directed him to the inner room in a flurry. She'd grown considerably since he last saw her.

Kim Shunpei ordered Hanako to lay out the futon for him. Hanako did as she was told, and Kim Shunpei set down his leather satchel and took a nap.

He was still lying down when Lee Young-hee and Sung-han came home, but he couldn't stomach the fact that Lee Young-hee dared to go to bed on the second floor, without him. It was the wife's duty to share her husband's bed on the night of his return. But she had rejected him. After waiting five nights for her to come to bed with him, he went to the Tobita red-light district to vent his sexual frustration, and he came back home drunk. He felt like Lee Young-hee had turned his own children against him. He could see hostility in Sung-han's eyes.

Kim Shunpei's violence got worse day by day. After three or four nights of escalating violence, he spared everyone his rampages for one night, and then the cycle started again. No one could stop him. The house was battered and could no longer undergo repairs. The broken front door dangled open on its hinges all day and night. Of course, no thief would want to sneak into this house and incur the wrath of Kim Shunpei.

"*Aigo, aigo,* every night he comes and wrecks the place up!" the neighborhood women whispered to each other in shock.

Lee Young-hee and her two children returned to the house every day at noon. While Kim Shunpei slept, they cleaned up the mess and set his dinner on a tray. Then

Lee Young-hee and Sung-han left for the black market. Regardless of the circumstances, they had to earn money.

Kim Shunpei went out at night. As he got more and more drunk, the same thoughts whirled in his head. His hatred of Lee Young-hee filled his blood and coursed savagely through his body. "That bitch!"

It wasn't just Lee Young-hee who rejected and defied him. His children, the neighbors, the whole world was hateful to him. His hatred burned in the crevices of his body like hellfire. He wanted those dark flames to scorch the whole world.

Kim Shunpei always returned home drunk. Lee Young-hee and the children waited on the second floor in the dark, wearing their air-raid hoods and not sleeping a wink. They used to do something similar during the war to prepare for enemy attacks, but Kim Shunpei prolonged the conditions of wartime. They sat stiffly and strained their ears for any sound. The children didn't understand why this was their fate to bear. They weren't the only ones. Even Kim Shunpei didn't understand the dark flames of hatred that burned in his core. That hatred was sprouting up in his children in a different form.

After midnight, the children fell asleep against Lee

Young-hee. Whenever Lee Young-hee closed her eyes, the memories came flooding back of when she and Harumi had moved from place to place, begging for pennies to escape from Kim Shunpei. *Should I run away again? Where could I go . . . ?* The answer was always the same: nowhere. And her children couldn't be homeless while they were still growing up.

Deep into the night, heavy footsteps were heard entering the house. It was Kim Shunpei. He walked without a sense of equilibrium. The sound of his footsteps was unmistakable. It sounded as though he were trudging through a swamp, dragging along something heavy— perhaps a dead body.

Lee Young-hee felt like her heart would jump out of her chest. She shook her children awake and said, "*Abeoji*'s here." The three of them snuck out through the back.

Kim Shunpei's violence settled down shortly before New Year's. During this period of deprivation, the neighbors kept up the tradition of making mochi on New Year's to sweep away the pessimism of the previous year, and Kim Shunpei may have been influenced by these celebrations. Then someone unexpected showed up: Ko Nobuyoshi. After getting evicted from the house in Nakamichi, he and his family had stayed with an acquaintance, and no word was heard from them after the air raids. It was unclear if they had lived or died. Lee Young-hee was concerned about them, but she was too busy to pursue the matter further. Ko Nobuyoshi looked skinnier and tanner, but still healthy. His visit also brightened Kim Shunpei's mood.

"Long time no see. I was worried," said Kim Shunpei, welcoming Ko Nobuyoshi in. The house was so devastated that there was nowhere to sit. Kim Shunpei, looking a little apologetic, cleared some space in the inner room for Ko Nobuyoshi.

The happiest one to see Ko Nobuyoshi was Lee Young-hee. She felt comforted by his warmth and sincerity. "It's been too long," she told him, serving him *sake* and appetizers.

"It really has. I've also been worried. But I'm glad everyone is well." Ko Nobuyoshi looked around the room and saw the aftereffects of Kim Shunpei's violence. He considered giving Kim Shunpei a piece of his mind, but as usual, he let him off the hook. Saying something would have just pissed Kim Shunpei off.

"The place we went to after the evacuation burnt up too. We were in Tokyo when the war ended, and we came straight back to Osaka. Right now we live in Miyukimori in Ikuno. My wife's renting a little barrack next to Miyukimori Shrine and selling dried goods there. I don't have a job right now, and we're just scraping by. The powers that be are still very controlling, and it's hard to buy what we need." Ko Nobuyoshi took a large sip of *shochu* and stuffed his mouth with pork. "Come over to our place sometime. You too, *ajumeoni*. The wife will be happy to see you."

The mood in the room felt a bit strange when both Kim Shunpei and Lee Young-hee were there. After Ko Nobuyoshi left, the thick walls were re-erected between them. The endless fighting, the brief moments of respite, the revolting violence—the war may have ended on the battlefields, but it never ended in people's hearts.

Several folks came over for New Year's, including the family's old neighbors from Nakamichi, Yoshie and Soon-myung. Ko Nobuyoshi, Akemi, Kim Shunpei's two nephews, and even Park Hyun-nam came. And of course, so did Harumi and Han Masahito. Everyone brought their children. The women wore *chima jeogori,* and the men wore suits. Lee Young-hee scrounged up what little money she had to host everyone and give the children cash for New Year's. Hanako and Sung-han received cash gifts from the friends and neighbors. Lee Young-hee wondered how many years it had been since such a lively celebration.

The men drank in a circle in the inner room. Kim Shunpei was generous and easygoing. The women were in the small two-*jo* room and in the kitchen and hallway, immersed in conversations long overdue. The children played outside. Only Hanako stayed inside, trying hard to be helpful as her mother chatted with her friends. The Jeju dialect filled the rooms.

Park Hyun-nam spoke, his forehead glistening with sweat. "A month ago I returned to Japan by the skin of my teeth. I thought I'd go back to my hometown in Korea and check things out there. If it looked like a livable situation, I'd call my family over. But not three hours after we left Osaka Harbor, the boat started sinking. Wasn't a storm, so we're not sure why we sank. What I think, though, is that they stuffed too many people on board, and it started tilting because of the waves. The boat must have capsized 'cause all of us, luggage included, were stuck on the tiltin' end. It was awful. I think most of the women and children and old people died. Me and two others held onto a big plank for dear life, and through some miracle, a fishing boat came and rescued us. But I dunno how many people died. It's a lucky thing I didn't bring my family with me, 'cause if I did, they would've drowned for sure. It gives me the creeps thinking about it. I couldn't save any of the women or children."

Park Hyun-nam's boat wasn't the only one that got shipwrecked on the way to Korea over the past several months. Japan had lost a bunch of ships in the war, and the ones that remained were in shoddy condition. So people borrowed fifty-ton fishing boats and loaded them over capacity with passengers and luggage, leading to various disasters.

"Now's not the time to go back. Right after the war I scoped out Seoul, Busan, Daegu, and Jeju, but there was nothin' to eat, let alone a place to live. Japan is a flaming shithole right now, but it's better than Korea." It was the first time Kim Shunpei told anyone his observations about Korea.

"I didn't know you went to Korea," said Ko Nobuyoshi,

impressed by Kim Shunpei's swift initiative.

"When did you go? What was the village like?" asked his nephew Kim Tae-su.

"Our relatives are all gone. And there's no land," said Kim Shunpei glumly.

The two nephews looked crestfallen and slumped their shoulders. What would they do if they had nowhere to return to? Jeju Islanders saw Jeju as their homeland, not Korea. It was hard to call Korea their homeland after years of discrimination and subhuman treatment by the mainlanders.

"Shunpei's right. We should wait and see. It won't be too late to go back after things calm down a bit. Korea and Japan are a mess right now, and none of us know what's up ahead."

Everyone wanted to return home. But there were a number of factors that prevented them from doing so. For one, quite a few Koreans had married into Japanese families. And people like Park Hyun-nam who miraculously survived a shipwreck were reluctant to risk their luck again. Was it worth courageously venturing home, only to be sacrificed to the waves? And after experiencing such hardships in Japan?

"Shunpei, whaddya think of running a *kamaboko* factory?" The depressed Park Hyun-nam wanted to change the topic.

"A *kamaboko* factory . . . ? How?" Kim Shunpei had never considered owning his own business, occupied as he was with boozing, womanizing, and fighting.

"I heard about it from one of the fishermen who rescued me. You know how *kamaboko* has been restricted. The Japanese government has a tight leash on commodities. But apparently, people are makin' *kamaboko* on the sly, and it's sellin' like hotcakes on the black market. You buy the fish straight from the fishermen. Even with the tariffs, if you get a license from the local office, you could make serious bank. Listen, the only *kamaboko* factories in Osaka right now are Taihei Industries and Kanetetsu. I looked it up. Only two places in all of Osaka. Worth a shot, eh? I'm a *kamaboko* worker. That's what I know."

Kim Shunpei and Ko Nobuyoshi were also skilled *kamaboko* workers. As far as the three of them were concerned, Park Hyun-nam's proposal didn't sound totally ludicrous. But they had no capital. And how would they get a license? Could Koreans even get licenses? All sorts of problems and doubts came up if one thought about it.

Ko Nobuyoshi wasn't excited about Park Hyun-nam's abrupt proposal. Besides, he couldn't imagine the drunkard Kim Shunpei managing other people. Essentially, the three of them would have to raise some money and make *kamaboko* that they could sell on the black market.

"We'd get arrested," argued Ko Nobuyoshi.

"That's why we give special favors to the cops so they'll turn a blind eye to us. Everyone is affected by the goods shortage, and all the Japanese are using the black market since they lost the war. Even the cops are buyin' black-market rice! You think we can live on our rations alone? What about y'all? You're eatin' *ajumeoni*'s forbidden pork and drinkin' forbidden *shochu*. I'm not sayin' we should steal anything."

Park Hyun-nam's assertions were indeed confirmed by reality. It was obvious that everyone was buying and selling on the black market, and various groups made underhanded agreements with the police. Ko Nobuyoshi couldn't refute Park Hyun-nam's logic based on these facts, but he suspected that buying and selling were different from manufacturing. Going mainstream on the black market meant circulating goods from point A to point B, and most of those goods—farmers' produce among them—weren't under a manufacturing ban. But a special license was needed to manufacture luxury items like *kamaboko*.

"Making *kamaboko* without a license sounds different from normal black-market stuff," said Ko Nobuyoshi, folding his arms and cocking his head to the side.

"Why are you always so uptight about things? Right now everything is just for show. The corrupt bureaucrats are lining their pockets like crazy. We just want a tiny piece of the pie."

Buying and selling on the black market was one thing, but Ko Nobuyoshi couldn't accept Park Hyun-nam's single-minded proposal.

"Shunpei, whaddya think?" asked Park Hyun-nam.

"Well, I see too many problems with it. It'd be best to get a license first."

Park Hyun-nam clicked his tongue at Kim Shunpei's unexpectedly tepid response, and he stopped pursuing the subject.

It was the first New Year's since the end of the war.

Much to Lee Young-hee's relief, friends and acquaintances showed up at her house for the first time since the war had scattered them in all directions. It was a busy five days, full of good cheer with friends, and Kim Shunpei refrained from violence even when he got drunk.

On the sixth day, Lee Young-hee and Sung-han went back to work at the Tsuruhashi black market. The udon, porridge, steamed bread, and sweet potato stalls thronged with people. Old women stood all day in shabby kimonos. The brown sweaters worn by American soldiers sold for high prices. Sometimes Lee Young-hee sold these sweaters. The demand for her items was high. She even thought about setting up her own store in Tsuruhashi as she continued to provide steady supplies of alcohol, meat, and tobacco to influential men. On the tenth day, though, the police conducted a massive raid without any warning. Sung-han saw the helmeted policemen approaching and swinging their batons, and he ran through the streets to warn his mother, but Lee Young-hee was already arrested, and her crate of goods was confiscated. Men dove under the stalls like dogs or cats, and the police kicked at their protruding butts. It was chaos. Opportunistic onlookers looted the stalls for goods left behind.

"I did nothing wrong! I did nothing wrong!" screamed a Korean woman in a *jeogori*, hugging the post of a food stand as a policeman tried to drag her with him. The post collapsed, bringing the stand down with it. The police were blowing their whistles and shouting furiously. One of them was yelling into a megaphone and trying to move everyone out, but the crowd kept swelling.

Sung-han made his way through the mass of bodies. He slipped through a tangle of legs until he reached the streetcar tracks, where the police had set up trucks and were corralling arrested people inside them. His mother was among them.

"Mom!" Sung-han shouted with all his might.

Lee Young-hee turned back. As soon as she did, she was pushed inside a truck. Sung-han was overwhelmed with grief, and his eyes filled with tears. He had to tell his sister. But when he went to get his bike, he saw that it had been stolen. Fuming with anger, Sung-han ran home.

Hanako was preparing dinner in the kitchen, and Kim Shunpei wasn't there. Sung-han panted for breath, his face ashen. "Mom was arrested by the police," he said.

"Are you serious?"

Hanako suspected that something like this would

happen. Removing her apron, she rushed to her brother-in-law Han Masahito's house, Sung-han following behind. They encountered Han Masahito in the *genkan*, right when he was about to leave.

"*Nii-chan*, Mom's been arrested," said Hanako calmly.

Han Masahito deliberated for a bit and then returned to the room. "Take out my suit," he told Harumi. As he changed into the suit, he asked Hanako, "Which police precinct?"

Neither Hanako nor Sung-han knew.

"Tsuruhashi is in Ikuno Precinct. Or maybe it's in Higashinari." It was hard to tell which ward the Tsuruhashi black market was in. "Probably Ikuno," he concluded as he put on a coat over his suit.

When Hanako and Sung-han went back to their house, they saw that Kim Shunpei had returned as well, earlier than expected. Hanako quickly started preparing dinner. She hesitated to tell her father about her mother's arrest. She knew she had to let him know eventually, but she feared what he would do in response.

She carried Kim Shunpei's special table into the room with rice and side dishes and timidly told him about the arrest.

"Tch! She got arrested 'cause she won't stop selling *sake*." Kim Shunpei opened his mouth as wide as a python and stuffed his face with rice. He then got up and went to the closet, from which he took out an earthenware pot of unrefined rice wine and emptied it outside. The smell of yeast permeated through the area.

"What are you doing?" Across the street, Mrs. Takamura was amazed at his indiscretion. Hanako held back her tears, regretting that she'd told her father anything.

"My wife Lee Young-hee's gettin' me wrapped up in whatever she's up to. No use going on like this." As if irritated by Mrs. Takamura's scruples, Kim Shunpei lifted the earthenware pot up and smashed it against the ground. He broke up the big pot into tiny little pieces.

Mrs. Takamura heaved a sigh and went inside. Hanako and Sung-han stood there and watched Kim Shunpei carry on with his ridiculous behavior. Afterward, he put on his jacket and went out. Hanako and Sung-han hurriedly picked up the shards of the pot and poured water over the ground to cover up the smell. Certain that their father would come back that night drunk and ready to attack, they gulped down rice balls and kept watch for their mother's return.

Around nine that night, Lee Young-hee returned with Han Masahito. The two children clung to her, relieved she hadn't been sent to prison. They looked up admiringly at Han Masahito for bringing their mother back. He was feeling pretty good himself. It wasn't terribly difficult to get the police to release Lee Young-hee. He had brandished his credentials as a leader of a Korean youth organization and was able to look the Japanese in the eye, assured that Korea was now liberated from thirty-six years of Japanese colonial rule. He made sure to let the Japanese know that they were on equal footing.

"They're in no position to complain if we Koreans got back at them for what they did. They know we wouldn't let it slide if they didn't acquit her."

Han Masahito's words were mostly bravado. He knew that just a year ago he'd put all his faith in Japan and the emperor. He realized now that they'd all been deceived. He was full of resentment. So many young Koreans had believed in the emperor. Some of his friends had even applied to be sent to battle. Now, Han Masahito was quite aggressive toward the police. He overlooked the fact, though, that the police saw no reason to make things more complicated for themselves over a single Korean woman.

Though Lee Young-hee may have been acquitted, Kim Shunpei's violence seemed inevitable. She felt nothing when her children anxiously told her about how he'd thrown out the rice wine in the closet and smashed the earthenware pot to pieces. Han Masahito didn't want to get involved in Lee Young-hee's marital troubles. He thought a married couple's problems were their own and that a third party shouldn't butt in. Kim Shunpei was family in any case, and Han Masahito didn't want discord between them.

Kim Shunpei would use this incident as an excuse to throw another fit. Lee Young-hee steeled herself for what was to come and ate one of Hanako's rice balls. At midnight, Kim Shunpei's drunken roar resounded through the house. On cue, Lee Young-hee and the children slipped out through the back balcony and went along the roof to the neighbor's house. The air was bracingly cold, and Lee Young-hee looked up at the sky. The beautiful night sky sparkled with stars.

Chapter 15

Spring seemed to rustle the world into action. The weak sunlight of winter became warmer and brighter and reached into the most shadowy parts of the Korean neighborhood. More and more children played in the empty lots beside the rowhouses. The children weren't ones to stay cooped up in their homes during the winter either; they devised creative games to play in the rain and snow. Everything could be turned into a game. Sung-han got everyone obsessed with a game of spinning tops. After laying a rush mat over a trash can and indenting it into a bowl shape, two players would swing their spinning tops down with kite strings. As the two tops approached the center of the bowl and violently collided, the one that got thrown out of the bowl was the loser. If both tops were thrown out of the bowl at the same time, the player who caught his top first was the winner.

The spinning tops came in various shapes and sizes. There were heavy ones, light ones, short ones, and tall ones, but the best kind was the six-pointed one. That kind came in different varieties, too, but it was superbly balanced in every way and far exceeded the other tops in both offensive and defensive power. The children bought basic models from the nearby candy shop and whittled them into the six-pointed tops they wanted.

Sung-han took his tops to the neighbor's foundry and whittled them with a grinding machine. It was difficult and dangerous to work on such a small object with the quickly revolving wheel. He had to keep a firm hold on the top and make sure his hand didn't slip; otherwise, his index or middle finger could meet the abrasive wheel, turn white in a moment, and then gush blood. The pain when that happened pierced through his whole body. But it was a challenge all the children were willing to accept to make their beloved spinning tops. They gave their tops names like "Red Dragon," "Blue Dragon," or "Giant," and losing a top to an opponent was devastating. They went to great lengths to win their tops back.

The tops changed hands constantly, but if children

from another neighborhood won, the loss couldn't be recouped so easily. So the children formed packs amongst themselves and went on grand expeditions to wage matches and re-matches. Sometimes money was involved, and many children were willing to part with a hefty sum (by their standards) for a special top. The whole area was rife with battles and ugly fights between packs. It wasn't uncommon during expeditions for boys to hide ball bearings and bicycle chains in their pockets.

Sung-han was the leader of his pack. Since he'd been held back a year, he was a year older than the others. For children, that made a big difference. As leader, he was expected to stand at the head of the pack and fight without flinching. If he lost a fight—or worse, ran away— he would be a laughingstock even among the girls. Their expeditions became turf wars, which hardly distinguished them from the adults.

The spinning tops game was the most militant, but other games with Japanese cards, marbles, and Western cards involved gambling of some sort. The *menko* cards in Tokyo were circular, but in Osaka they were rectangular. These cards were quite sturdy, and they came in bound stacks of three or four. When they got worn down, their

sentimental value increased, like old furniture. The
children also liked to catch dragonflies and play cops and
robbers. They gathered in the ruins of fire-devastated
areas between Taisei Street and Nakamichi Citizen's
School, capturing dragonflies under the reddening
sky. They tied small pebbles or screws with strings and
wrapped the objects in colored cellophane, which the
dragonflies took for food and flew toward. When the
dragonflies got tangled up in the string, it reminded
the children of fighter jets being shot down. When the
captured dragonfly was female, the children held it up
for the male dragonflies to swarm around so they could
capture the whole lot.

The games escalated in intensity. The cops-and-
robbers game was played at night. The children gathered
in an empty lot after dinner and divided themselves into
fugitives and pursuers. Naturally, money was at stake.
They bet on how many "robbers" would be captured
within a certain time frame. The game often turned into
an intense back-and-forth between the two teams. They
ran from alley to alley, and if a "robber" reached a dead
end, he or she clambered up a roof without any hesitation,
like little mice. The "cops" didn't hesitate to climb up after

them. Adults rushed outside when they heard their roof tiles cracking and yelled angrily, "Hey, you brats! What are you doing?" At that, the children disappeared into the darkness like the wind. They would hesitate if they could see the height they were jumping from, but in the dark they were bold. That kind of boldness was difficult to describe—perhaps it was human instinct. Naturally, uneven power relationships formed among these children as they chased and captured each other.

Sometimes the games took a brutal turn when the children faced off in abandoned lots with stones in their hands. They would use garbage can lids as shields and throw stones at each other across a set distance. One time, Sung-han hit eight-year-old Kunimoto Akio right on the forehead, but Akio got right back up with blood trickling down his face. While other children would have cried, Akio fiercely regained his fighting stance. Because of that, he was considered the leader of his pack.

The weak boys had to pay the strong boys tribute. Nine-year-old Takada Shuji was tall and looked strong, but he had a habit of losing his nerve at critical moments. One day he offered three pencils to Sung-han.

"What's this about?" barked Sung-han, knowing that

Shuji didn't have the money to buy these pencils.

"I filched 'em from the stationery shop in front of the school," replied Shuji proudly. From then on, shoplifting became a fad among the children. They often got into gangs of six or seven and kept an eye on the stationery shop. Women or elderly attendants were preferable to deal with. The children would enter the shop and pester the attendant with "How much is this?" or "How much is that?" while the others went around filling their pockets. Or they would ask for ten yen's worth of pulp paper and then steal items while the attendant was counting the sheets. They were clever in their tactics. But once they got a taste for petty thievery, they went around pilfering from toy shops, sports stores, and even the hundred-yen shop in Shinsaibashi. The children were nimble from their nights playing cops and robbers and could easily escape the shopkeepers who chased after them. The shopkeepers had no hope of pursuing the children who disappeared in all directions. Soon enough, the boundary between play and delinquency disappeared. Boys swaggered through the black market carrying weapons. They stole, blackmailed, and fought for the sake of their own egos and solved problems with violence. They knew violence would force the other person to submit to them. Such egotistical pleasures were leading them straight toward lives of debauchery and immorality. In a few years, a number of those boys would end up in gangs.

But in an unexpected turn of events, some of the boys' interests turned from thievery and fighting to more intellectual diversions.

One summer afternoon the middle-aged Kanemura (Mr. Kim), who lived in one of the back tenement houses, was idly sitting on a bench in the shade. It wasn't unusual to see Mr. Kim killing time there, abandoned by his wife and three children and binge-drinking for want of anything better to do. That day, too, he was hungover and staring drowsily at the neighborhood housewives chatting by the water pump. Just then, Sung-han was coming through the back alley with a group of boys. Whenever they were up to something, they used the back alleys instead of the front street.

The boys were caked in dirt and sweat. Mr. Kim stopped them as they passed by. "Hey, you know how to play *shogi*?"

"No clue." Sung-han turned away from the

neighborhood pariah Mr. Kim, but Mr. Kim caught hold of his arm.

"I'll teach ya. Sit down here." His grip on Sung-han's arm was strong.

Sung-han had no choice but to sit down on the bench. Mr. Kim smiled, showing his decaying teeth. He then brought out his plywood *shogi* board and pieces. "I'll teach ya how to use these things."

With hands gnarled from years of construction work, Mr. Kim laid out the pieces on the board clumsily. He explained how to arrange the board and what each piece did. His detailed account of each piece's life story and their relationship to each other went on and on, and by the time he was finished, the sun was setting.

"I get it," said Sung-han impatiently, numb from sitting for so long. He moved a pawn forward on the board.

"No need to rush. Listen carefully to what I'm tellin' ya. You're just a kid; don't take folks' words lightly," Mr. Kim lectured as he moved his pawn four paces. "Now, once you move a piece into the enemy's territory, you turn it over and it gets promoted to a gold general. Don't take pawns for granted, or you'll regret it. Understand?" He seemed to be talking about Sung-han personally. "Now, the knight moves different than the others. If you can master the ways of the knight, you'll be a *shogi* player to be reckoned with."

Under the heat of the setting sun, six sweating boys leaned into the shade, watching the game with interest. The song of cicadas accompanied the game, amping up the tension. Sweat trickled from Mr. Kim's graying hair into his thick eyebrows and ran into his eyes. He blinked rapidly and wiped his forehead. Something was strange. Sung-han was just now learning how to move the pieces, and Mr. Kim thought he could defeat the boy as easily as twisting an infant's wrist. Cocking his head to the side and folding his arms, Mr. Kim sat there thinking.

"It's your turn," pressed Sung-han.

It was quite provoking to see this kid glare at him like that. Mr. Kim couldn't lose his cool in front of these boys. But his head was all confused, and he started to panic. The *shogi* board in front of him looked like the edge of a cliff that would determine his fate.

"What are you doin', old man? Hurry up, will you?" Sung-han's bratty voice had no mercy in it.

Hopeless and humiliated, Mr. Kim stiffened his wrinkly, unshaven face and gave up. The boys cheered.

Sung-han beamed proudly. Mr. Kim, having lost to a ten-year-old beginner, slunk into his house and closed the door.

"What an idiot, that old geezer!" one of the boys shouted after him. The boys continued to shower poor Mr. Kim with all manner of abuse.

Grabbing the *shogi* board and pieces as the spoils of battle, the boys rushed to their customary meeting spot—an empty house—and began playing. Sung-han went over the rules with everyone and then went up against the eager Akio. After a game filled with trial and error, Sung-han won. Unable to accept the loss, Akio challenged him to another game.

"You lost, so it's my turn," cried Shuji, but Akio gripped the board and refused to let go. Shuji relented and said, "Well, it's my turn once you lose."

The frizzy-haired Akio kept his eyes fixed on Sung-han's every move, and his mind swam with calculations and strategies. When he placed a piece on the board, he hesitated to let go. "Let go, cheater." Sung-han moved his piece next and pondered his next move.

But Akio couldn't keep up with Sung-han, who was two years older than him. He bit his lips in frustration

when he lost again. Shuji pushed him out of the way.
Four or five games passed in this way until Sakamoto
Yosuke came into the house, wondering what the noise
was about. The boys were surprised to see Sakamoto
Yosuke, the eldest son of the only Japanese family in the
neighborhood and someone they encountered rarely.
Sakamoto Yosuke had polio: his neck was slightly twisted,
his fingers were stiff, and his speech was somewhat hard
to understand, but he could walk without any problems.
Twenty years old and docile in personality, he spent most
of his time shut up indoors. He joined the boys around
the *shogi* board, staring at the game between Sung-han
and Shuji. Sung-han won after twenty minutes.

"Can I play too?" asked Sakamoto Yosuke shyly.

The boys gaped in surprise. Sakamoto Yosuke's
disability was something they didn't understand. Sung-
han invited him to sit down.

"Know about *shogi*?" asked Sung-han brashly.

"Yeah, I do." The gentle Sakamoto Yosuke smiled.

Sung-han was brimming with confidence after his
consecutive wins, and he underestimated Sakamoto
Yosuke. The other boys watched Sakamoto Yosuke move
the pieces with a sluggish hand and were immediately

convinced that Sung-han would win. But the game didn't even last ten minutes. Sung-han and the other boys were dumbfounded by how quickly the game had gone.

"Let's play again." Needing to regain his honor, Sung-han carefully set the board. But Sakamoto Yosuke moved the pieces as though they were living things, and Sung-han had no room to even attack. Their second game also lasted under ten minutes. Thoroughly beaten, Sung-han studied Sakamoto Yosuke's gentle face. He had wise eyes. In fact, Sung-han had never seen eyes that looked wiser. He had a feeling that he was in the company of a different kind of human being. The boys found Sakamoto Yosuke's boundlessly gentle face quite mysterious—he was neither boastful nor humble about his skills. From then on, Sakamoto Yosuke was to be treated with respect.

The children were craving some intellectual stimulation. They became obsessed with *shogi,* as if it supplied much-needed vitamins for their minds. One day, Sakamoto Yosuke arrived with a foldable *go* board and asked Sung-han if he wanted to play.

Sung-han had seen the adults play *go* in Cho Myung-jin's office. He thought it would be impossible to play such a complicated-looking game on such a wide, finely lined board. The adults looked moody and dignified as they played it, and Sung-han doubted that it was a game for children. But he felt a special thrill as he placed a stone on the *go* board. After learning the basics from Sakamoto Yosuke, the children sensed that *go* required a different kind of mental skill than *shogi,* and they were curious to learn more. The sore loser Akio, above all, was enthusiastic about the game to the point of insatiability, which whetted the curiosity of the others, and soon, that empty house turned into something like a *go* dojo. The children's intellectual turn didn't stop at *shogi* and *go.* The three Ishihara brothers started carrying books around and reading them out in the open. The neighborhood girls were impressed and approached them with questions. Mrs. Ishihara boasted to the other women that her sons were going to be professors one day. The youngest son used to slink around with a constantly runny nose, but now he gave off an air of being the smartest kid on the block. The Ishihara brothers started going to an abacus cram school. To pay for it, the widowed Mrs. Ishihara jacked up the price of her black-market rice.

Hanako began her secondary courses and didn't play with the other children. With Han Masahito's help, she was admitted to National Foundation School, a private school for ethnic Koreans. For Koreans who had been barred from speaking their own language since the start of the war, ethnic education was now an urgent matter. The students at National Foundation School had a wide range of ages. Some of the students in the secondary school were adults with their own homes.

Hanako wasn't able to focus on her schoolwork. She spent most of her time outside the house to avoid being in the line of fire between her father and mother. But when she was at home, she was kept busy with household chores and had no time to study. Meanwhile, Lee Young-hee and Han Masahito went out to rural areas to acquire goods and earn money. They did this for extended periods, in part to stay far away from Kim Shunpei. They sent seafood, fruit, and flour back home. Han Masahito took advantage of his connections at the youth organization to acquire a truck, which he used to transport goods in direct violation of the restrictions. Lee Young-hee came back home two or three times a month to sell off all her items and then left again to replenish her stock. Kim

Shunpei would watch her leave with loathing.

One midnight, Han Masahito arrived home in a black car, pulling a truckload of Shikoku salt. No one was allowed to trade salt under the current monopoly conditions. It was a particularly tight ban in an era of tight bans. The truck contained over a hundred sacks of salt.

Kim Shunpei awoke and opened the door, amazed at the amount of salt piling up at his feet. Only fifty sacks would fit inside the dirt-floor *genkan,* and so they had to store the other fifty sacks in the empty house diagonally across from them. Sung-han was instructed to keep watch.

"Starting tomorrow, you can't play in there. We'll sell all that salt off in three or four days, but until then you have to stay home from school and keep watch over it. Understand? If anyone finds out about it, your *eomeoni's* gonna be in big trouble."

Sung-han nodded nervously. Han Masahito told Hanako the same thing.

Han Masahito then turned to the irritated Kim Shunpei and tactlessly gave him a task. "*Abeoji,* you can rest easy once we sort out this salt situation. We'll give you a cut of our profits too."

"What cut?" It didn't make sense to get a cut if he didn't help with the work.

"It won't be enough to rely on Sung-han and Hanako alone. We're counting on you."

Kim Shunpei couldn't refuse, if only because Han Masahito was his son-in-law.

Sung-han faithfully kept night watch over the salt sacks. The next day, he stayed home from school and sat on the bare dirt in front of the closed door. When his friends came back from school, he told them, "This place is off-limits for now. Go away."

"Why?" retorted Akio.

"None of your business. Now go away, or I'll clobber you."

Akio reluctantly withdrew. Sung-han sat there all day, and the neighborhood women gave him puzzled looks as they passed by. Sung-han was embarrassed by their stares, but he knew this had to be done to protect his mother. Hanako, for her part, kept peeking out the front door to check outside. Kim Shunpei restlessly moved in and out of his house. He knew that a hundred sacks of salt had cost quite a bit of money. Where did all that money come from? It must have been Lee Young-hee's doing. She was hiding all the money somewhere. Kim Shunpei thought she was making a fool of him by conscripting him into this large-scale operation without giving him any information.

That night, Han Masahito came by with two of his broker acquaintances. They took a look at all the salt and began negotiations. After ten minutes, the negotiations were resolved. One of the brokers took out a bunch of bills from his bag and counted them, saying, "We'll give you half today." Kim Shunpei watched the broker hand the bills to Han Masahito.

The two brokers backed their truck in front of the empty house and loaded the truck with the salt sacks.

"We'll come for the other half the day after tomorrow." The brokers shook hands surreptitiously with Han Masahito and left.

"Halfway through," sighed Han Masahito in relief.

"*Abeoji,* it isn't much, but here's three hundred yen."

"That's it?" said the disgruntled Kim Shunpei as he took the cash.

"I'll give you a little more later," said Han Masahito in an effort to appease him.

"What about her? How much is she raking in?"

This operation clearly involved hundreds of yen, and it was black market money, no less.

"You mean *eomeoni*? Her earnings are going to a fund, so we'll have to wait and see."

"Till when?"

"Till we wash our hands of this haul. If we get arrested, we'll lose more than our profits." Han Masahito skillfully dodged Kim Shunpei's questions and left. The three hundred yen in Kim Shunpei's hand was substantial, but it felt small compared to what he imagined Lee Young-hee was making.

Two days later, the two brokers showed up as promised. They paid Han Masahito and loaded the truck with the rest of the salt sacks. Kim Shunpei helped, wanting to finish the business quickly.

"Be careful. If a beat cop tries to stop you, just keep going. One or two of 'em won't be a problem," said Han Masahito.

The two brokers smiled in satisfaction.

When the truck left, Han Masahito gave Kim Shunpei seven hundred yen. Kim Shunpei wasn't displeased about the sum, but he was sure Lee Young-hee and Han

Masahito were keeping more for themselves.

Lee Young-hee left for a business deal at the start of August and came back in the middle of October. She had two large bags in both hands. The bags contained clothes and leather gloves for the children and a full suit for Kim Shunpei.

Hanako twirled in front of the mirror in her new blue flower-patterned dress. "I've always wanted something like this," she said happily, showing one of her rare smiles. Sung-han went around to his friends, showing off his expensive black-and-brown gloves.

"Let me try them on," whined Shuji. Each of the boys tried on the gloves one by one, feeling envious.

Lee Young-hee didn't forget to bring gifts for the neighbors either. It was her way of thanking them for housing her when she needed to escape from Kim Shunpei. Over the course of two days, women and children excitedly gathered at Lee Young-hee's house. Kim Shunpei was generous with everyone, having reaped benefits himself. He and Lee Young-hee didn't exchange a single word. On the afternoon of the third day, Lee Young-hee grinned and asked Sung-han, "Hey, should we go buy a bicycle?"

"Really?" Sung-han jumped for joy.

"And I'll get Hanako a watch, now that she's getting older."

Hanako was so moved she started crying.

Lee Young-hee brought the two of them to the watch shop along the main thoroughfare. Clocks and watches gleamed in the display window. Hanako was bewitched by the sight of them and didn't know how she could possibly choose just one.

"This one should do, right?" recommended the shopkeeper. When Hanako tried it on, she instantly felt like an adult.

After purchasing a watch for Hanako, Lee Young-hee led them to the bicycle shop three doors down. All the bikes there were secondhand. She bought the bike that looked the newest. "Please give us front and back locks," she requested. Even if a bicycle were locked in two places and put inside the house, there was still a chance it could get stolen. Thieves loved to target an expensive bicycle. "Make sure to lock it every time and keep it inside the house," Lee Young-hee reminded Sung-han.

"I know. I'll make sure it's safe," vowed Sung-han. The bitter memory of getting his bicycle stolen at the black market was fresh in his mind.

With those two purchases, Lee Young-hee prepared to head out of the city once more.

"You're leaving again?" said Hanako sadly.

"I'll be back by New Year's. I'm counting on you to keep the house in order. If it's just the two of you, *abeoji* won't get as violent, I think." She spoke as if they would be separated for an age. But the two children were still euphoric about their gifts.

Kim Shunpei wasn't happy. For Lee Young-hee to swoop in, splurge money on the kids, and swoop out in a matter of days, she was surely intending to spite him. The suit she'd gotten him was just another dig at him.

That night, he came home drunk. As he broke the glass doors and furniture, he howled, "You think you can leave whenever you feel like it? Insolent bitch!"

Lee Young-hee hadn't foreseen that Kim Shunpei would wreck the house even if she were away. The two children now had to bear the brunt of his mood swings. Hanako and Sung-han were petrified in front of their father. They still had a chance to run away, but they couldn't move or even breathe as their father viciously glared down at them. Kim Shunpei sat down on the wooden floor of the two-*jo* room. He lugged out a *shochu* bottle, filled his cup to the brim, and drank it down in one gulp. Exhaling, he once again fixed his gaze on Hanako standing before him.

"You're just a kid and you're wearin' a watch? Overpriced piece of shit!" Kim Shunpei tore the watch off Hanako's wrist and flung it against the wall. Hanako felt as if he'd torn off a piece of her body.

"And *you* can walk without a bike! You brat!" This time, Kim Shunpei lifted the bicycle from the dirt floor of the *genkan* and threw it through the cracked glass door, breaking the bicycle as the glass shattered around it. Then he tore up the suit Lee Young-hee had bought him. Hanako and Sung-han's hearts hammered in their chests as they watched him.

"Sit there now!" he ordered the children.

Hanako and Sung-han sat *seiza*-style on the wooden floor. Kim Shunpei's eyes burned with hatred. The children didn't understand what could possibly stir up such hatred in their father. They kept silent, hoping someone brave would come and rescue them.

"I know what you little shits are thinking. Oh, I know!" Hanako and Sung-han couldn't help feeling a twinge of guilt. It would be a lie to say they didn't hate their father. They stiffened, sure they were about to be punished for their lack of filial piety.

"Hanako, who do you think I am? I'm your *what*? Say it!"

It was an unimaginable question. Hanako felt the self-evident words constrict in her throat. Why did she have to confirm such a thing? She was confused.

"Say it, you little shit! I'm your *what*?"

"You're my father," answered Hanako in a small voice.

"Father? Stop with your bullshit. I'm not your father! I'm your *what*? Tell me!" He was asking for an affirmation and denial at the same time. It was as if he were prosecuting her in a witch trial. Hanako felt a lump form in her throat, and she couldn't speak.

"Say it! I'm your *what*?"

Hanako felt tears form in the back of her eyes. Sung-han, thinking he was next, racked his brain for an appropriate answer.

Hanako marshalled her courage and looked straight at her father as she said, "If you're not my father, who are you, then?"

"You little . . . Who am I? You brat . . ." In the next

moment, Kim Shunpei lunged toward Hanako and punched her in the face. Hanako slammed onto the wooden floor, her nose and mouth bleeding. Kim Shunpei hit her once more and then grabbed her by the hair and threw her into the *genkan*. Sung-han heard a loud thud. He turned his head and saw Hanako lying unconscious along the wall.

Baring his teeth, Kim Shunpei turned toward Sung-han and glared. Sung-han froze, unable to even swallow.

"You little shit. I know what you're thinking. Oh, I know!" Kim Shunpei took a swig from the *shochu* bottle. "Say it! I'm your *what*?"

He wouldn't stop asking that question. It was as if he wanted to extort from them an answer that would reject basic reality. Actually, it was something else. In order to get them to say he was their father, he was going to force them to reject their own identities. If he wasn't their father, who was he? Sung-han wanted to answer as his sister had. But he saw how she had paid the consequences.

"You're my father," he answered.

Sung-han never had much of an opportunity to call his father by that title, and when he said it out loud, it filled him with pain.

"Father? Stop with your bullshit. I'm not your father! Say it! I'm your *what*?"

Sung-han felt like a prisoner being tortured in a cage. He felt like he would be interrogated to death, bound to his father by the violence of kinship—a hatred just as fierce as love. What Kim Shunpei wanted was proof of a bond as strong as blood. Only blood would atone for blood.

Sung-han withdrew inside himself, not wanting to repeat the folly of his sister.

Kim Shunpei regarded Sung-han coldly and then said, "Bring a knife."

Unlike his father, Sung-han knew where his mother had hidden the knives. He couldn't refuse. He got up from his *seiza* position on the wooden floor and tottered a few steps with his numb legs. He came back with a knife. What was his father going to do with it? Cut up him and his sister? Crazy with fear, Sung-han broke out into a cold sweat all over his body. He felt so afraid he thought only coagulated white blood would leak out of his body if he were stabbed.

Kim Shunpei took off his shirt. His flesh rippled with countless fresh-looking scars from where knives and hooks had punctured it. The hair on his lower belly billowed in Sung-han's eyes like swarming insects.

Kim Shunpei grabbed Sung-han's arm that held the knife. "You hate me? You hate me, huh?" His bloodshot eyes were blazing. Sung-han looked away.

"Say it to my face!" screamed Kim Shunpei.

"No, I don't hate you," mumbled Sung-han.

"Lyin' brat. I can see what you're thinking. You hate me so much you wanna kill me. Then stab me with this knife. Go ahead and kill me!" Kim Shunpei moved Sung-han's arm and pressed the tip of the knife's blade to his own stomach. An orb of blood welled up and trickled down his stomach in a thin red line. "Stab me here! You don't even have the guts to do that?"

As if to provoke Sung-han, Kim Shunpei raised his fists threateningly. Sung-han stiffened. He was being tested. His father wanted to draw out the murderous hatred inside him. Sung-han's eyes filled with tears.

"Coward!" Kim Shunpei took the knife from Sung-han and threw it onto the floor. "When you have the guts, go ahead and stab me with that knife. I'm not gonna die." Kim Shunpei took another swig from his bottle, gargled the *shochu*, and spat it out.

"That bitch asked a shrine maiden to pray for my death. That's why this house is crawling with evil spirits. But I can take 'em." Kim Shunpei scowled at the ceiling and four corners of the room before lighting a cigarette. Suddenly, he yelled, "Sit down!"

Sung-han sat down without a second thought.

"Stand up!"

Sung-han stood at attention.

"Sit down!" "Stand up!" The orders continued another ten, twenty, thirty times, eternally repeating just like Kim Shunpei's unanswerable interrogations. He seemed to be training Sung-han to respond unthinkingly to any command. It was a way of instilling fear—the kind of fear that was inseparable from hatred.

Sung-han screwed up his face in pain as he was forced to sit and stand over a hundred times.

"At ease!" Kim Shunpei studied Sung-han's face closely, as if to discern how fast the boy's heart was beating. "You're hot, huh? How dare you sweat in front of me."

Sung-han didn't reply. If he did, his father would find a new excuse to prolong this torture. He concentrated all his strength on getting through it.

"You're just the same as that bitch. But you come from

my bones, understand?"

Silence was a form of resistance. In that way, the silent Sung-han resembled his mother.

Kim Shunpei ordered Sung-han to bring over a bucket of water. Kim Shunpei then poured the water over Sung-han's head. Sung-han stood there looking like a drowned rat as the water pooled across the floor.

"Don't you dare move from that spot. Not until I let you. If you move even an inch, you're dead meat." With that, Kim Shunpei stalked into the inner room and threw himself down on the tatami floor. His hulking body was like that of a mysterious beast.

The hands of the old grandfather clock marked time with each tick. It chimed eleven o'clock at night. It would be six or seven hours before daybreak. Sung-han needed to pee, but he stood rooted to the spot, his skin cold. He could no longer hold it in. The warm urine trickled down his legs to his feet and onto the floor. Sung-han thought it was truly absurd, peeing in his own clothes. It went without saying that his father was absurd too. Sung-han knew that whatever fear was beaten into him didn't change who he was.

Hanako rustled awake with a groan and turned over,

scrabbling up the wall to stand up. Her nose had bled all over her face, her lips were split open, and the area around her eyes was black from where she'd been slammed into the wall. She looked wretched. She turned her head this way and that and saw Sung-han standing in the two-*jo* room. She staggered toward him, but Sung-han put a finger to his lips, signaling to her that their father was sleeping in the inner room. Hanako beckoned to him and mouthed, "We should leave!" Sung-han shook his head. He wasn't certain if their father was asleep or awake.

Hanako crawled upstairs with her injuries and laid down on her futon.

Sung-han stood there for several hours. He strained to hear his father's breathing and carefully went to check on him. He kicked at the glass door to the inner room, but Kim Shunpei didn't stir. He kicked a little harder. Kim Shunpei was lying spread-eagled on the floor with his mouth open, fast asleep. Sung-han tiptoed closer until he could smell his father's alcoholic breath. He then picked up his father's shirt on the wooden floor and searched its pocket, pulling out a wad of bundled cash. *This is really bold, even for me,* thought Sung-han as he extracted a single one hundred-yen bill. If he was discovered, he wouldn't be able to escape. He put the shirt back in its place and went to the wall, looking for Hanako's watch. The watch crystal was cracked, but when Sung-han held the watch up to his ear, he could hear it ticking. He slipped the watch in his pocket. He would bring it to the shop the following day to get it repaired.

The bigger problem was the bicycle. The handlebars were all twisted, which made it hard for him to even mount it. If he left it in the house with the front door broken, someone could steal it. He brought the bike to Mrs. Ishihara next door for her to keep.

"*Aigo*, poor thing!" said Mrs. Ishihara compassionately.

The next morning, Hanako's face had swollen further and was covered in bruises. She couldn't go to school looking like that. Sung-han skipped breakfast that day and got ready for school. Kim Shunpei had evidently felt cold enough that night to lay out a futon for himself. His shirt hung on the wall of the inner room. Sung-han left the house nonchalantly.

After school, Sung-han came home in a state of suspense about the hundred-yen bill he'd stolen from his father's shirt pocket. He told himself over and over that he would deny all his father's accusations. He considered sneaking in through the back alley but then decided against it, thinking it would look suspicious. His heart beat faster as he got closer to the house. *What should I do?* When he reached his front door, Mrs. Takamura signaled to him from across the street. *He found out.* Sung-han's mind raced with possible escape routes.

"Sung-han . . ." said Mrs. Takamura meaningfully, her brow furrowed.

Sung-han made his way over to her.

"*Aigo* . . . Hana-*chan* drank rat poison and committed suicide. Harumi came and took her to the police hospital. Go quickly."

"Suicide!" Sung-han felt dizzy.

He threw his school bag inside the house and picked up his bike from Mrs. Ishihara's. Kim Shunpei was not in the inner room. Was he at the hospital already? He probably was. But this was no time to be scared of his father. He felt like he knew why his sister had done it. This was her way of getting revenge on their father. She should have stabbed him in his sleep while she was at it. A storm of dark feelings passed through Sung-han. His heart was roiling.

He secured his bicycle in the police hospital's *genkan*.

A long line of patients extended from the *genkan* all the way down the hallway. There was a long line in front of the reception desk as well. Sung-han cut to the front and poked his head over the counter. "I'm Kanemoto Hanako's brother. Can you tell me her room number?"

"Kanemoto Hanako . . . Ah, the girl who drank the rat poison. Room No. 7 on the second floor."

Sung-han was offended by the insensitive way the receptionist referred to his dying sister. "Stupid bitch!" he spat at her before running for the stairs.

"The hell?" The confused receptionist puffed up her cheeks.

The floors, walls, and ceiling of the old hospital all looked dirty, and the naked bulbs on the ceiling gave off a dull light. The smell of sanitizer, medicine, and sick people assaulted Sung-han's senses. A nurse was pushing a cart down the hallway with medical instruments on top of it. Their dry clatter made Sung-han feel sick.

There were six patients in Room No. 7, with three beds on either side of the room. Harumi sat next to Hanako's bed while holding her six-month-old baby. Hanako was asleep. With her bruised, swollen face, she looked dead.

"She gonna be okay?" Sung-han asked Harumi.

"She's okay now. They gave her a shot to stabilize her." Harumi looked around and then lowered her voice. "If I'd come in just a little later, she probably would've died. It was like a little bird told me, but I thought I'd check in 'round noon. The front door and inner door and cupboard were all broken. Father was sleeping in the inner room. I went upstairs and saw Hana-*chan* with her face all wrecked, and she was in a bad way. I asked her what was wrong, but she wasn't answering. She was coughing up blood, too. There was a bottle next to her. I knew it was rat poison; I recognized that bottle from when I was a kid. There wasn't a phone anywhere, so I went out into the street with the baby on my back and talked to the guard in the police box by the streetcar stop. He called the police hospital right away, and that's what saved Hana-*chan*. It was chaos. You think Father dares show his face here? He's a disgrace. She's his own daughter, but he just pretended he didn't know her and went off somewhere. Probably drinking as usual."

The memories of Harumi's own childhood came back to her, and her face clouded over.

"I sent Masahito a telegram, and he's coming back with Mom later tonight or tomorrow morning. I have to go home now to feed the kids, so watch over Hana-*chan* 'til they come, okay?"

Sung-han nodded.

Harumi sighed deeply and left.

Sung-han stared at Hanako's pitiful face. He felt pathetic for not being able to stop his father from hitting her. He needed courage to face his father's violence head on. But he didn't have any courage. Whenever he saw his father's gargoyle-like face, he froze.

He took out the watch from his pocket. It was ticking just fine. He put it next to Hanako's pillow.

Hanako finally opened her eyes during the night. She groggily lifted her head and noticed Sung-han beside her.

"You slept well by the looks of it," said Sung-han, smiling.

Hanako looked back at him hollowly. "Forgive me," she said with tears in her eyes.

Later, Harumi returned with her baby fast asleep on her back. "How are you feeling?" she asked her sister gently.

"Okay. But I feel like I'm gonna throw up."

"You're not well yet. The doctor said you'll be back to normal in a week."

It seemed to Harumi that she'd sent the telegram a long time ago. "They're late. I wonder if Masahito got my message."

The telegram had been sent to an inn in Shizuoka where Han Masahito was supposed to be staying, but she had no confirmation that he'd received it. If they didn't come tonight, she would send another telegram first thing the next morning. At ten, just when Harumi got up to leave, Han Masahito and Lee Young-hee appeared in the doorway.

Lee Young-hee rushed toward Harumi. "Is Hanako okay?"

Harumi nodded. Lee Young-hee went to Hanako's bedside and stroked her face.

"Forgive me, mom," sobbed Hanako. Lee Young-hee could imagine what Kim Shunpei had done to her from the bruises and welts on her face. Clearly, Hanako's suicide attempt was her last resort in the face of Kim Shunpei's violence. The reserved Hanako had tried to sacrifice her life to express her suffering.

"You're still a kid. Why do such a thing? If you die, it's the end. Don't try that again, okay?" Lee Young-hee held Hanako close as she scolded her. All those years ago, Lee

73

Young-hee had attempted to abort her by jumping from the second story of that inn, and now Hanako was paying for her sin.

Harumi and Sung-han were relieved that their mother was back with them. Han Masahito stood by silently, burning with hatred for Kim Shunpei. He had to speak with him tomorrow. If things kept going like this, something even worse could happen down the line.

Shortly after noon the following day, Han Masahito went to see Kim Shunpei. The broken front door hadn't been repaired. The inside of the house was in ruins. Sung-han had gone to school, while Kim Shunpei was in the inner room sleeping. Four or five bottles lay beside the futon. Han Masahito cleared the bottles away and sat down, facing Kim Shunpei's back. "*Abeoji*," he called.

Kim Shunpei turned his head, glaring. His whole body stank of alcohol.

"I'd like to have a word."

"'Bout what?" growled Kim Shunpei.

"Hanako . . ."

Kim Shunpei cut Han Masahito off and sat up to light himself a cigarette. "That little brat thinks she can copycat a suicide. What sorta kid does that? She should go ahead and die if she's so good at it. Life goes on."

Han Masahito couldn't accept such talk. "Have you thought about your kids' feelings? Why do you get drunk and wreck things like this? What did the kids do to deserve it? Why don't you just divorce *eomeoni* if you can't get along?" Han Masahito hadn't meant to say that last part, but it slipped out of him before he knew it.

"You think you can lecture me?"

"I'm just telling you what's reasonable."

"You're lecturin'! A divorce? Don't put your nose where it don't belong. Go home, rookie! I'll let you off the hook today."

Kim Shunpei looked like he was about to throw another fit, so Han Masahito had no choice but to leave. He regretted saying anything.

Hanako was discharged from the hospital a week later. Her face was no longer swollen, but her bruises remained. Kim Shunpei wasn't at home. He hadn't come to see her at the hospital once. He was likely avoiding her. Several of the neighborhood women visited and chatted with Lee Young-hee about this and that. Harumi also came by with her baby. Sung-han returned from school and made sure Hanako was fully recovered before he went outside to play with his friends.

When the women left, Lee Young-hee went to the carpenter who lived behind the bathhouse.

"Again? Your husband loves to break things, huh. But at least I get paid." The affable middle-aged carpenter laughed sarcastically.

February was almost over. Lee Young-hee deliberated about whether to go back to Shizuoka to finish up her business there. Hanako seemed to have recovered physically, but mentally she was still unstable. Lee Young-hee had to be completely confident about Hanako's condition before she could leave Osaka again. Han Masahito, busy with his organization activities, couldn't go to Shizuoka in her stead. He would have to stay there for over a month. Lee Young-hee decided to stop her operations in Shizuoka. She remained worried. Prices were going up, and it was a matter of time before her reserves dried up.

Apparently, Kim Shunpei had received something of a shock when Hanako attempted suicide, and for a few nights he went to bed without causing trouble, even when he drank. Hanako went back to school after waiting a month for her bruises to mostly subside. What didn't change was her dual role as housemaid and intermediary between her mother and father.

Chapter 16

Ten days after the new year, Lee Young-hee went to
Kyushu for business. The doors of the house were fixed,
the walls were painted over, and the *genkan*'s dirt floor
was replaced with cement. The repairs had cost about
two months' worth of living expenses, and the family
was strapped for money. Kim Shunpei kept demanding
that Lee Young-hee pay for his excessive drinking, and
everyone's nerves were worn down by the possibility of
violence breaking out at any moment. But foremost on
Lee Young-hee's mind was getting food on the table.

Han Masahito excused himself from accompanying
Lee Young-hee to Kyushu, saying he had a big transaction
to attend to in Osaka. But he spent all day with his
broker friends in Cho Myung-jin's office, playing *go* and
nitpicking over worthless subjects.

In February, Lee Young-hee delivered a bunch of mikan oranges and sweet potatoes to the house. Hanako and Sung-han had to get up at five in the morning to sell them. It was cold and dark at that hour, and the streets were covered in fog. They woke up to the crowing of the rooster in the *genkan*. For whatever reason, keeping chickens had become a fad in the neighborhood, and Sung-han had hatched three eggs of his own.

It was hard to wake up at five in the bitter cold. Hanako dragged herself out of bed. After throwing firewood on the hearth, she steamed sweet potatoes in one pot and boiled rice in another. In the meantime, she heated up the coals underneath the brazier in the two-*jo* room. When the sweet potatoes were done, she tried to wake Sung-han. "Let me sleep just a little longer," he groaned, clinging to his futon.

"If we don't leave now, we won't make it in time," said Hanako as she pulled on his arm and rolled his futon around him.

The half-asleep Sung-han stumbled downstairs and splashed his face with cold water. The two of them put the steamed sweet potatoes in a basket and set it on the bicycle carrier to bring to the Tsuruhashi black market.

The black market was crowded with people even in the cold, misty darkness of early morning. It was as if they'd sprung up from the ground like insects. Vagrants slept on the ground near the station, as unmoving as corpses. Some of them probably had frozen to death in the middle of the night, but no one seemed to care. Cripples in rags crawled along the alleys, surrounded by the legs of the crowd. Several of them begged for rice gruel at a stall, but the stall owner yelled, "Go away! You'll get trampled here!"

The black market seemed to be covered in a layer of steam from everyone's breath. The ground shook with the rumbling of hungry stomachs.

Hanako and Sung-han parked the bicycle in the alley and began selling the sweet potatoes off. Steam rose from the basket invitingly, and several people approached at once.

"Freshly steamed sweet potatoes from Kyushu right over here! Get them before they're gone!" called Sung-han. Hanako handled the money and wrapped the sweet potatoes in newspaper.

"Five sen for one sweet potato!" cried Sung-han shrilly.

A number of customers asked if they could buy half

a sweet potato. Sung-han cut the sweet potatoes with a knife. All the sweet potatoes were sold in less than one hour. Hanako and Sung-han then rushed back home. Sung-han dove back under the covers of his futon to catch a few more winks of sleep, putting off his departure for school until the last possible moment. Hanako couldn't sleep. She had to prepare breakfast. She set the food on her father's special table and brought it to the inner room when he woke up. Then she woke up Sung-han again, and the two of them hurriedly ate breakfast.

It took them a week to sell off the sweet potatoes, but after that came the mikan oranges. They didn't have to boil them, at least, but they still had to get up at six. They loaded two boxes of the oranges onto the bicycle and sold them at the Ueroku intersection. Mikan oranges were considered luxury items that weren't very filling, so few black market shoppers at Tsuruhashi would buy them. Hanako and Sung-han lined the oranges on top of the boxes and eyed passing pedestrians. They stood there patiently under the bitter winter sky. To rouse himself, Sung-han yelled, "Mikan oranges here from Wakayama! Sweet and delicious, and cheap too. Come get your mikan oranges!"

But the mikan oranges didn't sell well at all.

"It's no use. Why did Mom send us these things? I'm tired," grumbled Sung-han.

"But we have to sell them. Stop complaining," chided Hanako.

"Father's gonna take all the money we earn anyway."

"But what else can we do? We can't disobey him."

"What if we give him half?"

"We can't."

It was frightening to consider lying to their father's face. Hanako shuddered at the mere thought of her father's hammer-like blows.

"Lemme show you what I got." Sung-han took out a folded-up one hundred-yen bill from his pocket, making sure no one but Hanako saw.

"Why do you have something like that?" Hanako was shocked. It was rare to see even adults with a one hundred-yen bill. Sung-han slipped the bill back into his pocket and grinned, as if to tease her.

"Tell me. How'd you get that? You stole it?"

Sung-han's eyes glinted mischievously. "Yeah."

"Where? From who?" Hanako never imagined this could happen. A one hundred-yen bill was no trivial matter.

"I took it from Father."

"What? You're kidding." Hanako really thought Sung-han was making a fool of her. How could someone steal that much money from their monster of a father? Sung-han was surely just teasing her, but the one hundred-yen bill was undeniably real.

"Be honest with me. I won't tell anyone," said Hanako calmly. She had to make Sung-han realize the seriousness of this situation. If he'd stolen it, she had to convince him to return it.

"I really did steal it from Father. After he hit you, he poured a bucket of water on me and made me stand in that room for a long time. He fell asleep, so I stole a bill from his shirt."

Sung-han did seem to be telling the truth. Hanako felt a vague danger. "You think you can get away with that? If Father finds out, what do you think is gonna happen? He could kill you." Hanako's eyes were round with fear.

"This is from months ago. Father never realized it. If he did, I'd be dead already."

It seemed wrong to pretend like nothing had happened. But Hanako had no choice but to keep it a secret.

"Why'd you do it?"

"It's the price he has to pay for abusing us like he did. I can use this money to fix your watch."

"I don't need you to. You can't use this money. And don't tell anyone else. I'll keep the money for you."

"No. I'll need it when I run away."

"Stop being stupid. You think I *don't* want to run away? But we won't see Mom again if we do." Hanako's eyes glistened. Sung-han still refused to hand over the bill.

They sold barely anything that day. They'd endured the cold since six in the morning, but now they had to leave for school. As they walked along the alleyway, Hanako kept throwing Sung-han dark warnings. "Don't tell anyone. And don't use the money."

"What should we do with it, then? It's a waste not to use it."

"That's why I'm telling you to give it to me."

"No."

They argued back and forth until they turned the corner of the udon shop, where they fell silent. Hanako's heart beat faster. She was bad at keeping her face blank, so she avoided making eye contact with her father when she served him breakfast.

When Hanako and Sung-han came back from school, they saw a bunch of their neighbors in an empty lot, along with some Japanese from outside the neighborhood. The head of the neighborhood association called out, "Everyone get in line!"

A jeep was parked in the alleyway, next to which stood four conspicuously tall American soldiers. Two had blond hair and blue eyes, and two were black. They looked stylish and flashed charming white smiles as they smacked gum. After spraying the children with DDT, they gave them chocolate and chewing gum. The children stretched their arms up, greedy for even a single piece. Sung-han ran toward the crowd to meet the spray of DDT and get his share of sweets. He'd never tried chewing gum before.

"Sung-han," a silky-smooth voice called out.

He turned around to see Yasuko, the daughter of the same Mr. Kim who had taught him *shogi* all those months ago. It had been a year since she'd left, and now she was hanging on the arm of one of the soldiers. Her hair was permed, and her lips were painted red. Her clothes looked fancy, and she had high heels on. She was fourteen, the same age as Hanako, but she hardly looked her age as she walked around swinging her hips.

"You got big so fast," she told Sung-han, hugging him. Sung-han breathed in her scent and felt her breasts against his collarbone.

The neighborhood children gathered around Yasuko. The adults also watched from a distance. Yasuko gave the children chocolate, chewing gum, and biscuits, showing off her largesse. "I'm goin' to America with John, you know," she said proudly. Her eyes shone with hope.

"Wow . . ." said the children enviously. Akio turned to Sung-han while munching on a biscuit and whispered, "Yasuko's a pan-pan girl.* My mom told me."

"Pan-pan?" Sung-han only vaguely knew what the term meant, but he knew it meant something obscene. In any case, she was beautiful. After the American soldiers finished spraying the DDT, they smiled and drove away in the jeep with Yasuko in between them. The smell of Yasuko's perfume and the feeling of her breasts stayed with Sung-han for a long time. It was his first time feeling

---

* A term for teenage prostitutes after World War II known for soliciting American soldiers

so sexually aroused.

The family's revenue from black market sales was hitting a low point. The regulations had tightened, and Lee Young-hee sustained losses from a string of confiscations. The family was able to survive on the profits of the salt transaction for a while, but Lee Young-hee now understood the helplessness of not being able to read or write. Large-scale transactions required connections, knowledge, and capital. Han Masahito was tired of the constant cat-and-mouse games with the police, and he dreamed of hitting the jackpot as a broker. He spent all day discussing get-rich-quick schemes and government affairs with his friends. At this point, buying and selling on the black market was yielding no returns, and the reserves from the salt transaction were bottoming out. The family had to come up with another source of income. Lee Young-hee considered quitting the black-market trade and getting into the *sake* business. Unsure what to do, she returned home in the middle of February.

The kids were happy to see her. They felt safe against her warm bosom. The inner room was the domain of Kim Shunpei, while Lee Young-hee stayed on the second floor with the kids. Kim Shunpei didn't step foot on the second floor unless he was on one of his drunken rampages, and likewise, Lee Young-hee and the kids didn't step foot into his room unless they were bringing him a meal.

As the night got late and Kim Shunpei still hadn't returned, Lee Young-hee nervously turned off the lights in the house and made preparations to escape. But when Kim Shunpei did return, he went straight to bed. A few days passed without incident, and Sung-han wondered out loud, "What's wrong with him? Is he sick?"

"Stupid, what kind of sick person goes out drinking every night? He never gets sick," said Hanako.

"'He never gets sick,'" mimicked Sung-han. "Maybe someone could kill him for us," he said ominously.

"Hey, think before you speak," snapped the sanctimonious Hanako.

A few more days passed without incident until one day a sober Kim Shunpei called up to Lee Young-hee from the bottom of the stairs, "Hey, I want a word."

Lee Young-hee and the children shuddered. They thought back to anything careless they'd done recently that Kim Shunpei might find fault with. Sung-han dreaded the possibility that his father had found out about the one hundred-yen bill.

What could this be about? Lee Young-hee had no choice but to go down the stairs. Her body stiffened at the thought that he would force her to have sex with him.

Kim Shunpei was in the two-*jo* room, smoking a cigarette while sitting on the wooden floor in front of the brazier. Lee Young-hee maintained some distance from him and sat with her back to the kitchen hallway. She would need to flee in that direction if it came down to it. Kim Shunpei followed the smoke from his cigarette with his eyes. He and Lee Young-hee avoided making eye contact. When he abruptly cleared his throat, she readied herself to flee.

Kim Shunpei began speaking fretfully, sounding like phlegm was caught in his throat. "I'm thinkin' of settin' up a *kamaboko* factory."

Lee Young-hee lifted her face up and looked at Kim Shunpei. She then looked down again. She had a rough idea of what this conversation was going to be about. Money.

"I don't have any money. Lend me some."

Anger flared up inside Lee Young-hee at his selfishness. He thought he could just brush aside all his brutality against his family. The little money Lee Young-hee had was the family's lifeline. Kim Shunpei didn't understand the reality of that at all.

Kim Shunpei wasn't the type to change his cruel, violent behavior even if a natural disaster were to hit them. What was behind his about-face? Was he trying to get his act together now that he was approaching middle age? Or had he become self-conscious of how the world saw him? Both these questions sounded ludicrous to even ask. Lee Young-hee saw the shadowy underside to Kim Shunpei's show of respectability. Unfortunately, she couldn't refuse him. If she did, she would be subjected to endless violence. Of course, there was no limit to his violence even if she were to comply with his wishes. Lee Young-hee felt like she was caught in a stranglehold between two extremes. In any case, it would be extremely difficult to raise enough funds for a *kamaboko* factory. She had no faith that her lowlife of a husband would be able to raise his own funds.

Lee Young-hee raised her eyes from the ground and forced herself to ask, "How much do you need?"

Kim Shunpei estimated that he would need ten thousand yen to purchase two empty buildings nearby, five thousand yen to refurbish them, twenty thousand yen to invest in equipment, and five thousand yen for working capital, which amounted to about forty thousand yen altogether.*

"I'll return it for sure," said Kim Shunpei with a sincere look on his face.

Lee Young-hee had about four thousand yen. But there was no way she could give Kim Shunpei that money, which had to be preserved at all costs. In other words, she had to raise all forty thousand yen from scratch.

"Okay. I'll find a way somehow. Please wait four or five months. And then please make sure to return it."

"You bet." The power balance between them shifted, and Kim Shunpei roughened up his speech. His face relaxed, and he reached for Lee Young-hee's hand. But she pushed his hand away and resolutely left for the second floor.

Coming up with forty thousand yen was next to impossible. Lee Young-hee didn't know what led her to accept such a task in the moment. Perhaps by raising

---

* Equivalent to about JPY 3.6 million in 2020, or a little less than USD 350,000

all that money, she could put all those years of violence behind her. If she succeeded, her husband could turn over a new leaf. She believed this was the only way to ensure a peaceful domestic life. It was possible that Kim Shunpei would never return the money. In fact, it was highly likely. But Lee Young-hee didn't want to lose this one last glimmer of hope.

Kim Shunpei's mood improved, and his days got busy. He inspected the empty houses and planned refurbishments, and he observed the fish auctions in the central market. He also seemed to become more sociable. The problem remained whether he could acquire a special license for his *kamaboko* business. Under the current regulations, acquiring a license was exceedingly difficult. It wasn't as simple as going to the city office and submitting an application. After all, only two *kamaboko* factories were legally recognized by the Osaka government. No one else could enter the market. But if one could get a license, one could turn a huge profit. Kim Shunpei was finally doing what Park Hyun-nam had proposed to him in the past.

One night, Kim Shunpei showed up at Han Masahito's house with a bag of sweets. Kim Shunpei rarely visited his son-in-law, and Harumi was surprised to see him when she answered the door. Han Masahito was about to eat dinner. He, too, thought something was wrong when he saw Kim Shunpei's hulking body in their small house. The youngest child was asleep, but his five-year-old brother and three-year-old sister stared open-mouthed at their huge grandfather.

Harumi hurriedly put out a seat cushion for Kim Shunpei. "Have you eaten yet?"

"Yeah, I did."

Harumi was confused by Kim Shunpei's unusual calm. "I'll get the *sake*," she said, going to the kitchen.

Kim Shunpei looked at the grandchildren and put the bag of sweets on the table. He never brought sweets home for his own children. Han Masahito wondered what had gotten into him.

Kim Shunpei sat there smoking without saying a word.

"Anything you wish to talk about?" asked Han Masahito.

"Well, I'd like to consult with you about somethin'. I need your help."

It was unbelievable to hear Kim Shunpei—the same Kim Shunpei who solved all his problems with violence—

want to "consult" with him. It was almost enough to make Han Masahito drop his cup of *sake*. He leaned forward to check that this was the same Kim Shunpei. "What about?" Han Masahito felt uneasy. Something momentous was afoot.

"Truth is, I want to start a *kamaboko* factory."

"A *kamaboko* factory?"

So an alcoholic barbarian wanted to be an entrepreneur. Han Masahito hid his stupefaction and said, "That sounds great, but do you have the funds?"

"Lee Young-hee's comin' up with the funds."

"*Eomeoni* is . . . ?" It was unbelievable. Han Masahito and Harumi shared a look. "How much is she gonna raise?"

"Forty thousand yen."

"Forty thousand!" gasped Han Masahito and Harumi.

"How's she coming up with that?"

"Dunno. She just told me she would. Whatever else she may be, she's a woman who keeps her word."

The situation was beyond reckless. Harumi felt faint. Had her mother lost her mind? She said nothing more in front of her father, but she determined to confirm this situation with her mother as soon as possible. She feared they were opening a big can of worms.

Han Masahito thought similarly. For a husband and wife with enough problems already, this financial gamble would cause nothing short of a disaster. He had to stop them.

"So what do you want to consult with me about?" He would listen to Kim Shunpei for now and try to dissuade him later.

"I want you to get me a license."

Basically, Kim Shunpei wanted Han Masahito to use his connections as leader of the Zaihan Korean youth organization to put pressure on the Osaka municipal office. Postwar Japan owed Koreans a big debt. During the colonial period, Japan had used Korea however it wanted. Koreans had been subjected to misery and forced to make immeasurable sacrifices. Japan now thought it could get away with paying only a tiny sliver of its debt. Kim Shunpei went on and on explaining how he planned to run his business. As Han Masahito listened, his earlier suspicions were gradually dispelled. Kim Shunpei was no doubt an alcoholic barbarian, but he also possessed great powers of observation.

At a time when the starting salary of an average bank

worker was two hundred twenty yen, a roll of *kamaboko* cost twenty two yen. At that time, *kamaboko* was considered a high-class commodity, but it was also sought after by a lot of Japanese. If one could corner the market on *kamaboko*, he would make a fortune.

"If you help me get the license, you won't regret it."

For Han Masahito, who spent all day cooking up business ventures with his broker friends, Kim Shunpei's proposal sounded practical enough. It would be difficult to get a license, but the reward would be great.

Harumi cleaned up after dinner and was putting the kids to bed when she noticed Han Masahito nodding along to Kim Shunpei's explanations. She fretted at her husband's apparent willingness to humor Kim Shunpei. The two men seemed to already be discussing business particulars.

"I understand. I'll get on it promptly," promised Han Masahito. Satisfied, Kim Shunpei got up and left.

Harumi said hoarsely, "Is everything okay?"

The tipsy Han Masahito leaned toward Harumi. "We don't know yet what'll happen. But if we get the license, he'll succeed."

The die was cast when Lee Young-hee accepted Kim Shunpei's proposal. She decided to raise funds through a network of mutual financing associations. A tight-knit group of people, bound by years of trust, could amass large amounts of money by becoming dealers for several mutual funds that differed in size and scale. For example, if twenty people pitched ten yen into a fund, they would have two hundred yen. Small funds like these were mainly for show. Large mutual funds could call for shares of two hundred or three hundred yen apiece. Dealers were able to use the money in these funds without getting charged interest, but that was a privilege reserved only for dealers. On the other hand, if a non-dealer borrowed money and couldn't pay it back, the dealers would have to cover the cost. Thus, a single mistake could bring the whole association down. Dealers had to devise ways to prevent such a thing from happening. Lee Young-hee was going to be a wild card. She would play her hand at several mutual funds and conjure tricks to make something from nothing, but this house of cards could come crashing down in a single moment, and a lot of people could sustain heavy losses. But she couldn't think of any other way to raise forty thousand yen.

Before the war, it was common practice for Zaihan Koreans to use mutual financing associations as mutual aid networks. After the war, they were temporarily disbanded since the air raids and evacuations had scattered so many people, but in the following year they seemed to be making a comeback. In fact, Lee Young-hee was already investing in a fifty-yen mutual fund.

Lee Young-hee made her move. She went around to her neighbors and to her farther-flung friends and acquaintances, and she reached out to her contacts in the black market. Her funds expanded quickly. In the first month, she opened a ten-yen fund; in the second month, she moved on to a fifty-yen fund; and in the third month she suddenly upped the stakes with a three hundred-yen fund. In the fourth month, she opened a five hundred-yen fund. She raised the requisite forty thousand yen in five months. Kim Shunpei paid close attention to Lee Young-hee's energy, initiative, and trustworthiness. The house had become a revolving door for multiple mutual funds and their investors.

Lee Young-hee also started a *sake* business with several of her investors. It was her way of treating them when they visited her house, but it was also her way of securing working capital for her funds. People gathered at her house to sell silk, Korean brassware, and other goods amongst themselves. When Lee Young-hee opened a new fund, the area around the house became an open-air market. Exhibitions happened six or seven times a month, and the inside of the house was in constant disarray. Hanako had to sometimes skip school to keep up with the cleaning.

Kim Shunpei bought the two empty houses across from them. He also added a second floor to one of the houses. In the span of two months, the houses were refurbished and installed with equipment. Neighbors and investors came by to observe the progress. They were astounded by the size of the cutting board, which measured a foot thick, six-and-a-half feet wide, and thirteen feet long.

"This looks like the real deal," said one of the investors, impressed.

Kim Shunpei didn't say much at all. He just told everyone that his end goal was to make *kamaboko*.

Kim Shunpei started negotiations with the central market, but the supplier put up some resistance, doubting whether he could get a license or not.

"I'll get the license soon, trust me. I need the fish shipments as soon as I do. Here's the deposit." Kim Shunpei put down one thousand yen to get the other party to trust him. The supplier couldn't complain about the amount.

After the refurbishments and installations were completed, Kim Shunpei went to visit Ko Nobuyoshi in the Miyukimori Shrine neighborhood, an area heavily damaged during the war. The jam-packed houses propped each other up, and the alleyways crisscrossed like a maze. The road from Ichijo Street to Miyukimori Shrine was lined with Korean shops that sold textiles, brassware, grains, spices, seafood, and more, and the residents of the street were mostly Korean. The first time Kim Shunpei went to visit Ko Nobuyoshi, he got lost. He had no idea what lay at the end of the alleyways as he meandered through the haphazardly placed houses. Children were everywhere, and their mothers called shrilly after them. The neighborhood was a carnivalesque symphony of married couples fighting, children crying, and machinery running.

Kim Shunpei caught sight of Ko Nobuyoshi's children running through an alleyway naked. The children remembered that Kim Shunpei sometimes used to give them pocket change, and they looked up at him with their mouths hanging open.

"Is Dad there?" Kim Shunpei asked them.

"Yeah," they said, nodding.

"Where's your house?" he asked, handing them a few sen. The kids led him to their house with pattering feet. Ko Nobuyoshi lived in a wooden barrack-style hut along one of the innumerable alley intersections. His wife Akemi manned a little shop that sold miscellaneous Korean items and foodstuffs. Ko Nobuyoshi was on duty and stood there looking bored as his children came up to him.

"I've been lookin' for you," called Kim Shunpei.

Ko Nobuyoshi broke into a grin and said, "Ah, Shunpei. Good to see you here." Ko Nobuyoshi seemed to have aged noticeably in the short while they hadn't seen each other. Behind the shop was a single four-and-a-half-*jo* room.

"Is *ajumeoni* here?" Kim Shunpei looked around, taking in his surroundings.

"She went to stock up on supplies. No choice with this trade," said Ko Nobuyoshi with a self-deprecating smile.

"We don't have much, but want a drink?" He went to the inner room and brought out a bottle of *shochu* with two cups, as well as some dried beltfish. "You're here on some business, aren't ya," said Ko Nobuyoshi in Korean. Kim Shunpei never was the type to visit people just for the sake of it.

"A few questions, is all. I decided to open a *kamaboko* factory. I have the factory and equipment all set up. All I need are workers."

"I've heard the rumors. This is a big deal. I also heard your wife has her hands in a couple mutual funds. She's got quite the reputation here too. Quite the go-getter, they say." Ko Nobuyoshi spoke with a hint of irony.

Everyone vaguely knew the money had been raised through mutual finance associations, but Kim Shunpei didn't want to be implicated in those rumors. He made a disgruntled expression, and Ko Nobuyoshi asked, "Have any workers yet?"

"I'm lookin' for 'em now. Which is why I'm here. Would you want to work for me?"

It was rare to hear Kim Shunpei ask something in such a reserved way—using the words "would you," no less. Ko Nobuyoshi had no reason to refuse. In fact, Kim

Shunpei's proposal was like a lifeboat for the man idly watching over his wife's shop. He was also pleased to be asked first.

"'Course I'll come work for you."

Kim Shunpei keenly felt his friendship with Ko Nobuyoshi in that moment. He said, "I'll have four workers to start with. And I'll be one of 'em for the time being."

"You get a license, by the way?" asked Ko Nobuyoshi.

"Not yet. I'm countin' on my son-in-law to get it for me."

"When?"

"It's a matter of time. Masahito said he just needs one last push."

"Without a license you won't get to work your equipment."

"I know. But even if I don't get it by the end of the month, I'll start working anyway. I can't wait any longer than that."

He was determined to act first and ask for forgiveness later. Whether it was raising funds or acquiring the license, he felt like he was walking a tightrope. He needed a breakthrough at any cost. If he failed, he had no choice

but to flee in disgrace. Establishing a *kamaboko* factory
was Kim Shunpei's gamble of a lifetime.

Han Masahito continued negotiations with the
municipal office, but regulation of the food supply was
on the national agenda. Even if the municipal office had
the ability to grant a license, national policy couldn't be
ignored so easily. But after several rounds of negotiations,
Han Masahito was told that the matter would be looked
into. He was optimistic that the authorities just needed a
final nudge, but two months passed without any updates.
Kim Shunpei pressed Han Masahito for news, saying he
would start the machines at the end of the year—not to
mention that the mutual funds were reaching maturity.
This wasn't a time to fold one's arms and do nothing.
They had to circumvent procedure. Han Masahito and
his comrades at the youth organization got three hundred
members of the Zainichi Compatriots to demonstrate
in front of the municipal office. In the meantime, Han
Masahito tried to finalize negotiations with the hostile
licensors.

"We'll lose face if we give in to your coercive mob. No
way we're doing that," a representative said, not hiding his
disgust.

"We're not a coercive mob. The Zainichi Compatriots are an organization that advocates for Zainichi rights and the Zainichi way of life. There are six hundred of us. Do you think you can ignore an organization with six hundred members? Do you remember what you did to us during the colonial period? We're entitled to compensation from the Japanese government. Compared to that, what's the problem with giving us a license or two? We'll protest here every day until you give us one. Tomorrow there will be five hundred people, the day after that a thousand, and the day after that ten thousand. You'll see what shared blood can do. It's up to you."

Han Masahito's threats were mostly bluster. The protest slogans weren't centered on licenses. They said things like "Protect our rights," "Give us compensation," and "Put the war criminals on trial." This was in the midst of the International Military Tribunal for the Far East, which commenced on May 3, 1946, and was a big shock for the Japanese.

But the municipal office didn't budge. Rather, they dug in their heels. The protests escalated. A licensing problem was becoming a political one. The municipal office thought Han Masahito's threats were full of hot air, and he himself knew that a thousand protesters was a tall order. But contrary to his expectations, the crowds swelled with each passing day, and even members of the Communist Party and Socialist Party showed up. The number of protesters exceeded a thousand, so naturally the municipal office requested the deployment of the riot police, and a tense standoff ensued. The situation had far exceeded Han Masahito's expectations, but he couldn't predict where it would go from there.

"This has gotten serious." Han Masahito was so nervous he had trouble eating.

How had it come to this? Judging from initial appearances, he thought it would be short work to resolve the matter. But the energy of the crowd was being channeled toward something else, and the protests were turning into pure chaos. They bore a close resemblance to the "mayday for food supplies" protests that had happened a year earlier. War veterans joined the crowd. The masses surrounded city hall and chanted in unison, "Give us food!" There was the strange sense that a *kamaboko* factory license was connected to this demand. The shrewd Han Masahito entered city hall alone and requested a meeting with the mayor, saying, "We have an important matter to discuss." The flustered city officials granted this activist a meeting with the mayor in order to bring the situation under control.

The junior officials, department head, and section chief ostentatiously showed Han Masahito into the mayor's office. The mayor sat at his desk, looking upset.

Han Masahito bowed politely and handed the mayor his business card. The mayor took the card and glared at Han Masahito. "What do you think you're trying to do, fanning the flames like this? If the rioters and the police clash, what do you think will happen?"

No one could have expected that the situation would magnify into such a crisis over a single license. The junior officials and department head sent Han Masahito dirty looks.

"I warned the section chief plenty of times. But none of you listened. You don't care about our urgent concerns. We had no choice but to use force."

"What are your urgent concerns? A single license?"

"Yes. A single license. Will you grant it to us?" Han Masahito applied pressure at the critical moment.

"How ludicrous. How can a license be so urgent? I'm speechless. So if we grant you a license, you'll break up the riots?"

"Yes, we will."

"All right. The department head will give you one. How tiresome." The mayor looked at Han Masahito like a dirty object and gestured at the section chief to take the man away.

Han Masahito left the office quickly, without having to be ushered out. He joined the protest and told the Zainichi Compatriots to fall back. He didn't know what would happen next. He'd ignited the whole thing, but the municipal office would be the one to clean up after him. Even after the Zainichi Koreans fell back, the communists and socialists and labor unions pressed on with their demands, showing no signs of leaving. A year ago, the mayday protests had been forcefully shut down by Douglas MacArthur, and the leftists wanted their revenge. But their ongoing protests were all the pretext the authorities needed. In the middle of the night, they arrested union leaders one after another. By the next morning, the leftists felt as if they were on a boat without a helmsman, and they vanished like the mist.

The spontaneous protests didn't bring about any kind of effect. During the mayday protests, the labor unions still worshiped the emperor and saw him as the ultimate authority, and they'd sent him a formal appeal. They were like farmers during the Tokugawa period, sending an appeal to the shogunate even if they had to die for their audacity. The leftists' tactics for this protest were just as thin. The police decided to target the unions even after the protest ended. But the police didn't extend their offensive to the Zainichi Koreans. They perhaps thought it unwise to rile them up so soon after they'd been liberated from colonial rule.

Ten days later, Han Masahito visited city hall and received the license from the section chief. All the while, the section chief regarded Han Masahito with an annoyed, scornful expression.

Kim Shunpei was overjoyed by the news. He could start factory operations under clear skies.

"You did well. Good lad, you are." Kim Shunpei rarely complimented anyone. "You can treat yourself with this." Kim Shunpei handed him a one hundred-yen bill.

Han Masahito was offended. Was that one hundred-yen bill what Kim Shunpei thought of the work it took to mobilize the Zainichi Compatriots, bring in the Japanese labor unions, and even face off with the dangerous riot police to get that license in his hand? It was worth hundreds of yen. It was the necessary precondition for Kim Shunpei's business. Han Masahito was no errand boy, and Kim Shunpei was just being stingy. Han Masahito refused to accept the bill, his pride wounded. Kim Shunpei couldn't just let the bill hang there, so he turned to Harumi awkwardly and said, "Use this to buy the kids some new clothes or something."

Han Masahito was loath to let his wife accept the money, but they had no other choice.

"Thank you," said Harumi, bowing her head meekly. But the tension in the air didn't go away. Lee Young-hee watched the exchange anxiously. She was about to get more *sake* when Han Masahito announced, "We'll be leaving now." He stood up from the table. Harumi hoisted her child on her back and followed him out.

"What nerve! Actin' all high and mighty. Who does he think he is?" Kim Shunpei looked as if he wanted to tear the license up.

As the days passed, Lee Young-hee felt as if they were walking on thin ice with the maturing mutual funds. If they dallied on production and couldn't pay dividends to their shareholders, they would be ruined.

She anxiously hoped the tiff between Kim Shunpei and Han Masahito wouldn't turn into something bigger. She couldn't make out what Kim Shunpei's intentions were when he told Han Masahito to "treat himself" with the one hundred-yen bill. There were definitely other ways to repay him. She didn't know what Han Masahito was expecting, but she understood his feelings. It was likely that Kim Shunpei had offered the one hundred-yen bill as an afterthought. He surely would need Han Masahito's help as he continued with his business, considering that he couldn't read or write. But the two men were digging themselves into a ditch over this trivial difference in opinion.

Han Masahito lashed out at Harumi when they returned home. "Why'd you accept the money? I'm not an errand boy. I didn't run around like that for the money. I want everyone to be just a little better off, dammit. That guy may be big and tall and all, but he has no balls. I've never been this pissed off."

"Well, what else could I have done? Not accept it? What then?"

"What then? You're saying he'd hit me, right? What can a scoundrel like him do to me? He knows how to be violent and nothing else. Your father has ice running through his veins, not blood."

"That man isn't my *abeoji!*" cried Harumi.

The child on Harumi's back started crying, alarmed at the sharpness of her voice. Harumi's tone expressed years of resentment against Kim Shunpei.

Han Masahito knew that Kim Shunpei wasn't Harumi's biological father. A friend had told him about that after his formal marriage interview, but it was never a matter of great concern to him. Once he saw the beautiful, gentle Harumi, he knew he wanted to make her his wife. Harumi did have a truly gentle disposition. She never spoke maliciously about other people, and she never grumbled even when they were as poor as dirt. Harumi showed more consideration and kindness to Kim Shunpei than a normal daughter would. That same Harumi had just said that Kim Shunpei wasn't her *abeoji*. This was proof that she still was thinking about her real father, the one she'd never met.

Harumi took the crying child in her arms and breastfed him. She was surprised at herself for letting her mouth run like that. Tears flowed down her cheeks.

Chapter 17

On the first day of production, Kim Shunpei woke up at four in the morning. He put on a brown shirt over brown pants, latched his cherry tree club to his belt, put on a felt hat, and took a hook with him before leaving for the central market. It was as if he were heading out for battle. He took the first train to the market and spent some time observing the riverside fish auction. The auctioneer's hoarse voice was unbearably alluring to Kim Shunpei. It reminded him of the open-air markets in Korea. But Kim Shunpei moved away from the auction and headed for Naniwa-*ya*, the fish supplier for his former workplace Toho Industries. He needed a lot of fish, and Naniwa-*ya* would be a more efficient way of getting them than attending an auction. The prices were cheaper too, since one could buy directly from the fishing boats. Naniwa-

ya also undertook the shipping. The three-wheeled cart was filled to the brim with fish, and Kim Shunpei sat in the passenger seat, urging the driver on toward the new factory.

The dark early morning sky turned gradually into a dazzling blue. The area around Taisho Ward was a vast field of burnt wreckage. Shanties dotted the landscape here and there. A man stood at an earthen charcoal brazier in front of his makeshift hovel, staring after the cart. From the passenger seat, Kim Shunpei could look around at his leisure, and he didn't see a single proper building. The buildings that the fires had spared stood out from the landscape, stark and eerie. Starving people were everywhere. As Kim Shunpei and the driver passed through the Tsuruhashi black market area, the number of starving people multiplied, and the cart got stuck in the crowd. The wholesale goods store for seafood and paste products was in a separate block of land linked to the Tsuruhashi black market area, accessible from Tsuruhashi Station. Bicycles, bicycle trailers, and horse-drawn carts threaded their way through the maze-like streets.

"Stop the car 'round there and wait for me."

There wasn't any room to park on the narrow street.

The driver had no choice but to back up and go out onto the road that ran along the tram tracks.

Kim Shunpei got off and went to the wholesale goods store to follow up about his production schedule.

"You're finally licensed, eh. That's no joke. The people at Manada-*ya* and Mikawa-*ya* must've gone to city hall a hundred times to get a license, but they were always turned away at the gates. Amazing that you could manage it. In any case, looking forward to doing business with ya. Not much of that stuff to go around, is there? We're counting on you to think of us first."

With a cunning twinkle in his eye, the owner of Yamato Wholesale Goods laid out some advance cash. Neither of them knew yet if the *kamaboko* would sell well or not, but Kim Shunpei counted the amount and grinned broadly. This was just the beginning. The Manada and Mikawa stores also gave him advances. After visiting eight wholesale stores, Kim Shunpei had four thousand yen. He couldn't stop shaking. The world was full of people who toiled and toiled for just ten yen. Was there any other trade that could get him four thousand yen in a single day? Added value accrued to products that appeared to be of high quality. While a lot of people were starving, plenty of rich people were eager to lay their hands on fancy *kamaboko*. The value of *kamaboko* increased all the more because the city produced so little of it. The high-class restaurants frequented by black-market profiteers spared no expense for it.

When Kim Shunpei returned to his factory, he unloaded the dozens of crates of fish by himself. He didn't get tired. The four thousand yen in his shirt pocket kept him going.

He ate lunch and took a nap. When he went back to the factory at two in the afternoon, he saw the new cutting board laden with fruit, rice cakes, and flowers, and a shaman was sprinkling *sake* around the bathroom, the equipment, and the delivery truck. Lee Young-hee had asked a shaman to bless this factory as it embarked on its journey. Kim Shunpei didn't believe in gods or demons, but he understood why Lee Young-hee did, and he stood by respectfully.

Ko Nobuyoshi showed up a little later. He saw the piles of fish and said, "Time to get to work. How many years has it been since I held a knife?" He unwrapped three knives from his rolled-up newspaper and inspected them closely.

"Come up with a name yet?" asked Kim Shunpei. The provisional name of the factory was written on the license, but he'd wanted to change it ever since things got awkward with Han Masahito.

"I did. How about 'Asahi Industries'? Makes you think of the energy of the rising sun."

"Energy of the rising sun, eh. Not bad."

The four thousand yen in his shirt pocket indeed felt like the energy of the rising sun. Ko Nobuyoshi wrote "Asahi Industries" on a piece of scrap paper and gave it to Kim Shunpei, who had a sign made at Isshinto, a nearby workshop. He hung the sign above the factory entrance and looked at it with satisfaction. Kaneko Yu (formerly Kim Yu) and Kimura Masayuki showed up for work shortly after Ko Nobuyoshi. The stout, square-faced Kaneko had a hangover. As soon as he arrived, he dunked his face and head under the water spout.

"Again? You think you can show up to work like this?" complained Ko Nobuyoshi. He was the one who'd introduced Kaneko to Kim Shunpei.

"Whatever. I'm always hungover," said Kaneko defensively.

"And where's your knife?" asked Ko Nobuyoshi.

"Sorry. Don't have it," said Kaneko, hanging his head sheepishly.

"Don't have it, huh. Had it stolen from you at the gambling den, I s'pose?"

Kaneko scratched his head.

"You're amazing, you are. You think you can call yourself a *kamaboko* worker without a knife?"

Normally, *kamaboko* workers had three or four personal knives on hand. Ko Nobuyoshi had carefully prepared three knives for himself the day before. But Kaneko had to use a factory knife.

Kimura Masayuki was a Japanese worker recruited by Kim Shunpei. He'd been deployed to Yamaguchi Prefecture during the war and returned to Osaka after Japan lost. A month ago, he crossed paths with Kim Shunpei at the Tsuruhashi black market. They were old gambling friends. He had a short temper, but he was a reliable and skilled worker.

The four workers began their shift. They dumped the fish onto the cutting board and removed the guts. The fish were then washed and fed to the compressor. The sound of the springy new machines was pleasing to the ear. For grilling, the workers used high-grade charcoal produced from ubame oak. Kim Shunpei was choosy about his charcoal. The workers ate at six in the evening, midnight, and five in the morning. Lee Young-hee and Hanako's job was to make the workers' meals. Hanako worked until midnight and left for school the following morning.

Kaneko was an alcoholic. He chopped fish with one hand and drank rice wine with the other. He cleansed his palette with a bite of kimchi. But within two hours he was back at his drink. By the end of his shift he was quite drunk. It was Kaneko's style of work. The other workers also drank during their shift. They could hardly lift their noses from the grindstone once work started, and rice wine was a pleasant distraction.

At four in the morning, the workers started transporting the *kamaboko* to the wholesalers. That was when Kim Shunpei awoke Sung-han from his deep sleep.

"Sung-han, get up! And I mean now!"

Sung-han looked up blearily at his father.

"You'll do calculations for me."

"What kind of calculations?"

"Just get a pen and notebook. And follow me."

Sung-han did as he was told and followed his father downstairs. His mother was in the kitchen making breakfast for the workers. All the other houses in the neighborhood were dark. Sung-han felt the illusoriness of the early morning hour.

The workers in the factory were packing the *kamaboko* into boxes.

"Sleepy, huh? Must be tough for you, kid," said Kaneko drunkenly.

"Sung-han, write down what I say. Mikawa-*ya*, two hundred rolls, 22 yen for each roll. How much is it?"

Sung-han wrote down what his father said and calculated the total as 4,400 yen. Kim Shunpei tore off the note and handed it to Kimura, who was in charge of transportation.

"Now jot down the names and amounts for the others."

Ko Nobuyoshi noticed Kim Shunpei's sloppy way of handling things, but he kept silent, knowing that the man disliked meddlers when it came to money.

Kimura piled the truck bed with boxes of *kamaboko*, bound them tightly with a rope, slipped the "bill" into his breast pocket, and drove off. It took about twelve minutes to drive to Tsuruhashi from Taisei Street. For eight stores, the process lasted about two hours. Kimura came back grumbling about how tired he was. Kim Shunpei decided he had to buy another truck.

Another problem was getting a phone. Kim Shunpei counted on Naniwa-*ya* to supply fish for him, but the fish varieties differed by the day, and Kim Shunpei had to go to the central market every morning. A phone would save him a lot of time and energy, but according to the phone company, he would have to wait up to a year and a half to have the wiring installed on the premises. Kim Shunpei instead dished out an exorbitant amount for a black-market phone. Though his expenses were piling up, so too were his sales.

Every morning, Sung-han was forced to get up by his father to write out the bills, and when he returned home from school, he had to write out the receipts as Kim Shunpei counted the amounts in front of the wholesalers. Sometimes Sung-han had to go collect the money himself.

"Impressive for a kid, aren't ya? But be careful. Carrying around this much cash puts a big red target on your back," warned the Yamato-*ya* owner.

A month after the start of production, the factory was bringing in over four hundred yen per day. Their sales rivalled those of a *kamaboko* factory with sixty or seventy workers.

Orders increased by the day, and after three months two more workers were hired. The factory still couldn't keep up with demand, and after another three months, three more workers were hired. The small, cramped factory was practically buried in fish and finished products, so a long, narrow warehouse was annexed to Kim Shunpei's property for charcoal storage. The owner of the warehouse was terrified of Kim Shunpei and didn't oppose him. There was no place to store all the fish and commodities unless he expanded the factory grounds, which meant constructing a new factory. But Kim Shunpei didn't listen to the opinions of his workers. The factory was literally overflowing with fish: crates of them were stacked in two or three rows and spilled over into the narrow alleyways, filling the air with its stench. Mr. Kang, who lived further down the alleyway and kept pigs in his *genkan,* complained to Kim Shunpei one day. In response, Kim Shunpei emptied out ten crates in front of Mr. Kang's door and said, "Feed your swine with this, then!" Since then, the neighbors withdrew silently into the shadows.

The production quotas grew and grew, and Lee Young-hee and Hanako toiled without end. It was no ordinary task to feed nine hungry workers three daily meals. They fed the workers the same kind of fish that went into the *kamaboko*, but the menu couldn't stay the same day in and day out. Lee Young-hee became sleep-deprived after months of having to shop and cook fresh meals from three in the afternoon to five in the morning. She thought she would soon collapse from overwork. But she didn't complain. Until she could liquidate the funds she'd raised, she had to grit her teeth and work. Hanako helped her, often past midnight.

Ko Nobuyoshi sometimes came in for a bottle of rice wine during his shift and asked with a concerned look, "Everything alright?"

"Yes, I'm fine," Lee Young-hee replied, smiling.

Lee Young-hee's body was showing her age and her accumulated fatigue. She thought it impossible at this point to change the course of her life, which was headed straight toward her own decrepitude. *I'll have to start preparing for my journey beyond* . . . . she thought to herself. Would she reach the Pure Land? Could she rely on the mercy of Kannon to release her from the drudgery of this world? When would that day come . . . ?

Lee Young-hee nodded off as she stared at the fire in the hearth.

Lee Young-hee opened a number of mutual funds weekly, and about twenty investors held shares in each fund. Both floors of the small house would be packed with people talking and laughing, bringing liveliness into the house when otherwise there was none. Lee Young-hee was always hospitable to the investors and gifted them with *kamaboko*, much to their delight.

"You must be so pleased with your husband's success! It makes me envious," said one of the investors.

"It's quite something. No one could've expected an alcoholic like him to turn it around like this. You really stuck it out."

From the outside, it did look like Lee Young-hee was to be envied. Rumor had it that Kim Shunpei was a millionaire and that Lee Young-hee was living a life of ease. The number of people interested in buying her shares increased. But Lee Young-hee wasn't inclined to set up any more mutual funds. Instead, she wanted to settle her accounts as soon as possible. It would take another three years for that to happen. Kim Shunpei was thus far repaying his loan in installments, but he could change his mind at any given moment. She knew his personality well, and it was a constant source of anxiety. She could see the signs of something untoward happening already.

Since starting the factory, Kim Shunpei had stopped drinking himself to oblivion and curbed his violent behavior. One could say he was now too busy to get drunk, but it was also clear that he was pouring himself into his one chance to succeed in life. By the half-year mark, his business was going according to plan. However, his abnormal fixation on money was making his family recoil. The ravenous workers consumed as much as fifteen gallons of rice in a single day, and the amount of vegetables and other foods Lee Young-hee had to buy increased dramatically. Mrs. Ishihara next door supplied Lee Young-hee with rice, but when Lee Young-hee presented Kim Shunpei with the food bills, he would screw his face up and yell, "What, you ran outta rice already?"

This pattern extended to the children's school bills as well. Kim Shunpei raised a fuss when his children needed money for tuition, school meals, and school supplies.

One day, Hanako showed up in Kim Shunpei's inner room and meekly requested money to pay for her tuition.

"Money, money, money! You think I'm a money tree, don't you!" he screamed, rolling up a wad of cash and throwing it at Hanako. She picked up the cash, crying silently. Soon after that, Hanako withdrew from school altogether. When Lee Young-hee tried to persuade her to at least graduate from middle school, she firmly refused. Just as when she'd attempted suicide, it was her way of getting back at her father.

Lee Young-hee never asked for money to cover their living costs. Living costs were separate from the cost of feeding the workers, which was supposed to be included in the factory budget like the workers' salaries. But Kim Shunpei was convinced that all the money he earned was being eaten up by his family. He had no conception of family responsibility. He never used to buy his children clothes or gym shoes. Why did he have to pay for them now? He voiced this reasoning every time his family needed money. He would quickly yank back the money he'd held out and give the other person a hard look, deliberating. He sometimes wore a look of confusion. Lee Young-hee or one of the children felt a twinge of guilt at such moments. They knew the only thing binding them to Kim Shunpei was this economic transaction. It was a relationship everyone reluctantly endured.

Kim Shunpei suspected that Lee Young-hee was spending some of the money on rice wine. "You dare use the rice for my workers to make rice wine?"

Tired of Kim Shunpei's groundless accusations, Lee Young-hee started paying for half the rice bill herself, and eventually she stopped charging him completely. Of course, this placed a heavy burden on Lee Young-hee. She had hoped that the factory would make her more secure, but the household finances were on fire. For two months, she fed the workers from her own pocket to avoid angering her husband, but the situation didn't improve. Lee Young-hee gave up hope, feeling like she couldn't go on for much longer. Hanako became more and more bewildered. By this point, Kim Shunpei was once again drinking and behaving violently. But he couldn't satisfy himself with the level of violence he'd committed in the past. He was now the manager of nine workers, and their daily sustenance was non-negotiable. If he destroyed the house the way he used to, he couldn't expect Lee Young-hee to make the workers their meals. Not to mention that the repairs and the work slowdowns would cost him money.

Lee Young-hee turned to hawking Korean clothing, pottery, and other goods. Hanako, no longer a student, offered herself up as her mother's replacement. She worked in the kitchen day and night as if she had no other choice. She appeared to be working herself past the point of exhaustion. Some of the neighborhood women took pity on her and started helping her out. Kim Shunpei loathed Hanako's willfulness.

Whenever Sung-han returned from school, he left again with a handbag to collect money from the eight wholesale stores. He spent some time chatting with the shopkeepers, who were mystified by the fact that no one mugged Sung-han for the heaps of money he carried around.

Sung-han squirreled away twenty or thirty yen from each haul. It wasn't particularly difficult, considering that a day's sale could amount to forty thousand or fifty thousand yen. Sung-han took advantage of his father's illiteracy by fudging the sales slips. He used this money to lavish his friends with gifts, and sometimes he gave Hanako spending money too. Hanako was aware that the money wasn't technically Sung-han's, but she accepted it anyway and used it to buy side dishes for the workers' meals. In that way, part of the stolen money was recycled back into the factory.

The rationing system for food establishments was now lifted, and restaurants and noodle shops could finally operate freely. Sung-han frequented the noodle shop on the corner of the main thoroughfare. The shopkeeper told him, "Hey, Sung-han-*chan*, could you supply me with some *kamaboko*? I can give you free meals here in return."

Sung-han was happy to oblige. He brought four or five packs of *kamaboko* to the noodle shop every day.

Prices sharply increased due to inflation. A bowl of udon used to cost six sen in 1944, but now it cost fifteen yen. The *kamaboko* Sung-han smuggled into the shop more than sufficiently compensated for his free meal. The meals at home were the same for him and Hanako as it was for the workers. Sung-han was tired of Hanako's hodgepodge stews and ate udon at the shop every day. He also started diverting packs of *kamaboko* into the black market by way of the shopkeeper. Sung-han would wait for Kim Shunpei to leave and then boldly carry away up to twenty packs of *kamaboko*. The other workers didn't pry into Sung-han's affairs, nor did they report him to

Kim Shunpei. They knew that if they did, Sung-han's father would beat him until he could no longer stand. Sung-han was able to save up three thousand yen. He showed the thick roll of cash to Hanako and said, "Hana-*chan*, with this, we could run away from home whenever we want."

"I really wish I could be as carefree as you," she said enviously.

The *kamaboko* factory was prospering. Now wholesale stores outside of Tsuruhashi were also putting in orders for four a.m. deliveries. Some of them made deals with the workers beforehand and reserved whole batches for an extra two yen per roll. For this reason, the workers would secretly set some *kamaboko* aside, and the kickbacks they got were used for the purchase of alcohol. They were frightened of Kim Shunpei, of course, but they covered for each other and had clever tricks up their sleeve. Only three workers, including Ko Nobuyoshi, didn't engage in these underhanded dealings. Ko Nobuyoshi had no inclination to expose the others and pretended not to notice anything. It would be a different story if their profits started to fall, but there was no sign of that happening. In the past year, Kim Shunpei was reaping massive profits, which would likely multiply in the future. The workers thus had no qualms about earning some drinking money for themselves. In fact, the workers' salaries were too low. They tried a few times to negotiate a raise, but Kim Shunpei stubbornly refused every time. Kim Shunpei would yell, "If you little shits wanna complain, come forward! I'll settle the score with you!" He would then stab a knife into the cutting board and glare at them all. None of the workers dared to quit either. The economy was in poor shape, and there were no guarantees that another job would be waiting for them. Kim Shunpei ruled Asahi Industries by fear.

One day, Kim Shunpei appeared at the factory with a seedy-looking woman. She looked like she was in her early twenties and was wearing a worn-out shirt over work pants. Her short hair accentuated her narrow, inset eyes and her pug nose. She scratched incessantly at her stick-like arms.

"Here's the new cooking girl," Kim Shunpei announced to Hanako in the kitchen.

"Nice to meet you," said the girl nervously, tipping her head forward in a slight bow. She avoided looking at Hanako directly. Her eyes resembled a blank sheet of glass without any focal point. Her sticky hair clung to her head, and she looked like she hadn't bathed in several days. Hanako immediately wondered if the girl would be a live-in worker. Where would she sleep? Her question was answered the next day. Kim Shunpei had a carpenter build a two-*jo* room next to the *genkan*. Construction took three days, and then the girl moved in.

Lee Young-hee was repelled by the sight of the girl. Even her way of speaking was dirty. She suspected that the girl was giving Kim Shunpei sexual favors.

The girl took a bath and put on new clothes. She forced out a smile when she saw Lee Young-hee, showing her gums and stubby teeth. She looked like someone Kim Shunpei had picked up from the streets. He must have hired this starving, forsaken girl to be a kitchen maid. Lee Young-hee clearly saw what Kim Shunpei's intentions were. Since Lee Young-hee refused to sleep with him, he'd brought this girl here under the pretext of employing her. What he really intended to do was spite Lee Young-hee.

The girl's name was Misako. Misako was responsible for preparing the midnight and morning meals, so Hanako only had to prepare the afternoon meal.

Hanako's heavy burdens were eased. But now the house had turned into a love shack for her father and Misako. Misako was always waiting for Kim Shunpei like a bitch in heat. Ever since her first night in the house, she didn't bother to stifle her moans as she had sex with Kim Shunpei in the inner room. She moaned so loudly that the others wondered if the neighbors could hear her. Lee Young-hee plugged her ears on the second floor, full of shame, but she also felt something like jealousy over the girl, who could apparently climax multiple times in sequence. Lee Young-hee's long-lost memories of sexual pleasure came back. Such feelings humiliated her and reminded her of the pain of being a woman. What were her children thinking, in any case? She peeked at them to make sure they were sleeping.

Hanako knew that sex was a normal adult activity. She heard Misako's animal-like groans and felt sorry for her, assuming Misako was a victim of her father's bullying. But Misako didn't sound like she was being abused; her groans rather sounded like exclamations of joy.

Kim Shunpei enjoyed Misako day and night. She wasn't a pretty girl, but she gradually took on a coquettish luster. Her eyes in particular shone more than before.

She never used to say anything or look anyone in the eye, but now she chatted with the workers and sometimes convulsed with laughter in front of them. The workers were aroused by her vulgar laugh and her bowlegged strut.

"Just like the ass of a pig," said Kaneko, lecherously following Misako with his eyes as she walked away from them.

"Have a go at her. She'll do it with anyone," urged Kimura.

"Get real! The boss would kill me," said Kaneko, giggling.

Misako barely stayed in the two-*jo* room that was built for her. When she wasn't working in the kitchen, she was ready to receive Kim Shunpei at any moment. After sex, she slept in the inner room. She was Kim Shunpei's live-in mistress.

Misako always woke up past noon. After washing her face, she applied makeup using her hand mirror. She spent a long time at it. She spread copious amounts of white powder on her face as if she were painting a wall. She gazed at herself in the mirror, flashing a smile with her bright red lipstick and then hanging her head and looking sad. She put on various performances in order to make herself more enticing for Kim Shunpei. She role-played various scenarios and practiced all kinds of facial expressions. She could even make her face drip with tears. Then she left for the market, humming happily.

As if to show the workers that she belonged to Kim Shunpei, she wheedled at him like a child. "Hey, Boss, I want *geta* sandals. Could you buy a pair for me? Please?" The workers watched Kim Shunpei for his reaction. Misako was acting without any shame, as if she wanted to seduce the workers as well.

Kim Shunpei looked disgusted and said, "Go away!" He wasn't really angry at her, though. He wanted to make it look like he disapproved of her antics.

Lee Young-hee occasionally bumped into Misako inside or outside the house. When that happened, Misako would turn her face away in a huff. She was getting more arrogant by the day and making Hanako do her shopping for her.

"Hana-*chan*, mind gettin' the eggs for me?" asked Misako as she combed her hair. When Hanako returned with the eggs, she said, "Could you go get the tofu too? And the cabbage and onions while you're at it."

135

At this point Misako had taken charge of the food expenses and decided on the menu. Hanako had no power to complain.

"Why should I follow her orders? It's ridiculous. Mom, you really plan on living like this? I can't stand it. We can't even go outside, it's so embarrassing. Sung-han keeps saying we should run away, and I agree with him at this point." Hanako vented all her frustrations onto her mother. She was at a sensitive age, and she couldn't understand her mother's complacency. How could her mother let this stranger intrude on the family like this, even if her marriage was loveless?

"That's enough. Hana-*chan*, I know you want to go to dressmaking school. How 'bout I pay for it? Without a job you'll end up like me, you know. I'm excited to see you grow up."

Lee Young-hee couldn't give Hanako a straight answer. Nor could she be expected to. This wasn't Kim Shunpei's first affair. What Lee Young-hee couldn't stand was that he was having an affair in her own house. But she guessed this situation wouldn't last long. Misako hadn't yet gotten a full idea of Kim Shunpei's cruel, unpredictable personality. Not just anyone got to see what he was truly made of. Misako had taken one step inside his world, but soon enough she would come face-to-face with his violence and get a taste of the kind of fear that would drive her nearly mad. It was only a matter of time.

The streets baked in the summer sun. Heat curled off the surface of the streets even in the shade. Everyone splashed themselves with water, but it just clung to their skin, gathering heat.

Lee Young-hee left early in the morning to peddle her wares, and Sung-han and his friends went to the Yamato River to swim. And Kim Shunpei left for the central market, as he did two or three times a month, to survey fish varieties, discuss market prices, and deliver down payments.

Misako went to bed at seven in the morning, after clearing the dishes from the workers' early morning meal. She no longer bothered to wash the dishes, making Hanako do it instead. Misako laid out the futon, changed into her nightclothes, and waited for Kim Shunpei to come back. This was the daily routine. When Kim Shunpei came into the room, he looked down at Misako, who lay there with her robes untied and her thighs spread out. He took off his clothes and groped her all over. Her young, supple body demanded sexual pleasure to the point of greed. When his penis entered her, she arched back and screamed, "Ah!"

Misako put her fleshy lips to Kim Shunpei's chest and sucked on it like a leech. Once he started thrusting, she climaxed immediately. "I can't take it. You'll make me die if you keep goin'," she muttered incoherently, wrapping her arms tightly around him. "Do it from behind. Make me feel filthy."

Misako's appetite for sex was nearly bottomless. Only Kim Shunpei could satisfy it.

The neighborhood women were drawing water from the pump and doing their washing. The streetcars and buses rumbled down the main street, causing the old tenement houses to tremble slightly. When Misako first arrived here, she thought the rumble of the streetcar was an earthquake, and she ran outside in a panic.

Misako and Kim Shunpei fell back on the futon, exhausted. Misako fell asleep with her robes left open, but Kim Shunpei got up shortly afterward to change clothes and return to the central market.

The sun was shining brightly overhead. The voice of a goldfish peddler cut through the strange silence of noon, stirring in Kim Shunpei a faraway memory. No one else was out on the streets. Kaneko crept out of the factory and went into Lee Young-hee's house with an innocent expression on his face. He passed through the kitchen and glanced toward the inner room before going out the back. The glass door was shut, but the back door to the room was flung wide open to let in the air. Misako was sleeping with her robes splayed around her and her thighs spread open. Kaneko had a clear view of her black thicket of pubic hair. Her breasts looked like sand dunes, rising and falling with each breath, and her nipples were full and round. Kaneko crawled on all fours into the room. After taking off his clothes, he put his tongue to Misako's crotch. Misako awoke at the sensation. Then she felt something penetrate her. She twisted her body around to get this unfamiliar body off her, but the thing inside her body seemed to fuse itself to her. She was overpowered.

"It's me." Kaneko looked down at Misako.

"Stop," said Misako. "If the boss sees this, he's gonna kill you."

"It'll be fine. He won't come back 'til evening."

"But what if someone else catches us?"

"They won't. Look, I'm head over heels for ya, see?"

Kaneko bent down and stuck his tongue into Misako's mouth. She didn't resist. The kiss was long and wet. Misako breathed harder.

"You really like me?" asked Misako.

"You bet." Kaneko moved his hips and checked Misako for a response.

Misako moved her hips in turn. "You really do? No one's said that to me before." It was hard to believe him. But she wanted to believe him.

"I mean it. I really do," Kaneko whispered into Misako's ear, delivering the coup de grace.

"You really do, huh . . . ." Misako's voice came out like a whine, tinged with both doubt and deep emotion.

Hanako went down to the first floor to wash the pots and dishes from the previous meal and begin preparations for the three o'clock meal. She then heard some unexpected moaning. The glass door to the inner room was translucent except for the top pane, which Hanako peeked through. Misako was on all fours, and Kaneko had her in a nelson hold. Hanako's breath came up short, and she started to feel dizzy. The man and woman looked like dirty animals. Hanako ran outside, where the sunlight blazed in her eyes. Both the sunlight and the image of the two copulating animals were burnt into her retinas. Why did human adults have sex like that? And why was Misako doing it with Kaneko? She thought Misako belonged only to Kim Shunpei, but did she belong to Kaneko too? Impossible. Misako was a cheating slut. Hanako couldn't forgive her. But she couldn't tell anyone. She couldn't admit that she'd seen something forbidden.

After some time had passed, Kaneko snuck out of the house and innocently went back to the factory. What was Misako doing now? Hanako felt like even seeing Misako's face would disgust her, but she went back inside and started washing the dishes. Misako appeared in the kitchen wearing a new *yukata*.

"Sorry 'bout that, I'll wash 'em," said Misako kindly.

"It's fine. You can leave." Hanako kept put, not wanting to get close to Misako.

"Is that so? Well, I'll go shoppin' for the food, then." Misako put on her new *geta* sandals and left through the back door with her shopping basket. As Hanako squatted over the dishes, the image of the two copulating animals wouldn't leave her mind. She felt an urge to tell her father what she'd seen and watch everything get smashed to pieces.

Kim Shunpei returned in the late afternoon. He looked a little tipsy, but he also looked pleased about whatever transaction he'd completed.

"Welcome home," crooned Misako, clopping over to Kim Shunpei in her *geta* sandals. Hanako was delivering dinner to the workers in the factory and stared hatefully at Misako sidling up to Kim Shunpei. Her duped father also looked ridiculous. He'd bought Misako nice *geta* sandals with red straps, but he'd never bought his own children so much as a pair of socks. Hanako remembered how he'd thrown a roll of cash at her head when she asked him for tuition money. It served him right to get cheated on.

Throughout the night shift, Misako joked and laughed with the workers as usual, but she avoided looking at Kaneko. She was terrified by what would happen if any of the other workers caught on to their affair and ratted them out. But she and Kaneko were so driven by lust that they met up behind Kim Shunpei's back. When Kim Shunpei came home drunk, Misako fed him more alcohol and soothed him with pretty words until he fell asleep. After making sure that he wouldn't wake up, Misako snuck out of the house and went behind Benten Market to wait for Kaneko in a small storage room beside the dumpsters.

Kaneko stepped out in the middle of his shift, saying he needed a quick drink. None of the others thought this was unusual. Kaneko used to raid the rice wine in Lee Young-hee's house right under her nose, but Lee Young-hee had since quit the *sake* trade, and now the workers had to bike to the liquor shop a kilometer away. But this bought Kaneko more time. He and Misako had hurried sex while standing half-naked in the storage room. The smell of the dumpsters in the tiny storage room only sharpened their lust for each other. But no matter how careful they were, they couldn't cover up their own affectations. Something was clearly off when Misako and Kim Shunpei had sex. Misako expressed herself slightly differently when her heart wasn't in it. At some point, sex with Kim Shunpei started to feel like a chore. Kim Shunpei didn't fail to notice this subtle change. Smoking a cigarette on the futon, he asked casually, "Not feeling so great, huh?"

"It's not that . . . ." said Misako, but she felt Kim Shunpei bristle. It wasn't that Kim Shunpei had proof of anything, but the seeds of doubt had now been sown.

Misako felt his eyes on her. Those sharp eyes seemed to easily read what was in her heart, and she wanted to confess to him right then and there.

Later that night, Misako met Kaneko in the storage room and told him that Kim Shunpei suspected her.

"No way. You sure it's not all in your head?"

"I'm sure. He suspects me."

Kaneko looked grave. It was dangerous for them to be meeting tonight.

"Is the boss sleepin'?"

Misako nodded.

Now wasn't a time to be careless.

"What do we do?" Misako's voice trembled.

Kaneko held his breath and strained his ears for any noise outside. The rotten smell of garbage filled their noses. They couldn't move, terrified of Kim Shunpei's shadow. Kaneko regretted ever seducing Misako. She looked ugly to him.

"Go home," he said.

"I can't. I don't know what the boss is gonna do to me."

"What else can you do? Run away? You have no money. Where you gonna go?"

"I have money. The boss gave me an allowance to buy

food with."

"How much?"

"Twelve-hundred yen." Misako pulled out her wallet from the sash in her kimono and showed him the money.

They were convinced that Kim Shunpei had woken up and was tracking them. This was no time to dawdle. Kaneko had never meant to get together with Misako, but twelve-hundred yen could sustain them for two or three months.

The moon flickered among the moving clouds. Misako and Kaneko waited for the clouds to darken the area before they left the storage room. They set out for Tsuruhashi Station. It was past midnight, and the area around the station was full of vagrants rummaging through the black-market trash. Kaneko's mind whirled. Where should he go, west or east? In any case, he had to leave Osaka as soon as he could.

"Where are we going?" asked Misako uneasily.

"Dunno. East? To Tokyo?"

"Tokyo?"

"That's right. No jobs in the countryside, are there? But Tokyo has 'em. And the boss won't chase us all the way there. Too many people in Tokyo."

When they reached the station, they had to wait another two hours for the first train.

"It's dangerous to wait here. Let's walk to Tamatsukuri or Morinomiya."

They walked for the next two hours until they made it to Kyobashi Station. Around this station, too, the vagrants wandered, picking their way through the remains of the black market there. A woman sat at the end of the road, breastfeeding her baby. Kaneko and Misako weren't sure if the skinny man lying next to her was alive or dead.

Misako bought two tickets for Osaka Station, and they passed through the gate. About forty people were on the platform waiting for the first train. Everyone looked like they were on supply runs—everyone except Misako and Kaneko, who only had the clothes on their backs. Soon the train arrived. Misako and Kaneko melted into the crowd and boarded the train.

Chapter 18

"I really don't get those two. Behind the boss's back? Since when?" said forty-two-year-old Tanimoto, looking around carefully as he separated fish guts.

"I knew something was up. Kaneko wasn't even at the *sake* shop when he said he'd be. Guess he was fucking Misako instead," said Kakizaki thoughtfully as he fed minced fish parts into the mixer along with salt, sugar, and flour.

"But where were they even doin' it?" wondered Son Fumiyo.

"You could do it anywhere if you wanted to," said the older Tanimoto, as if he were speaking from a wealth of personal experience.

"Like on the streets?" asked Son Fumiyo bluntly.

"The streets are fair game as any. I'd know that," said

Kakizaki, sneering at Son Fumiyo's naivete.

"Kaneko must've been really horny. I don't think I could've gotten it up for that ugly cow," said Son Fumiyo bitterly.

"You don't get it, do you? You can't judge a woman based on how good her face looks," snapped Kakizaki.

Son Fumiyo had nothing to say in response.

"Go back to work if you have nothing good to say. If the boss overhears you . . ." warned the manager Ko Nobuyoshi.

Since Kaneko and Misako's "elopement," Kim Shunpei was spending every night getting drunk. In fact, the story was a standing joke in the neighborhood. Soon enough, the intoxicated Kim Shunpei appeared on the factory floor and said, "I know you little shits are laughing at me. Oh, I know!" Glaring around at them, he smashed the fish crates against the floor. Then he picked up a charcoal brazier with his bare hands and hurled it at the workers.

"Boss, please stop!" screamed the workers, scattering. Work was over for the day.

The next day, a group of wholesale store owners came by the house and knocked until Kim Shunpei woke up.

"Please, Kim-*san*. We have a lot of orders to fill. This

isn't just your problem, you know. Is a girl worth getting this worked up over?" The Mikawa-*ya* owner naturally wanted to censure Kim Shunpei more harshly. It was unacceptable for a tradesman to throw everything to the dogs because of a personal problem. He almost felt like demanding compensation from Kim Shunpei for the lost revenue.

"Just forget about her!" said the Manada-*ya* owner with a serious look on his face.

Kim Shunpei was full of embarrassment in front of these merciless shop owners. He was a laughingstock among the tradesmen. It was clear that violence didn't work in business.

When Yae had deceived him, he felt like a sharp knife was cutting his chest into ribbons. He felt no such pain with Misako. The only thing he regretted was that she'd run away with the cash he'd entrusted to her. She wouldn't have run away if he'd never given her that cash.

Kim Shunpei had his own self-respect to think about. Who was idiotic enough to throw away his own profits? Plenty of women were ready for such idiots. A hungry woman threw herself at any man with enough money. There was nothing in this world one couldn't buy with money. At the foot of the Shinsaibashi Bridge, men stood with signs around their necks that said, "I'll sell my life for money." If a man sold his life, what could he possibly do with money? Clearly, men needed money even then.

Kim Shunpei left the management of the factory to Ko Nobuyoshi. The other workers trusted him, and Kim Shunpei saw him as his only true friend. It had been a while since the two had shared a drink after work. Ko Nobuyoshi knew how to comfort him when his spirits were low.

"We're both nearin' fifty. Fifty years passes by like a dream, they say. Now that you made it big, why not settle down and spend more time with your family?"

Kim Shunpei had no intention of doing such a thing. His family was like a stone weight he had to drag around. He considered women mere sex objects, while children were worthless investments. All humans were alone in the end. Having a family was a matter of weighing advantages and disadvantages. And he couldn't let himself get taken advantage of.

"Look. If I don't have money, who's gonna talk to me? My kids won't even look at me if I don't have money to give 'em. I could have any number of children with my money. But if I croak, that's the end."

Kim Shunpei's egotism ran deep. He didn't have faith in anything. Gods, Buddha, the underworld—they were all illusions, nothing more than drivel. What was this thing called life? What did humans live for? Kim Shunpei had no answer. Most humans lived for the sake of it and then died. Nothing more. It was useless to find any profound meaning in life. Its joys and sorrows were all ephemeral phenomena. As far as Kim Shunpei was concerned, if he disappeared, the whole world would disappear with him.

Ko Nobuyoshi was struck anew by the overwhelming presence of Kim Shunpei's tireless body. That body would one day perish, but Kim Shunpei believed in his body alone, and no words could change that.

Kim Shunpei eventually regained his presence of mind, and business progressed without any problems.

Ko Nobuyoshi hired an apprentice to replace Kaneko. Won Yoshio was twenty years old and had little experience, so for the time being he handled chores and other odd jobs. He loaded and unloaded crates, disposed of the fish bones, did the cleaning, and transported goods.

Kim Shunpei's nephew Kim Yong-su ran a hog farm in Nishinari, and he periodically came by with a bicycle trailer to collect the fish bones to use for pig feed. A cleaning company had formerly disposed of the fish bones for a fee, but now Kim Yong-su paid Kim Shunpei for them instead.

"Charging for the fish bones is overkill," warned Ko Nobuyoshi.

"That guy makes a living off pigs. Why shouldn't he pay for his feed?" said Kim Shunpei stubbornly.

Kim Yong-su grumbled to Ko Nobuyoshi in private. "Everyone's happy to have me pick up their food waste. It's just Uncle who wants money for it." But no matter how much Kim Yong-su grumbled, he was unable to challenge Kim Shunpei face-to-face. And he knew that if he stopped the arrangement, Kim Shunpei would pick a fight with him over that too. "How much do you think I earn from one pig? I can only get by if the feed's free," said Kim Yong-su shrilly. He looked sad and pathetic in his shabby clothes, which stank from the food waste he handled. But Ko Nobuyoshi couldn't do anything to help him.

That summer, Kim Shunpei brought home a pig

weighing about a hundred kilograms. The pig had reached adolescence and was firm with meat and fat. Kim Yong-su preferred to ship out piglets, but every year he owed Kim Shunpei a choice pig as part of the interest on the loan he'd taken out to establish his hog farm.

The pig was bound with rope inside the truck. Kim Shunpei took the pig out and carried it himself to the back part of the house with the concrete flooring. As women and children looked on, Sung-han brought out a large aluminum basin, while Kim Shunpei held the struggling pig by its knees and cut its throat with a sashimi knife. Fresh blood spurted out from the gash, and the pig flailed and screamed as it died. Meanwhile, Sung-han collected the blood in the washbasin. The whole thing was a bloody spectacle.

Kim Shunpei expertly took the pig apart. Not a single drop of blood was wasted. Finely chopped onions, green onions, salt, pepper, garlic, ginger, and vegetables were tossed in the blood and then made into sausages. Lee Young-hee and Hanako had the help of the other neighborhood women for this task. In a rare show of generosity, Kim Shunpei gave the neighbors a share of the meat. And of course, the workers got plenty of pork with their subsequent meals. Kim Shunpei stored the rest of the pork in his own special way. He cut the meat into thin slices and layered them in an eighteen-liter drum with medicinal herbs, garlic, ginger, peppers, and other spices. Three of these drums, packed with meat, sat in the shade behind the house until the meat started rotting. Within days the whole area swarmed with flies. The outhouse was only a few steps away, and maggots crawled up from the toilet, forming a trail to the drums. House visitors had to leave within minutes, their eyes watering at the stench. But Kim Shunpei ate the rotting pork with gusto. He casually blew away the maggots that latched onto the meat. This special recipe was supposed to prevent summer fatigue. No one knew how effective it was, but it could hardly be called edible.

"He's really goin' at it, isn't he? Makes me wanna throw up."

"How is he not sick yet? His stomach made of iron or something?"

"A normal person would die from eatin' that."

The workers found Kim Shunpei's pork recipe disgusting enough, but his appalling health regime didn't end there. He acquired a sample of infant feces from a midwife, which he soaked in water for three days before he drank it. From an animal shelter, he brought back about a hundred dog bones, which he simmered in a pot for three days and drank like a soup. He then crushed the dog bones into a powder, which he smeared all over himself with cold water. From the pickled vegetable shop at Benten Market, he brought back daikon leaf scraps, which he crushed into a solution and drank. Downy deer horns from the freezing steppes of Siberia, tiger testicles, fur seal penises, the blood of Chinese soft-shell turtles, anything that could replenish his sexual power he ingested, along with his various medicinal concoctions. He was like an alchemist from medieval times. Perhaps because of all this, his skin took on a pink hue, and his cuts and injuries healed quickly. There was nothing Kim Shunpei couldn't eat. His body might even have been able to find some virtue in poison, were he to drink it.

The apprentice Won Yoshio was stronger than the average worker and had a penchant for violence. His personality showed on his stern-looking face. He was quick-witted and disciplined at work, but if someone got on his bad side, he was unmanageable. That same Won Yoshio was as docile as a cat in front of Kim Shunpei.

One day Won Yoshio left for the wholesale store with a truckload of *kamaboko* and came back on foot.

"What on earth?" said Ko Nobuyoshi.

"The truck got stolen," said Won Yoshio, hanging his head.

The truck was indispensable for business, and it had cost eight thousand yen.

"Well, shit," said Ko Nobuyoshi, holding his head.

Kim Shunpei was sure to raise hell. Won Yoshio gulped in dread. A lost truck wasn't something the workers could hide.

"Couldn't you put in a word for me, Manager? Who knows what'll happen to me if I go tell him myself?"

There was no way Won Yoshio could avoid punishment. If he went to Kim Shunpei alone, he would get beaten up until his limbs snapped and he could no longer stand up. Ko Nobuyoshi was reluctant to mediate between them, but he couldn't look the other way either, so he accompanied Won Yoshio to Kim Shunpei's room. It was six o'clock in the morning, almost closing time, and Kim Shunpei had just gone to bed.

"Shunpei, we need to talk," said Ko Nobuyoshi quietly.

Kim Shunpei opened his eyes and saw Ko Nobuyoshi

standing there with Won Yoshio behind him. Kim Shunpei sat up on the futon, reached for the ashtray, and lit a cigarette. Such was his habit when he was woken up unceremoniously.

"So, Won Yoshio had the truck stolen from him."

Kim Shunpei didn't wait for an explanation. "The truck stolen! Stop fucking with me! A gambling pal of yours must've stolen it, huh? You little shit!"

His hand reached for the abacus beside his pillow and flung it at Won Yoshio's forehead.

"Forgive me, Boss!"

Kim Shunpei grabbed Won Yoshio's legs, dragged him forward, and banged the abacus against his forehead once more. The abacus shattered. Warm blood flowed down Won Yoshio's face.

"Forgive him! It wasn't his fault!"

Kim Shunpei couldn't hit Ko Nobuyoshi of all people, so he sat back down, lighting another cigarette. Won Yoshio, his face covered in blood, stared at Kim Shunpei with fear and hatred in his eyes.

"I'm lowerin' your monthly wages, you hear?"

The fierce-tempered Won Yoshio could only bite his lips and submit to the humiliation.

"Getting hit was inevitable. You did lose the truck,"
said Ko Nobuyoshi as a reminder, wary that the boy
would hold a grudge.

Won Yoshio had to get seven stitches on his forehead.

Over the next two years, regulations on the *kamaboko*
industry were lifted, and new *kamaboko* producers
opened for business in the Higashinari and Ikuno wards.
Independent businesses were ready to burst through the
red tape that had lasted for years. *Kamaboko* workers
were being recruited left and right.

One of Kim Shunpei's workers didn't appear for his
shift one day. "Shit! A headhunter must've gotten him. I'll
kill him!" Kim Shunpei clenched his teeth and stamped
his feet in frustration. But within the next two months,
four more workers quit, seeming to steal away in the
middle of the night. Kim Shunpei couldn't go so far as
to monitor his workers during their off-hours, and he
bitterly watched the world change around him. In the
four years after the war, prices increased tenfold, and
protests for proportionately higher wages increased as
well. Many workers saw their demands met, but Kim
Shunpei continued to exploit his workers with low wages.

Kamaboko factories were popping up all over Osaka and Japan as a whole. The labor shortage prompted recruitment on a mass scale, and workers naturally flocked to the places that offered higher wages. Kim Shunpei had to bump up his workers' wages accordingly. But he couldn't bump up the prices of his *kamaboko*, as the wholesalers would vehemently oppose him if he did.

"This is the end," said Kim Shunpei, as if he were ready to scrap his whole factory.

"Well, *kamaboko* was too expensive before. Now it's sure to sell even better," said Ko Nobuyoshi.

Ko Nobuyoshi estimated that Kim Shunpei had earned no less than twenty million yen during the past two years of his *kamaboko* monopoly. After a year of watching Kim Shunpei wake Sung-han up at three in the morning to write the bills, Ko Nobuyoshi felt sorry for the boy and took on part of the responsibility. That was how he knew about Kim Shunpei's earnings. Far from there being excessive competition, consumer demand still exceeded production. The proof was in Asahi Industries' sales, which continued to rise. On a good day, profits broke the one hundred thousand yen mark. Ko Nobuyoshi thought the workers' wages were too low given these conditions.

The factory didn't have a ledger for income and expenditures. The bills were written the day of and converted to cash that afternoon. Taxes now entered the picture, but Kim Shunpei refused to entertain the idea of paying them, no matter how much Ko Nobuyoshi insisted.

"Why should this country take the money I earned with my own sweat? Stop being stupid. That law has nothin' to do with me."

"Every business has to pay taxes to the government according to its profits. You'll get punished otherwise," said Ko Nobuyoshi.

Kim Shunpei didn't budge. "Bring it on, then. Send me to jail. My money is my money." He vowed that he wouldn't part with a single sen on behalf of anyone. When it came to the workers' meals, Kim Shunpei gave Hanako only enough money to purchase the food she needed for that day. He doggedly went over the price for each item she would order.

Sung-han was now a middle school student, and he asked for tuition money from his mother instead of his father. Sometimes he swiped a crate of *kamaboko* from the factory and sold it through his own networks. Sung-han knew how to exploit his father's weaknesses. Unlike Hanako, he was always prepared to run away from home. Whenever Kim Shunpei came home drunk and violent, Sung-han disappeared for days or even weeks at a time. He'd had a habit of playing hooky since elementary school, but as he grew older, he wandered further out for longer periods of time. He would sometimes leave for school and then not come home for several days. The first time this happened, Lee Young-hee and Hanako searched for him in a panic, but eventually, they got used to it and let him be.

"I don't know what's going through that head of his."

Kim Shunpei noticed with displeasure that Sung-han would wander off where he couldn't be reached. Just the other day, Kim Shunpei, out for blood, marched up to the second floor where Sung-han was studying, but his son back-flipped off the balcony like a young samurai warrior and leisurely walked away. He didn't return until four days afterward.

Sung-han traveled along the routes he'd once taken during the wartime evacuation. He went to Gojo in Nara, Ueno in Tokyo, Okayama, Miyazaki in Kyushu, and elsewhere. If he felt like it, he stayed with a fisherman or a farmer and helped them out in exchange for a few days' room and board. He was a charming and capable boy, well-liked everywhere he went. When people asked him where he was from, he said he was from Osaka, but he also didn't hide the fact that he was Korean. People thus thought that his parents had abandoned him, and they treated him with compassion.

One day, his homeroom teacher unexpectedly visited the house to address Sung-han's truancy. Kim Shunpei was unsure how to act. Homeroom teachers made house calls if the student was doing poorly, and Kim Shunpei found this most dishonorable. He'd never met Sung-han's thirty-year-old teacher before, and he treated him with meek courtesy. Sung-han joined them at the table, meekly sitting in *seiza* position.

"Thank you," the teacher said to Hanako, who brought out the tea.

The air turned solemn. The teacher glanced at Sung-han before speaking. "Kanemoto-*kun* got top marks in elementary school, so he's a smart kid. He's lively and athletic, and he can do anything he sets his mind to. However, he's missed two months of class since he entered middle school. He's not keeping up with the curriculum.

His grades are low, of course."

The hulking Kim Shunpei shrank in embarrassment.

"My sincere apologies."

"I hear you're quite attached to your drink."

Kim Shunpei was thrown by this sudden twist.

"Well, I . . ."

The young teacher went straight to the point.

"Kanemoto-*kun* told me that you drink every night, and that it leads to violence."

Kim Shunpei's face turned red. Lost for words, he lit a cigarette. Sung-han glanced at his confused, inarticulate father and felt a glimmer of satisfaction.

"The home environment is important for a child's studies. Kanemoto-*kun* has told me that he can't study in his home environment. He says he hates being at home, which causes him to spend his time elsewhere. If what he's saying is true, you need to do some hard thinking as his father. Please reconsider your drinking habits. Boys grow up watching how their fathers act. At this rate, Kanemoto-*kun* will get into trouble down the line. A boy his age is highly impressionable."

As Kim Shunpei listened to the teacher lecturing him, he understood that Sung-han was the one who'd requested this home visit. Or else he'd induced the teacher to visit through some other ploy. Kim Shunpei raged inwardly at the way he was being shamed.

"I think that once Kanemoto-*kun* stops skipping school and applies himself, his grades will improve. There's high school to think about too, so he'll need to start focusing especially in his second year."

"Yes. My sincere apologies." Kim Shunpei could only lower his head and say the same thing over and over. He acted as if he were pleading guilty in front of a judge. It was the first time this young teacher had visited the home of a Korean family, and he'd come with a sense of purpose, as well as a set of hackneyed phrases that could hopefully make the thuggish Kim Shunpei realize his fatherly duties.

The teacher's visit lasted an hour. At the end of it, Kim Shunpei gave him ten rolls of *kamaboko*. The teacher accepted the gift with pleasure.

"Take care," the teacher said.

As soon as he left, Kim Shunpei yelled, "Sung-han, come 'ere!"

Sung-han was forced to sit *seiza*-style in front of the brazier in the two-*jo* room. As his knees bit into the wooden floor, he watched his father's every move, ready to escape at any moment.

"How dare you slander me in front of your teacher. I've never been this embarrassed in my life. I'll burn you alive."

Kim Shunpei picked up a hot piece of coal with his thumb and forefinger, and it sizzled against his skin as he held it up to Sung-han's face. Electrical currents ran through Sung-han's body, and his face twitched uncontrollably. Jumping onto his feet, he ran through the kitchen and out the back door. As his father chased after him, he turned a corner, slipped into a secret passageway he remembered from his days playing cops and robbers, and climbed up on the roof to check where his father was. Kim Shunpei lost track of the nimble Sung-han and gnashed his teeth. "Damn it! Once I catch you, I'll snap your neck like a chicken!"

That night, the drunk Kim Shunpei broke the doors and furniture as he always did and went up to the second floor to hurl Sung-han's desk and notebooks outside. The desk's legs broke on impact, and the notebooks' pages flew everywhere. Kim Shunpei sat in the two-*jo* room chugging a bottle of *shochu*. Lee Young-hee and Hanako fled. At a total loss for what to do, Sung-han ran toward the police box. Soon the guilt of reporting his father to the police caught up with him. As he paced back and forth in front of the police box, the guard on duty looked up from his papers and said, "What are you doing at this time of night? Go home." It was then that Sung-han decided to tell him. The guard huffed in annoyance and folded his arms.

"Please do something! Please!" said Sung-han over and over. "My mom and sister might get killed." He said this last part to jolt the guard into action.

The guard had to respond. Sung-han led him to the house, upon which the guard saw the desk, papers, and books scattered across the street, as well as the broken front door. Deciding that this was indeed out of the ordinary, the guard walked briskly inside. After noticing more broken doors and broken furniture, he caught sight of the imposing Kim Shunpei sitting in the two-*jo* room with a bottle of *shochu*. The guard flinched back and gripped his baton. "Whatcha doin' over there?" he called out.

Kim Shunpei turned his fierce gaze toward the guard. "Who the fuck are you?" he thickly.

"This is the police. What's goin' on here?"

Kim Shunpei didn't appear to have heard what the guard said, and he kept drinking. He never was particularly responsive to the presence of policemen.

"Where's your wife and children?" The guard searched the rooms to check if they'd been killed.

"No one's here! The fuck you doin', sticking your nose where it don't belong? Go away!" His speech was slurred, but his meaning was clear.

"Your son alerted me. Where's your wife and daughter? Are they safe or what?"

"My son . . . ? That piece of shit, sellin' out his own father to the cops. I'll kill him!" Kim Shunpei smashed the *shochu* bottle against the floor.

Sung-han was listening from the other side of the corner, and once he heard the glass shatter, he turned and ran as fast as his legs could carry him. He didn't return for a week.

Family affairs were like a game of whack-a-mole, with Kim Shunpei holding the club. Lee Young-hee, Hanako, or Sung-han popped up at different times for him to beat back down. But these days, they disappeared faster than he could bring down his club, and his anger grew by the day. Sung-han could clear out at a moment's notice and not return for days. Kim Shunpei was swinging at nothing but air. He had no way of knowing where Sung-han lurked about, and whenever he tried to extort an answer from him, Sung-han dug in his heels. Even when Sung-han did come home from school several days in a row, he avoided the house. He spent all day hanging out with friends and sneaking in late at night. No one in the family knew what hours he kept. Kim Shunpei inwardly gave a start whenever he encountered Sung-han for the first time in several days. Sung-han seemed to be growing bigger and stronger with each encounter. His cheeks and jaw looked more sculpted, and his eyes burned with youthful energy.

"That brat was raised all wrong. The bitch spoiled him. He's cocky and disrespectful, that little shit . . . . It's too late for him. Next time I have a son, I'm raising him myself."

When Ko Nobuyoshi heard Kim Shunpei talk about his children's upbringing, it was as if Kim Shunpei were speaking about an alternate reality. In fact, Kim Shunpei talked about his children like the German shepherd he'd kept all those years ago. When someone expressed interest in buying the German shepherd, Kim Shunpei sold it off without a second thought. He would surely do the same with his kids if he had the chance. And what did he mean by "next time I have a son"? Lee Young-hee couldn't possibly bear him another child. Who would, then? Perhaps Kim Shunpei was already putting his plan into action. There were women he'd lived with, as well as women he'd raped. It wouldn't be a surprise if Kim Shunpei had fathered several children out of wedlock. But whether or not he'd actually intended to have a son (and only a son), a young man showed up at his door in the middle of November.

The rain that day was torrential. A shaman was performing an exorcism in the kitchen at Lee Young-hee's request. She lit candles all along the hearth, laid out yarn across a brass pot full of rice, prepared an offering of fruit, and chanted in a low voice while ringing a bell. Lee Young-hee and Hanako were praying. The shaman instructed Lee Young-hee to put money on top of the rice; the money was the shaman's fee. Lee Young-hee called Sung-han down from the second floor and asked him to break her one hundred-yen bill. Meanwhile, Kim Shunpei was in his room drinking. The sound of the pouring rain blended with that of the machines running in the factory. The night was strangely calm.

Sung-han stepped out from the *genkan* to break the bill at the nearby sweets shop when a young man stopped him from under the eaves. Tall and well-built, he wore a shirt over work pants and Japanese thonged sandals without any socks. He looked quite shabby.

"Your old man there?" he asked.

"Yeah." With that, Sung-han was on his way, running through the streets without an umbrella. When he returned from the sweets shop, the young man was in Kim Shunpei's room, sitting in the *seiza* position. *Who is he?* Sung-han handed the bills to Lee Young-hee and was about to go back up to the second floor when his father called him. Sung-han nervously made his way to the inner room.

"Sit there," said Kim Shunpei tipsily, gesturing to a spot next to the young man. Then he looked back and forth between them, comparing their faces. Scratching his groin and frowning, he said, "This guy's your older brother."

Sung-han was thunderstruck. Unsure how to respond, he looked at the nervous young man sitting next to him.

His crew cut and handsome features didn't resemble Kim Shunpei. One could say, perhaps, that he'd inherited Kim Shunpei's sharp eyes and large frame. He looked to be in his mid- to late-twenties, about twice Sung-han's age.

Kim Shunpei stood up and helped himself to another two or three glasses of *shochu*. Lee Young-hee was in the kitchen, perturbed by this young man who'd appeared out of nowhere, the son of a different mother. She couldn't pay attention to the shaman's prayers. When that man had stepped into the house, Lee Young-hee couldn't believe her eyes. He was like a carbon copy of Park Kyung-hwa. Back when Lee Young-hee lived in Jeju Island, she'd seen Park Kyung-hwa a few times, though always from a distance. Park Kyung-hwa was known as the most beautiful woman on the island. Lee Young-hee had to admit that she was enchanting. This young man was undoubtedly her son. Shortly after Lee Young-hee got together with Kim Shunpei, her friend had told her that Kim Shunpei was the father of one of Park Kyung-hwa's sons. Lee Young-hee found that hard to believe. Park Kyung-hwa was married, and she was ten years older than Kim Shunpei. It appeared, though, that the rumors had been true.

The drunk Kim Shunpei acknowledged for the time being that the young man was his son, but he had to look at him again and again to find some physical characteristic that resembled his own.

"What's your name?" he asked.

"Takeshi," said the young man curtly.

"Takeshi, huh . . . Age?"

"Twenty-seven."

Kim Shunpei ground his teeth together, trying to think back to what he'd been doing twenty-seven years ago. He was unsure how to treat a son who'd come into his life just now, after twenty-seven years.

"Whatever. You can sleep in the two-*jo* room over there."

As Takeshi stood up, his height and stature seemed to rival Kim Shunpei's.

The room originally built for Misako was now Takeshi's. Korean families typically stocked a reserve futon or two for guests, and Lee Young-hee laid a new one out for Takeshi.

"Sorry for the trouble," said Takeshi, bowing.

Lee Young-hee was in a dither about how to handle the unexpected arrival of her husband's son. It was already hard enough to breathe in this house, but Takeshi felt like a foreign object.

"Is he really Father's son?" muttered Hanako.

"I think so," said Lee Young-hee without conviction.

"Wait, so he'll be our older brother?"

"Your dad's his father, so that would make him your older brother, wouldn't it?"

"And you'd be his mom?" asked Hanako fretfully.

The shaman was still chanting. Her voice seemed to be knocking on the doors to Lee Young-hee's heart—as was Park Kyung-hwa's departed spirit. The candles flickered, and the room was filled with a mysterious energy. Lee Young-hee clapped her hands together and prayed with all her might.

That night, Kim Shunpei lay on the floor, going through his dim memories of the past. Park Kyung-hwa had once lived in the same village as him. He was fifteen, and Park Kyung-hwa was twenty-five. Kim Shunpei was enraptured by the sight of her walking along the village paths with her husband, her white *chima jeogori* fluttering in the wind. Kim Shunpei was known in the village as a bully, but every time he encountered Park Kyung-hwa, he gave a little bow, and his heart thudded in his chest. He was kept awake at night by his desire for her. Park Kyung-hwa eventually left for Japan with her husband. Soon after that, Kim Shunpei headed to the Korean mainland, spending five years there as an itinerant worker before leaving for Japan himself. In Osaka, Wakayama, and Hyogo, he went back and forth between the construction work camps and gambling dens. Then he started working as a *kamaboko* worker in Amagasaki, spending his free time gambling, drinking, and brawling. Within three months, he quit that job to work as a longshoreman in Hiroshima. It was there that he coincidentally met Park Kyung-hwa's husband, Kwon Jung-ik. In fact, it seemed more like an inevitability than a coincidence. At that time, work was being done to expand Hiroshima's naval port, and Korean workers were being recruited all along the Hanshin Industrial Belt. Kim Shunpei and Kwon Jung-ik answered the call, attracted by the high wages on offer.

Kim Shunpei and Kwon Jung-ik had known each other on Jeju Island, but due to their age difference, they were only distant acquaintances. In the foreign country of Japan, though, it was natural for two people from the same village to become close. Five days after they met at the docks, Kwon Jung-ik invited Kim Shunpei to his place in an old tenement house. Park Kyung-hwa welcomed Kim Shunpei in, looking more beautiful than ever. They had a nine-year-old son, and even though they were poor, they kept a bright and cheerful home.

"We don't have much of anything except fish." Park Kyung-hwa served Kim Shunpei dinner and smiled with her white teeth. Kim Shunpei burned with desire.

He couldn't sleep. He would dream of Park Kyung-hwa and ejaculate in his sleep. His lust for her intensified by the day. He even mulled over the possibility of killing Kwon Jung-ik without anyone noticing. Or he could abduct her. His lust stirred up dark, outrageous thoughts. The cruel cogs of fate turned in only one direction. There came a day when Kwon Jung-ik left for Jeju Island to visit his ailing mother. Kim Shunpei had an evil premonition of what was to come. This would be his only opportunity to do what he wanted to Park Kyung-hwa.

On the night following Kwon Jung-ik's departure, the drunk Kim Shunpei showed up at Park Kyung-hwa's door with a bottle of *shochu*. He acted as if he'd come to share a drink with Kwon Jung-ik.

"His mother fell ill, so he left to see her yesterday. He

won't be back for another ten days, I think."

"That so? Too bad. I brought this *shochu* for us to drink together."

"I'm sorry you had to come all this way." They were at the front door, and it didn't look like Park Kyung-hwa would invite Kim Shunpei in. It was considered a deviation from Korean morals for a woman to host another man in her husband's absence. Park Kyung-hwa wasn't particularly wary of Kim Shunpei, but when he stepped into the *genkan* and closed the door behind him, she froze in shock. This man had gone too far. "What are you doing?" she said harshly, sensing Kim Shunpei's intentions. He pulled out a handkerchief from his pants pocket and stuffed it into Park Kyung-hwa's mouth. He tied her hands behind her back with a rope. He'd moved so fast that she didn't even know what had happened to her.

Her son was in the inner room, sleeping. Kim Shunpei rammed her against the front door and ripped off her drawers. She struggled against him, but she was helpless against his overwhelming power. He wet her vagina with his spit and thrust into her. She opened her eyes wide, unable to breathe. Kim Shunpei's thick penis was invading her body. Tears ran from her panic-stricken eyes.

Kim Shunpei accomplished what he'd come to do and untied Park Kyung-hwa's hands. She threw the handkerchief at Kim Shunpei. "You brute!" she spat.

"Stop squealing. From now on, you're mine! Got it?"

"Enough with your selfishness. I'll tell everyone what you did!"

"Go ahead and try. Be ready for me tomorrow night!"

Park Kyung-hwa broke down crying as if she were about to lose her mind. Feeling a bit rueful, Kim Shunpei disappeared into the night. He put Hiroshima behind him that very night.

Takeshi was born as a result of that terrible event. After his birth, Park Kyung-hwa became gravely ill. She confessed to her husband what Kim Shunpei had done to her, and then she died. Kwon Jung-ik directed all his hatred toward Kim Shunpei's son. He gave Takeshi barely any milk, thinking he was better off dead. The neighbors persuaded him to give the baby up for adoption.

Twenty-seven years later, Takeshi found Kim Shunpei. Why did he wait until he was twenty-seven? Judging from his shabby appearance, he'd gone broke. His eyes weren't the eyes of a normal person; they belied some savage emotion bottled up inside him. The ever-suspicious Kim Shunpei couldn't sleep until dawn, trying to puzzle out what brewed behind those eyes.

Kim Shunpei went out with Takeshi shortly after noon the next day. One could spot a family resemblance between them not from the front, but from the back. It was enough to make one think that two versions of Kim Shunpei were walking around.

They went to a Western clothing store in Tsuruhashi, where Kim Shunpei ordered a suit and coat for Takeshi. Then they went to a shoe store, but none of the shoes there fit Takeshi, and Kim Shunpei had to order those too. Then he gave Takeshi one thousand yen to use for spending money. He almost never did something like that. The money was a kind of atonement for never having given a second thought to the kid he'd conceived twenty-seven years ago.

Lee Young-hee also figured she had to do something for Takeshi, so she bought him an expensive watch.

"Thank you so much," said Takeshi humbly.

The neighbors found out about Takeshi that very day, and they, along with the *kamaboko* workers, showed up at the house nonchalantly to get a look at him. Within three days, the rumors had spread to Ikuno, Joto, and Yodogawa, and a slew of people went out of their way to see him.

In the inner room, Nishiyama Haruo (formerly Jang Haruo) was sharing drinks with Kim Shunpei when he said teasingly, "Seems like a good lad. How's it feel to be a new father . . . of a twenty-seven-year-old?"

All the men in the room roared with laughter, and Kim Shunpei looked half-embarrassed, half-disgruntled. He was forced to think about past events he would rather have forgotten. Everyone peered into the two-*jo* room as if Takeshi were an animal at a zoo.

As the men drank in the inner room, the women gathered on the second floor. Mrs. Kinkai said, "With this twenty-seven-year-old around, won't Kim Shunpei stop with his violence?"

"Yeah, your new son would stop him for sure," said Mrs. Takamura giddily.

"That'd be nice." Lee Young-hee didn't buy into the women's careless speculations, but she let herself hope that Takeshi would at least act as a deterrent, since he looked like he might surpass Kim Shunpei in strength.

The circumstances surrounding Takeshi's birth were a public mystery, but no one asked about it out loud. The problem looming in everyone's minds was how a father ignorant of his son's existence for twenty-seven years could now share the same roof with him and not have anything go wrong. The more malicious among them whispered that father and son would kill each other. As a matter of fact, Lee Young-hee felt oppressed just knowing that these two large men were in the house. While it was true that she barely interacted with Kim Shunpei other than when she brought him meals, she sensed dark currents of emotion that could easily break out into a fight between the two men.

After meals, Takeshi would leave the table with a quick "thanks" before going back to his futon in the two-*jo* room. Takeshi was so tall he had to sleep diagonally to stretch his legs out. Spending his days twiddling his thumbs, he got Sung-han to buy him weekly periodicals and magazines, which he read from cover to cover. As Mrs. Kinkai had predicted, Kim Shunpei was acting quite tame, even when he got drunk. He appeared to be avoiding Takeshi. Perhaps that was because his son was the spitting image of Park Kyung-hwa.

Takeshi was a forceful presence for his half-brother Sung-han, who ran from store to store getting Takeshi magazines, periodicals, beer, *sake,* and snacks. Sung-han was allowed to keep the change. Takeshi was quite generous. When Won Yoshio came over to hang out in his room, Takeshi freely gave him a hundred or two hundred yen. Won Yoshio called Takeshi *aniki* and acted like he was Takeshi's sworn younger brother. The one thousand yen Kim Shunpei had given Takeshi was gone in less than a month.

Then a woman showed up. She had on a beige coat over a purple suit, wore purple high heels, and carried a crocodile-skin bag. Her clothes and accessories were of the highest grade. It was clear from a single glance that she was no ordinary woman. Smiling with her thick makeup, she said, "Excuse me!" and opened the front door.

Takeshi's room was right beside the *genkan,* and he let her in, saying, "You're late!"

"I wanted to come earlier, but some things came up. I'm sorry." She spoke to him sweetly. As she was taking off her high heels, Kim Shunpei arrived home. He looked at this gaudily dressed woman from head to toe, his eyes sharp and critical.

Without a moment's delay, Takeshi said, "Hey old man, this is my fiancée."

The woman took off her coat, straightened up, and bowed. "I'm Sanae," she said.

"Fiancée . . . ?" Looking like he'd just been tricked by a fox, Kim Shunpei turned on his heels and went out the door.

Chapter 19

Kim Shunpei had two hours to spare before work. As he rode his bike, he pictured Takeshi's fiancée in his mind's eye. In these times, someone with clothes as high-grade as that either came from wealth, worked as a hostess at a fancy club, or else enjoyed access to a highly unusual financial source. Judging from his own experience, Kim Shunpei was certain she was involved in the nighttime entertainment business. He could tell from her flirtatious facial expressions and posture. Was she going to live in that cramped two-*jo* room with Takeshi? No, it wasn't possible. He abruptly realized that he was approaching Miyukimori Shrine, where Ko Nobuyoshi lived. He always used to get lost on his way to Ko Nobuyoshi's house, but when he was absorbed in thought, he didn't miss a single turn.

Ko Nobuyoshi was probably asleep, but he decided to drop by anyway. Akemi greeted him. "He's at a meeting," she said.

"A meeting? What meeting?"

"A Korean association district meeting."

The purpose of the meeting was to denounce the Korean War, which had broken out in the early dawn of June 25 that year. But Kim Shunpei wasn't interested in such things.

"He said he'd go straight to work after the meeting. Everything alright?" said Akemi. It wasn't common for Kim Shunpei to call on them before work.

"Everything's fine. I was just in the area."

He had wanted to vent his frustration about the woman to Ko Nobuyoshi, but he turned around and rode away. Deep in thought, he made his way slowly through the alleyways, which spooled this way and that like giant intestines and then emptied him out onto the former evacuation route. He decided to head toward one of the wholesale stores to settle a bill and was crossing the road when he encountered a large group of demonstrators marching toward him. A truck led the way, bearing a dozen or so young people yelling into bullhorns and holding signs and banners.

"Americans out of Korea!"

"We'll never forgive the traitor Syngman Rhee and his supporters!"

"Overthrow the Yoshida Shigeru cabinet!"

"All hail the Tiger of Mount Paektu, General Kim Il-sung!"

Chants in both Japanese and Korean thundered through the streets, and not a few spectators joined the march from the roadside. Kim Shunpei stopped his bicycle and stared at this protest, the first one he'd seen. He knew that the Korean Peninsula was divided into North and South, and that war had broken out. But he didn't know why the two sides were at war, nor why Korea had been divided in the first place. It was all the same to Kim Shunpei. He had no conception of nation or fatherland. He did nurse sentiments for his native land, Jeju Island, but words like "country," "nation," or "fatherland" were on a completely different scale for him. Long ago, he'd spent five years wandering Korea from Busan to Daegu to Daejeon to Seoul. He was held in contempt by the mainlanders, discriminated against, and shut out of work. They laughed at his Jeju Island dialect and told him to squeal like a pig.

Jeju Island was known for its pigs. Of course, Kim Shunpei fought with the people who insulted him. They trained him for a lifetime of fighting.

He noticed women in *chima jeogori* marching in the demonstration. It was truly bizarre to see these women raise their fists and chant. Policemen stood along both sides of the street, on the lookout for any trouble.

"Why are you shutting us in like this?" screamed a woman. Whenever any of the protesters bulged out toward the edge of the road, the policemen mercilessly pushed them back with their batons.

Ko Nobuyoshi was also at the march. His normally warm and gentle face looked fierce. There was a severe beauty to humans when they were fighting for what they knew was just—their right to self-determination. And behind that severe beauty was seething rage. The march was headed for Manadayama Park, where they planned to disperse. But all of a sudden, a truck in the opposite lane rammed into the truck at the head of the march. Two or three of the activists on the truck bed were thrown to the ground from the impact. Two more trucks followed the first. Dozens of men jumped down with wooden rods and beams of timber and attacked the crowd. They also attacked the policemen who tried to stop them.

Kim Shunpei didn't understand what was happening. But he couldn't just stand there. Was Ko Nobuyoshi alright? The woman from before fell down, her white *chima jeogori* stained with blood. Protestors and onlookers alike started fleeing the scene. Ko Nobuyoshi, lips bleeding, moved toward the attackers with his sign.

"Nobuyoshi! You okay?" called Kim Shunpei.

Ko Nobuyoshi was surprised to see him. "Shunpei— what are you doing here?" He thought Kim Shunpei was part of the group of thugs attacking the protesters.

"Coincidence."

"Coincidence?"

"I went to your house to see you. I was on my way back. What's goin' on around here?"

"Those bastards are gang members hired by the Syngman Rhee camp."

Just then a man approached Kim Shunpei swinging a wooden plank. Kim Shunpei stopped the plank with his arm, and it splintered in half. The man looked up at the giant Kim Shunpei and gasped. "*Hyeongnim!*"

"Shosuke, what are you up to in a place like this?"

"We're just carryin' out orders." Kim Shosuke glanced at Ko Nobuyoshi, whose face was turning dark with bruises.

"Both of you come 'ere." Kim Shunpei led the two men away from the fray and walked to the nearby commercial quarters, where they entered a café. Ko Nobuyoshi and Kim Shosuke silently followed him in, sulky about being forced together when they'd just been fighting as antagonists.

Kim Shosuke belonged to the same Kim clan as Kim Shunpei. He was fifteen years younger than Shunpei and saw him as an older brother of sorts. After the war, Kim Shosuke had joined a violent far-right gang that rapidly consolidated power across the black markets in Kyobashi, Tsuruhashi, Tennoji, and the area around Osaka Station. He was now the leader of the Kanemoto-*gumi,* which was based in Umeda and thirty men strong. But he was no match for the likes of Kim Shunpei. Their age difference was one factor, but he also knew how terrifying Kim Shunpei was. He'd lived in Nakamichi during the war years, and the image stayed with him of Kim Shunpei fighting dozens of thugs at once like a titan. It was downright weird how Kim Shunpei never joined any factions and acted alone in everything he did, trusting no one. Kim Shosuke himself was a seasoned fighter—one had to be in the syndicate he was part of—but a single glare from Kim Shunpei was enough to cow him.

Kim Shunpei took a sip of coffee and screwed his face up at the bitter taste. "Shosuke, you know who Ko Nobuyoshi is?"

Kim Shosuke had a vague sense that he'd heard the name before when he lived in Nakamichi. "Naw, I don't." He looked sideways at Ko Nobuyoshi. He had a fine, graceful face with a straight, angular nose.

Kim Shunpei lit his cigarette. "Ko Nobuyoshi's aunt is the wife of your oldest uncle on your father's side."

"You're serious?" Kim Shosuke had no recollection of these details from his distant past. Ko Nobuyoshi didn't know anything about this family connection either.

"Don't that make us cousins or somethin'?"

Ko Nobuyoshi now looked at Kim Shosuke. His face was round and his eyebrows thick, and he sported a thick mustache. He reminded Ko Nobuyoshi of a *dol hareubang.*[*]

---

[*] Stone statues found on Jeju Island, considered guardian spirits

"Don't know him. And don't care to, meetin' him like this," said Ko Nobuyoshi in annoyance, speaking now in the rougher Osaka dialect. "Why'd you come after us again? We march peacefully and you attack us with clubs and planks and God knows what else. Your own compatriots. Unforgivable! And hittin' women too." Ko Nobuyoshi wiped away the blood on his lips and massaged his shoulders and legs.

"Just followin' orders, man," said Kim Shosuke. He was telling the truth; he figured that Kim Shunpei would be able to tell if he were lying.

"From the Syngman Rhee crew, right? Syngman Rhee and the Americans were the ones who started this war. You think it's okay to side with those immoral bastards?"

"I dunno much about the politics side of things. But they told us the North attacked first."

"Idiot. Why would the North do that? The Americans and Syngman Rhee attacked first to crush Kim Il-sung. Those bastards said they'd take over the North in a week. But the war's been goin' on for half a year. The Chinese and Soviets joined, so Syngman Rhee and the Americans are gonna lose by the look of it. We're one country. We have to be united." Ko Nobuyoshi's impassioned speech made him seem like a different person.

"No point hashing this out here. Work's about to start." Kim Shunpei looked at his watch. "By the way, Shosuke, you wouldn't know a guy named Takeshi, would you?"

"Takeshi? What's his last name?"

Even if Takeshi was Kim Shunpei's son, he'd likely taken on his biological father's family name, Kwon.

"Kim, or Kanemoto. Or else Kwon, or Koyama. Not sure."

Kim Shosuke thought for a moment and then replied, "None of my bros have that name. He's no one I know. You lookin' for him?"

"No. Leave it."

Ko Nobuyoshi had returned to his usual taciturn self. He wondered why Kim Shunpei was asking about Takeshi.

As they parted ways, Kim Shosuke told Kim Shunpei, "Hang out with us in Umeda sometime."

"I'll go when I go." Kim Shunpei watched Kim Shosuke saunter away in his *jikatabi,** riding breeches,

---

* Japanese-style split-toe boots

and traditional Japanese short-sleeved coat. "That son of a bitch can't be trusted," he muttered. Though Kim Shunpei could hardly be a judge of that.

The violence on the former evacuation route came to an end. The demonstration couldn't piece itself back together. Planks and signs were strewn all over the road.

"I'm going back home to clean my face up before work," said Ko Nobuyoshi.

"Alright. I'll stop by the Tsuruhashi wholesale store, then."

As Kim Shunpei got on his bicycle, Ko Nobuyoshi remembered to ask why Kim Shunpei had come all the way to Miyukimori Shrine. "You needed something from me, right?"

"Don't worry 'bout it. I was just annoyed earlier. He had a girl over—no ordinary girl. Somethin' was off about her."

It wasn't strange for someone Takeshi's age to have a girlfriend. It was fine for her to come on occasion, but if she got too comfortable in that room, she was going to be a pain in the ass. There was only one thing Kim Shunpei could do. It was impossible for two alpha males to live under the same roof. He would have to make Takeshi rent his own place. But he obviously had reservations about that too. He didn't want to waste money on Takeshi. Kim Shunpei was the type of person who refused to yield an inch in a dispute. Generosity was the same thing as weakness in his mind. It was his belief that being generous didn't solve much of anything. Ko Nobuyoshi wanted to give Kim Shunpei some advice, but the willful Kim Shunpei often did the direct opposite of whatever Ko Nobuyoshi advised.

Sanae visited the house once in November, but by the time December rolled around, she was basically a regular. She smiled with her thick makeup and greeted Lee Young-hee, Hanako, and Sung-han with various gifts, and she brought Kim Shunpei imported whiskey. Kim Shunpei of course refused to accept it. He wanted her gone, but she was Takeshi's fiancée. Could he kick out the fiancée of a son he'd neglected for twenty-seven years? Normally, he would have made them get married. He would never have let his son bring home a girl without his consent. But he couldn't say anything, if only for the fact that he had no standing with Takeshi as a parent.

Sung-han spent hours after school in Takeshi's two-*jo* room. This was not to Kim Shunpei's liking. He thought

Takeshi was ensnaring Sung-han with cash handouts.
Hanako also seemed to look upon Takeshi favorably. Kim
Shunpei felt like he no longer belonged to his own home,
and he spent his nights drinking and walking around.
And he couldn't resort to violence to deal with Takeshi's
inexplicable existence. Takeshi was the revenant of Park
Kyung-hwa. It was as if she'd come back to haunt Kim
Shunpei, twenty-seven years after he'd raped her, twenty-
seven years after he'd brutally satisfied his craving for the
village beauty.

By the beginning of the new year, it appeared that
Sanae was there to stay. She and Takeshi spent all day
on the futon, tangled up like vines. They set up a small
foldable table right on their futon and made Sung-han
and Hanako bring them sashimi, snacks, beer, and fruit.
When they felt like it, they dressed up and went out.
They would come back home drunk after everyone else
had gone to bed, and Sanae would rush through Kim
Shunpei's room in her nightgown to get to the toilet. Kim
Shunpei had to rub his eyes to make sure he wasn't seeing
a phantom. Whenever Sanae drank alcohol, she had to
pee at unpredictable times. In an emergency, passing
through Kim Shunpei's room was faster than passing

through the kitchen hallway. He could barely contain his rage.

Takeshi and Sanae spent all day in their little love nest, and Sanae's exclamations of pleasure could be heard at night too. She sounded as if she were dancing the mambo. Kim Shunpei couldn't take it anymore. One day he stood over the sleeping Takeshi and Sanae and yelled, "Flirtin' and messin' around day and night! Fuck off to an inn if you have to! And stop walkin' around in that thin chemise. I don't run a whorehouse. I hate girls with no common sense. What are you two playin' at, huh?"

Even Kim Shunpei's explosive anger didn't work on them. Sanae got into *seiza* position and bowed, placing three fingers from each hand on the floor. "Sorry, Papa Kim. We'll be careful from now on," she said. Her theatrical performance incensed Kim Shunpei further.

"That's why you should get us a place of our own, old man. We can barely move in here." Takeshi was openly provoking him. He seemed to be hinting that even if Kim Shunpei bought a house for him, it wouldn't make up for twenty-seven years of neglect.

"What did you just say? You think I have that kind of money? I won't pay a single sen for your house.

195

Freeloaders like you think you can say anything.
Shameless brat! If you don't like it here, get the fuck out!"

Sanae's plump flesh protruded from her slip. Even looking at her made Kim Shunpei feel dirty, and he slammed the glass door on his way outside.

"His face changes color when he talks about money, huh," said Takeshi.

"He has so much cash it's rotting in his stores. But he doesn't want to give you a single sen. He shunned his own son for twenty-seven years, and he thinks he can talk to you like that?" Sanae drank from the whiskey bottle and gave Takeshi some whiskey from her own mouth.

Lee Young-hee didn't intervene in this matter at all. She didn't think it was her place to intervene. The relationship between Kim Shunpei and Takeshi looked highly unpredictable. Twenty-seven years was too long for the two men to consider each other father and son. And there was something about Takeshi that Lee Young-hee couldn't grasp.

Two men visited Takeshi one day. They looked to be about Takeshi's age. They sat right on the futon and huddled in to talk in low whispers. Normally Takeshi would have made Sung-han or Hanako go shopping, but this time Sanae went out to get the men *sake,* sashimi, and ham. Takeshi and the two men talked as if they didn't want anyone else to hear, and Sanae stood outside the room as if she were standing guard. An hour passed, and the two men left.

The two men met up with Takeshi several more times, always going over some secret business. When they encountered Kim Shunpei they said politely, "Sorry for intruding."

Kim Shunpei pretended like he didn't notice anything. He took stock of the two strangers but avoided prying into Takeshi's affairs. He had nothing to do with it. Kim Shunpei knew the ins and outs of the criminal underworld, even if he moved as a lone wolf. But he was the indirect cause for Takeshi ever getting involved in that world. For someone who'd lost his mother and been abandoned by his father, there weren't many life choices available. Kim Shunpei was aware of that, which made him wary of the possibility that Takeshi would kill him in his sleep. Regretting ever letting Takeshi into his house, he had the feeling each night that his karma would come back to bite him right then and there. He'd also just found out that one of his workers, Miyamoto Haruo, was the one who'd brought Takeshi over in the first place. Miyamoto Haruo was Kwon Jung-ik's son—Takeshi's older half-brother. How had that happened? The earnest Miyamoto Haruo was a replacement worker, hired by Kim Shunpei through an intermediary. This couldn't be mere coincidence. Kim Shunpei suspected that the two half-brothers were plotting something, and he kept watch over them silently.

When Sung-han returned from school, he threw off his backpack and barged into Takeshi's room as usual. Takeshi, Sanae, and Won Yoshio were sitting in the room. It was a day off at the factory. Won Yoshio was excitedly watching Takeshi disassemble a handgun. Takeshi polished the body of the gun and the bullets with oiled paper, and then he revolved the chamber and adjusted the balance. Then he took aim at a spot on the wall and pulled the trigger. The gun clicked. Sanae slid up close to Takeshi and watched, spellbound.

"*Aniki,* lemme touch it," said Won Yoshio, eyes glinting.

Takeshi smiled coldly and gave him the handgun. Won Yoshio felt the weight of the gun in his hands and, like Takeshi, aimed at the wall and clicked. "Incredible!"

He gazed admiringly at the lustrous gun.

"Lemme touch it too," whined Sung-han.

"It's off-limits for you," said Takeshi.

"Oh, let him. Can't hurt, can it?" said Sanae, amused.

The moment Sung-han took the gun from Won Yoshio, a thrill came over him. It was as if he were suddenly bathed in sunlight and carried away toward a distant horizon of pleasure. A savage feeling also came over him. He let the gun go without even realizing it.

From that day on, Sung-han saw Takeshi as a being from a different world. But his hands tingled with the memory of the gun. Sung-han guessed that Takeshi would be leaving the house soon. Why else would he get a gun? It turned out that Sung-han predicted correctly.

The evening Takeshi left, it was pouring rain, just like the evening he'd arrived. Takeshi took this opportunity to ask Kim Shunpei for money.

"Lend you money? I don't have any. Not a single sen."

That was Kim Shunpei's stock phrase. No matter who he said it to, he loved saying, "Not a single sen." Everyone knew, of course, that Kim Shunpei had made huge profits during his three-year monopoly on *kamaboko* production. But he always insisted that he didn't have a single sen.

"That bitch is the one with all the money."

In other words, he thought that the money raised from Lee Young-hee's mutual funds had been sucked away somewhere. In actuality, the shareholders were getting their dividends from the larger mutual funds, but not from the smaller ones. That was Kim Shunpei's proof that there was "no money." He was giving Lee Young-hee a hard time over the way she was managing the funds. Kim Shunpei could make something appear true just by asserting it strongly enough, but after a point Lee Young-hee had started to delude herself into thinking that Kim Shunpei really had no money.

Takeshi had enough. He marched into Kim Shunpei's room and tore vigorously at the wallpaper, revealing dents in the wall. He took from the wall several bundles of one hundred-yen bills, which altogether amounted to a few million yen.

"I have eyes, you know. Stashin' your money here, huh? You left me to fend for myself all my life, and you think givin' me a one hundred yen or two hundred yen could cover your ass?" Takeshi reached deeper into the wall and pulled out more bundles of cash.

"You dirty thief!"

At last the fight ensued. The two large men grappled each other and threw each other against the glass door. They knocked down the storage cupboard and fell over each other into the *genkan*. They fought skin to skin, bone to bone, and the house echoed with the sound of scuffling bodies and breaking objects. Baring their teeth and bellowing, they hurled themselves outside into the downpour. Sanae watched with her face drawn tight. Sung-han was at the cinema, and Lee Young-hee was out for business. Hanako rushed to the factory to alert the workers. In the meantime, Takeshi dunked Kim Shunpei's face into the gutter, which was overflowing with dirty rainwater. Struggling, Kim Shunpei pushed himself up and headbutted Takeshi in the face. Takeshi staggered backward, his nose dripping blood.

"*Inom gaesekki!* I'll kill you!"

This time, Kim Shunpei dunked Takeshi's face into the gutter. The nine workers rushed over and tried to pull them apart, but the two men's taut bodies didn't yield. Finally the workers broke in between Takeshi and Kim Shunpei as they snarled and cursed at each other.

"Get outta my house, you little bastard!" Kim Shunpei

was disavowing the fact that Takeshi was his son.

"I'm gonna avenge my mother someday!" shouted Takeshi bitterly.

Sanae packed up all their things and handed the sopping wet Takeshi his suit and overcoat to change into. Takeshi flung them both onto the wet ground, as well as his shoes. Then he and Sanae left without even an umbrella between them.

Kim Shunpei's bowels were seething. He grabbed Miyamoto Haruo's collar. "I've known all along you're Kwon Jung-ik's son. Why'd you bring that bastard here? I see *right* through you. Both you bastards are after my assets!"

The mild-mannered Miyamoto Haruo stiffened. "No, no! I just wanted Takeshi to meet his real father." His eyes filled with tears.

"Quite a show you're puttin' on, aren't you. How'd you find out he's my son? What's your proof? You're not welcome here either! Get outta my sight!"

And Miyamoto Haruo left as well, running through the rain in his factory uniform.

The workers came up with conflicting interpretations of what happened. Some sympathized with Kim Shunpei, while others sympathized with Miyamoto Haruo.

Won Yoshio was especially critical of Kim Shunpei's mercilessness. "He left him to the streets twenty-seven years ago, and now he's done it again. What kind of parent is he?"

Ko Nobuyoshi thought differently. "Everyone knew he and his girlfriend had it coming. Actually, I'm amazed the boss let 'em off the hook like that. I don't think Takeshi and Miyamoto had any plans to pull something off, but Miyamoto shouldn't have brought Takeshi here. It never was a father-son relationship to begin with."

As Ko Nobuyoshi expertly piled *kamaboko* onto the board, he suddenly remembered what Takeshi had said: "I'm gonna avenge my mother someday!" When would that "someday" be? And what was the grudge about? Even without Miyamoto, Takeshi might have found a way to reach Kim Shunpei.

Hanako and Sung-han felt fresh danger now that they were suddenly bereft of their breakwater against Kim Shunpei. Lee Young-hee's feelings were more complicated. Her sympathy toward Takeshi didn't translate to anything like love. No one asked for sympathy from a distance, and her relationship with Takeshi had been cool and transparent. Lee Young-hee affected an air of disinterest after Takeshi left. She simply wished for Takeshi to find happiness wherever he went next. Her parting wish for him turned out to be an empty promise: ten days later, Takeshi died.

Takeshi's death came up in the human-interest page of the newspaper. Ko Nobuyoshi was the one who found out. Takeshi's picture was printed next to a headline that read, "Hiroshima's gang wars have reached Osaka." "At ten o'clock p.m. on XXX, the head of Hiroshima's Yamaki-*gumi*, Arai Takeshi (formerly Park Takeshi), was drinking at Club Kai in Soemoncho when two men came in and shot Arai seven times with a pistol. Arai was killed, and his two killers escaped."

So Takeshi had used his mother's last name.

Ko Nobuyoshi learned that Takeshi used to be a gang leader in Hiroshima. The war he was waging with another gang had spread from Hiroshima down to Shikoku and Kyushu. Takeshi ended up assassinating three members of the opposing gang, who were of course looking for their revenge. For half a year, Takeshi had moved undercover from place to place, and he decided to take advantage of his half-brother's invitation to hide in Kim Shunpei's house until the dust settled. But things got dangerous there too, so he left. All this Ko Nobuyoshi found out confidentially from Miyamoto Haruo. But behind all that was the fact that Takeshi wanted to avenge his mother. Takeshi had told Miyamoto that he was going to kill Kim Shunpei with a gun. Miyamoto had tried to stop him. Ko Nobuyoshi couldn't tell Kim Shunpei about any of this. If he did, Kim Shunpei would go on a rampage.

When Kim Shunpei was notified of Takeshi's death, he spat, "That guy was no good for the world."

Sung-han overheard this and thought the same was true for Kim Shunpei himself.

The shock of Takeshi's death faded into just another incident. In a matter of days, it seemed that everyone forgot Takeshi had ever existed. No one was more forgotten than the dead. Everyone lived just to eat for the day, and those without shelter starved to death. One early morning, Mrs. Kinkai was approaching the water pump when she noticed two stray dogs pawing at something in the empty lot. The dark lump turned out to be the corpse of a cripple. He was clothed in little more than rags, and his rag-wrapped hands and knees were cut and swollen.

In the dead winter of February, his body had frozen solid. His death wasn't documented in the newspaper's human-interest page.

"It's a harsh world," said Ko Nobuyoshi as he chopped off fish heads.

"Tomorrow's payday. How 'bout we go to Tobita and fuck around?" said the young Won Yoshio.

"You owe me money first," said Kaneyu.

"Hey, you lot can use your money to gamble or drink or buy a prostitute or whatever. But thousands of our compatriots are gettin' killed in the war—ever think about that? Or is that too much for those brains of yours?" Ko Nobuyoshi had had enough of these workers and their ignorance.

"Sure, but what if they make *us* go to Korea to fight? Who'd take care of our families then? Would Ko-*san* do it for us?"

Most of the workers agreed with Kaneyu.

"When did I say you had to go to Korea to fight? I never said anything like that. All I'm saying is we should do what we can while we're here." Ko Nobuyoshi was tired of spelling everything out for the simple-minded Kaneyu.

"What are we supposed to do, then?" said Kaneyu as he emptied a crate of fish onto the cutting board.

"There's an assembly at Katsuyama Park in Ikuno tomorrow. We're gonna ask ourselves the hard questions: what the war's for, who's to blame, and how we end it. If there's anything we can do, we'll do it."

Ever since becoming a committee member of his regional organization, Ko Nobuyoshi had often talked about these kinds of things. He took great pains to convince even one of his fellow workers to attend these assemblies.

"Sounds dumb. If I had that kind of time, I'd catch up on sleep," said Won Yoshio.

"You have no idea what you're even talking about. You're just gonna watch as your Korean brothers and sisters get killed every day?"

Won Yoshio's sharp eyes seemed to be laughing.

"They're gettin' killed, alright. But aren't they doin' it to each other?" said Kaneyu.

"No, it's the Americans' fault."

"You gonna go to America and start a war there, then?" said Kaneyu mockingly.

Just then, Kim Shunpei appeared before them, looking

like he wanted to punch someone. The workers shut their mouths and concentrated on their work.

"You little shits think your quota's lower 'cause Miyamoto quit? Stop fucking with me! The quota's the same as ever. There are more than enough of you here. Now get to work!" Kim Shunpei banged on the cutting board with his cherry tree club. Won Yoshio instinctively reeled back. The memory of getting hit on the forehead with the abacus came back to him.

The output of *kamaboko* fell by about ten percent after Miyamoto Haruo left. Kim Shunpei claimed there were "more than enough" workers to meet the quota, but in fact the opposite was true. Even with Miyamoto there, the workers had been pushing themselves to the limit to meet their quotas, but now there was a gaping hole in the flow of production. Pushing themselves any further meant hours of overtime work, and a good number of the workers were sure to quit. That was what Manager Ko Nobuyoshi was afraid of.

Once Kim Shunpei was out of earshot, the workers started grumbling amongst themselves.

"We've been workin' ourselves to the bone here. And now we have to do *more*? Does he wanna kill us or what?"

Tanimoto flung his knife onto the board as if he were ready to quit at that moment.

"Tanimoto, what's with that attitude? If the boss sees you like that . . . ." warned Ko Nobuyoshi.

"He's basically tellin' us to work overtime! Manager, could you get us overtime pay?"

Tanimoto was right to make that request. And the other workers murmured in agreement. But only Kim Shunpei could assent to giving his workers overtime wages.

"I'll talk to him," said Ko Nobuyoshi. But he couldn't make any promises that Kim Shunpei would give the workers what they wanted.

"Why don't you take the boss with you to Katsuyama tomorrow? He could come out of it with a different mindset," said Tanimoto sarcastically.

"Yeah. If the boss goes, we'll go," said Kaneyu, smirking. He knew Kim Shunpei would never go to such an assembly. What he didn't know was that Kim Shunpei would never grant them overtime pay.

The next day, Ko Nobuyoshi proposed to Kim Shunpei that he at least give the workers half their usual wages for overtime work.

"Wages for overtime? *Kamaboko* workers never get paid for overtime work. Doesn't matter how long you work, what matters is if you're good enough to finish the job. Those good-for-nothing bastards. They make me sick!"

Ko Nobuyoshi said nothing to convince Kim Shunpei otherwise. It was true that *kamaboko* workers traditionally didn't get overtime pay. Most owners and workers had no conception of what overtime even meant.

When Ko Nobuyoshi told the workers what Kim Shunpei thought, they smoldered with discontent. Some workers resigned themselves to the situation, but Tanimoto, Kaneyu, and Won Yoshio refused to accept it. The drunk Kim Shunpei appeared at the factory floor around midnight and looked at the workers threateningly. To intimidate the workers, he threw fish around on his hook, drove a long spike through a wooden plank with his fist, and picked up a charcoal grill with his bare hands.

Commotion broke out just before dawn. Sung-han awoke to screams and angry shouts. He looked out from the balcony to see Kim Shunpei and Won Yoshio facing off in the morning fog while the workers and neighbors watched in horror. Won Yoshio held several knives in his hands.

"Yoshio, stop! Stop right now!" screamed Ko
Nobuyoshi. But he couldn't step in between them—
otherwise Won Yoshio might stab him.

"You little fuck! You dare oppose me?" Kim Shunpei's
thundering voice seemed to send shockwaves through
people's bodies and into the ground.

"You're not worth shit!" The short but burly Won
Yoshio looked like he was ready to kill. He threw the
knives at Kim Shunpei one after another. But the knives
couldn't pierce Kim Shunpei's leather coat. With his last
knife, Won Yoshio slowly closed the distance between
him and Kim Shunpei.

"Quick! Cut him down!" screamed Sung-han.

Kim Shunpei slowly turned his head toward the
balcony. Right at that moment, Won Yoshio lunged and
stabbed Kim Shunpei in the guts. Kim Shunpei's huge
body shook violently. He took one step forward, grabbed
at the knife handle with his left hand, and swung his
club with his right arm, hitting Won Yoshio in the head.
Everyone heard something being crushed, and Won
Yoshio staggered back, groaning and vomiting blood.
Kim Shunpei also tottered backward and collapsed with a

thud.

"This is mad," said Kaneyu, appalled. Ko Nobuyoshi bent down and extricated the knife from Kim Shunpei's stomach. The drunk Kim Shunpei moaned and moaned. Won Yoshio was holding his head and writhing in pain. One of the workers, Kimura Masayuki, used the phone to call the police. The onlookers drew in closer. Lee Young-hee and Hanako were at a loss for what to do and waited for Ko Nobuyoshi to give them a signal.

"*Ajumeoni,* bring some cloth. We need to stop the bleeding."

Lee Young-hee brought out some bedsheets. Ko Nobuyoshi tore off some strips and pressed them to Kim Shunpei and Won Yoshio's wounds.

"*Aigo, aigo,* how frightful!" cried the elderly Mr. Kang as he tottered away with his hands behind his back.

"Both of 'em might die," said Tanimoto, clearly stimulated by the bloody spectacle.

Meanwhile, Sung-han kept close watch from the balcony.

An ambulance arrived, along with three policemen on bicycles. The ambulance promptly took Kim Shunpei and Won Yoshio to the police hospital, but the policemen stayed behind to collect information from the eyewitnesses. The interviews took over an hour, but no one mentioned what Sung-han had said.

Lee Young-hee packed Kim Shunpei's clothes in a bag to bring to the hospital. Then she turned to Sung-han, who was sitting absentmindedly at his desk.

"Why did you say that?" she asked.

Sung-han was wondering the same thing. Why *had* he let something like that slip? "I don't know," he said.

Lee Young-hee didn't inquire further. She sensed that Sung-han was in pain. "I'm going to the hospital. You come too."

"No."

"Why not?"

"I'm leaving. Father is probably gonna kill me."

"Stop with that foolishness. Just come with me to the hospital and apologize," said Lee Young-hee sharply.

Sung-han felt like his chest was going to burst.

Lee Young-hee got on the back of the bicycle and had Sung-han take her to the police hospital near the Imazato traffic circle. Sung-han wondered if his father was alive. He lifted himself up from his seat and pedaled hard against the oncoming wind, and he thought about how he could only blame himself if his father died. He couldn't forget what he'd seen on the balcony—the look of surprise in his father's eyes.

When they reached the hospital, Sung-han went up to the reception desk. "A man named Kim Shunpei was brought here just now in an ambulance," he said.

"Are you his son?" asked the nurse.

"Yes, I am. And this is my mother."

"He's about to undergo surgery. Please fill out this form with the patient's name, address, age, and occupation."

Sung-han did as he was told.

Doctors and nurses hurried through the hallway preparing for the surgery. No other emergency patients were around this early in the morning. Soon Ko Nobuyoshi rushed in.

"Did the surgery start yet?" he asked Lee Young-hee, who was sitting on the bench.

"It's starting now," she answered calmly.

The surgeon, in his late middle age, came out and looked at Sung-han. "Are you the son?"

Sung-han nodded.

"Your dad's asking for you. He's drunk, but we can't do much about that. He's a bit too big for our table. You can hold his head up." The surgeon quite looked the part with his hooded eyes and thick eyebrows.

When Sung-han followed the surgeon into the surgery room, Kim Shunpei looked up from the table. He was so drunk that the anesthesia wasn't working effectively, and he was fully conscious. Sung-han went to the table to support his father's protruding head.

The surgeon inserted his scalpel into Kim Shunpei's upper belly and cut a line down his abdomen. The nurse quickly mopped up the blood with gauze. The surgeon worked through Kim Shunpei's thick flesh with the scalpel. Soon he had a view of the intestines. The three layers of flesh and fat looked just like the meat of a pig. The surgeon casually took out the intestines, which expanded and contracted with each breath. He then suctioned up the internal bleeding.

"Still not done? Hurry up, you fraud!" said Kim Shunpei, his consciousness clouding.

"Quiet! What kind of patient is this? I see heavy internal bleeding. I'm amazed you survived this far."

"Hurry up, you fraud! Ugh . . . you wanted to kill me . . . . Ugh, ugh . . . You want to kill me . . . ." Kim Shunpei glared up at Sung-han. "You wanna see me dead, huh?

Try it, then. I'll take you on. Be ready. You wanted to kill me, huh! Ugh . . . Answer me!"

The surgeon was astonished by Kim Shunpei's ranting and raving.

"This area's torn." The surgeon started stitching up the part of the intestines that the knife had pierced. Then he casually put the intestines back in.

The surgery lasted about two hours. Sung-han was mentally exhausted by the end of it. The nurses brought Kim Shunpei to a private room on the second floor.

"Is he okay?" asked Lee Young-hee.

The surgeon took off his mask and spoke through his mustache. "I've never had a patient like your husband before. His physical resilience is extraordinary. He'll recover very soon."

Won Yoshio remained a problem. His skull had caved in. Ko Nobuyoshi asked about him worriedly.

"As for him, recovery will take a while. But his life isn't in danger, and I don't think he'll suffer from any side effects."

"He's not getting surgery?"

"He doesn't need it."

Ko Nobuyoshi felt himself relax at the surgeon's lucid

explanations. Like Tanimoto, he'd thought both men would surely die.

Every two days, Lee Young-hee brought Kim Shunpei a change of clothes, but she didn't exchange a single word with him. Hanako and Sung-han also came by twice, and neither of them said a word. It was as if a thick, transparent wall separated them from their father. Ko Nobuyoshi visited Kim Shunpei twice during his work shifts and checked in on Won Yoshio, too.

As the surgeon had said, Kim Shunpei's recovery was amazingly swift, and he was discharged in ten days. He felt feebler than usual, but his condition wasn't much different from before. The neighbors and workers were in fearful awe of his tenacity. But Kim Shunpei didn't go back into the house. Instead, he moved to a room on the mezzanine floor of the factory. He employed a female cook to make the workers' meals from then on. He seemed to have separated from his family for real.

Chapter 20

After Kim Shunpei moved to the factory's mezzanine floor with his travel bag, the others wondered what new incidents would unfold. The days passed sluggishly, but Kim Shunpei was like the center of his own magnetic field. If anyone drew too close, they would get sucked in.

Kaneyu was cutting off fish heads on the factory floor and looking up periodically toward the mezzanine floor. "It's like he's breathin' down our necks. I can't even work," he said.

"Yeah. Even when he's not around, I feel like I'm being watched. It's fuckin' exhausting." Kakizaki kept drawing from the stub of his cigarette. After one last puff, he pushed the stub into a fish's eye.

"Why'd he even move up there?" said Tanimoto.

"Like I know! No one understands how the boss

thinks," said Kimura.

Kaneyu lowered his voice, unabashedly eager to gossip. "I heard Takeshi found a heap of cash behind the boss's bedroom walls. Wonder where he'd hiding it this time."

"Didn't he bury it somewhere? Can't even trust a bank, can he?"

Ko Nobuyoshi quickly refuted Kakizaki's hypothesis. "He has money in the bank. Now stop with all this stupid talk and get back to work."

The workers shut up. But Kimura was right: even Kim Shunpei's manager and close friend Ko Nobuyoshi didn't understand what went through Kim Shunpei's head. It wasn't like Kim Shunpei ever opened up to him. It was as if Kim Shunpei had a second eye, always glinting from behind his pupils and searching through people's hearts. He always seemed to want something from people, even while he pushed them away. He was in his own little isolated world.

The one who found Kim Shunpei's move hardest to comprehend was Lee Young-hee. She never predicted that he'd be the one to move out of the house first, instead of being the one to drive *her* away. This move also felt different from the times he'd left with his travel bag to wander around aimlessly. Was he now going to break ties with his family completely? Lee Young-hee had no objection to that. After spending years and years flailing desperately under Kim Shunpei's shadow, she wanted to be released from his curse. But he hadn't really left; he'd just moved across the street. At the same time, the relief of no longer living under the same roof as him felt hard-won. She and her children could move and talk more freely in the house without him there.

But Kim Shunpei's violence wasn't over. As always, he would get drunk, break down Lee Young-hee's front door, and march in. Not only did nothing seem to change, but with Kim Shunpei lurking so close by, a new unnatural kind of nervousness pervaded the house. Lee Young-hee tried not to think about him. Besides, money was getting tight. She eked out a living from selling Korean silk, brassware, and ornaments, but her financial situation was deteriorating. Her debts were on the rise, and she was teetering on the edge of bankruptcy. Hanako wanted to go to dressmaking school, and Sung-han was set on going to high school. Lee Young-hee thought over what to do until she could think no longer. She had to go back into the *sake* business. She threw herself into *sake* production,

knowing that Kim Shunpei wouldn't like it. Her first
batches were inevitably sold to the *kamaboko* workers,
who went behind Kim Shunpei's back to drink in the
middle of their shifts. Then her son-in-law Han Masahito
started bringing his friends over for drinks, and old
friends and acquaintances showed up as well. It was easier
to act than sit and worry endlessly. More and more people
started showing up at Lee Young-hee's door—people
whose very presence could deter Kim Shunpei from
attacking for a little while.

Every time the seedy-looking, sad-eyed Hong Byeong-
saeng came to visit, he stayed for three or four nights.
He made his living swindling peasants and fishermen all
over the country, while his family remained in Tochigi.
Sometimes he sent his family a remittance when he made
a successful deal, but most of the time he just scraped by.
When he ran out of money, he took shelter at temples and
farmhouses, and if he was in Osaka, he nursed back his
strength at Lee Young-hee's house. Lee Young-hee had
to feed him at her own expense. Some of his fingers were
missing from when gangsters wanted to settle scores with
him. Hong Byeong-saeng's one source of pride was that
he'd graduated from a university under the old system.

But it was also something for which he was ridiculed.

There was another man named Ito (a.k.a. Yi Takane), about sixty years of age, who was sponging off Lee Young-hee at the same time. He was the leader of a small gang in Sakai with ten other members, but he went into hiding after he couldn't pay back a debt to another gang. Lee Young-hee had hidden him for over a month, but there was no sign of him leaving anytime soon. He and Hong Byeong-saeng spent their days sitting around, gossiping, and playing cards. Of course, neither of them had money to bet on. They just needed something to do. And at night, they drank from Lee Young-hee's stores with impunity.

Men came through her house one after another. After Yi Takane finally left, the house became a watering hole for young activists. Inflation was spiraling out of control, and the penniless activists had nowhere to live. They constantly sniffed around for food like starving dogs. They held meeting after meeting at Lee Young-hee's house, and when she was gone they would raid her stores of rice wine and help themselves to liver and pork in the refrigerator. Sometimes they would wolf down Hanako and Sung-han's food as well. One of the activists told Sung-han, "Marx said that religion is the opiate of the masses. When we establish a socialist society, religion will disappear. In fifty years it'll be extinct."

These young activists always had to show off how smart they were, but Sung-han saw how they ate and drank with the utmost entitlement. He thought they were the most ignorant people on earth. Could these ignorant, arrogant assholes really bring about revolution?

The Korean War was entering its third year, and the activists spent a good deal of time discussing the war.

"The Syngman Rhee camp has recruited over five hundred Zainichi Korean volunteers. Those bastards are connected to the Japanese right-wing thugs. No one's volunteering for us. We'll have to fight for our country ourselves," said Park as he passed around the *sake*.

"You're right, of course, but how are we gonna join up with our comrades in the Democratic People's Republic? The right-wing bastards are leaving for Korea from Sasebo on American warships. We don't have anything like that," said Kang impatiently.

"We'll set off from Hokkaido for Nakhodka, then go through China toward the Tumen River. If they have five hundred, we'll have five *thousand*—no, *ten* thousand volunteers," said Park, sounding elated.

Baek raised an objection. "I understand how you feel, but how the hell are we gonna ship ten thousand volunteer soldiers to Nakhodka? It's impossible with the Japanese police and self-defense forces on the lookout for people like us. We should figure out what we can do here in Japan. We can resist the American imperialists, we can resist the Syngman Rhee puppet government, we can resist the Yoshida cabinet's complicity in the war and its obsession with re-militarizing Japan. We can mobilize the masses and crush the right-wing bastards that way. We can prepare for armed conflict in a different context."

With frothing mouths, the activists discussed and argued until late at night. Lee Young-hee found the presence of these activists reassuring. They woke up the next afternoon hungover and hungry. If nothing was in the refrigerator or storage cabinet, they went out to wash down their hangovers with more drinks.

Many of Lee Young-hee's guests were destitute and couldn't pay Lee Young-hee for her drinks. She considered discontinuing her *sake* business and going back into the peddling trade. But hadn't she resorted to selling *sake* because peddling wares didn't earn her enough money? It wasn't like anyone wanted to employ a fifty-year-old

Zainichi Korean woman. Then a middle-aged man named Chang Chan-myung stumbled into her life. He was the son of the elderly Changs, the Yodokawa couple who had housed Lee Young-hee twice: once when she was on the run from Kim Shunpei, and once when she and her family lost their homes to the air raids. He was a calm and cultured man, but he was wanted by the police for dealing methamphetamine. Park Yoshiko had hidden him in the past. In a strange turn of events, Lee Young-hee agreed to participate in Chang Chan-myung's meth ring, deciding that certain scruples had to be sacrificed. Making and dealing meth was a family operation. Lee Young-hee didn't want her children to get involved, but Chang Chan-myung convinced her otherwise. No one suspected children, and they were sure not to tell anyone. Lee Young-hee also kept up her *sake* business for appearances, so that no one could wonder how she was making a living.

The meth was made on the second floor of the house. Sung-han and the dexterous Hanako helped with production, and Lee Young-hee, per Chang Chan-myung's instructions, acquired the ingredients and made deliveries. Sailors were their main clientele, and a single order could earn her tens of thousands of yen. With two or three deliveries in a single month, Lee Young-hee was able to pay back her debts. Could she quit the trade at this point? She now nursed some wicked aspirations. Meanwhile, Chang Chan-myung didn't leave her house once. Once a week, his wife visited to bring him new clothes. Like her husband, she didn't speak much, and she hurriedly left with each visit. The cultured Chang Chan-myung pored over his books. He was interested in socialism: Marx, Engels, Lenin, Stalin, Mao Zedong, Kim Il-sung, and the like. His influence on Sung-han was not inconsiderable. Sung-han didn't have a clear understanding of what Chang Chan-myung talked about, but he came to believe that justice lay in socialism. For a middle school student, this belief was absolute. It wasn't a contradiction to produce meth and believe in socialism at the same time. A human had to feed himself first and foremost. This new way of life was full of danger but also felt strangely fulfilling. It was a challenge of the will to keep secrets and hold one's own counsel under the dreadful eye of the authorities. Sung-han also learned that trusting others in these circumstances called for a spirit of self-sacrifice. But particularly strange was the fact that the neighbors *knew* Lee Young-hee's family was involved in an illicit drug trade. So did the men who came to drink her *sake*. But no one said anything out loud.

After three months passed, Chang Chan-myung announced one day, "You've taken good care of me. I'll be taking my leave today. Please make sure to get rid of any evidence after I'm gone." With that, he disappeared like a ghost under the noonday sun, just as he'd arrived.

Lee Young-hee had no idea why he left, but she did as she was told, throwing the ingredients into a pot and burning them all. She looked meaningfully at her children, and they all relaxed, as if they'd woken up from a bad dream. She then took out her thick rolls of cash and counted them again and again, amazed that they were hers.

Park Yoshiko visited a few days later to thank Lee Young-hee for hiding Chang Chan-myung.

"No, I should be thanking you. I thought I'd get arrested for sure, but nothing happened, thank heavens. He left so suddenly, though. It's got me quite worried. He's not going home, is he? Where is he now?"

Park Yoshiko looked like she wanted to give a whole speech, but she just said, "I don't think he's in Japan anymore."

"If he's not in Japan, where could he be?"

"I don't know. All I know is he's not in Japan."

Lee Young-hee didn't pry further.

Sung-han, listening in, guessed that Chang Chan-myung had gone to North Korea. It seemed to fit Sung-han's image of him.

That summer, Kim Shunpei bought the old two-story house on the corner. One had to pass in front of this house to reach the main road. Kim Shunpei refurbished the whole place and moved in. Lee Young-hee's house wasn't even thirty meters away. He could have bought a house that was more out of the way, even by a few hundred meters, but he chose to have Lee Young-hee and his children right under his nose. No one knew what Kim Shunpei was thinking, nor what he was sensing in the air. Ever since moving to the mezzanine floor of the factory, he hadn't spoken with his family once. When his family encountered him on the street, they scurried away. Now the chance of running into Kim Shunpei increased all the more. Hanako and Sung-han made sure to take the back alleyways and detour through Benten Market in order to reach the main road.

One day toward the end of the summer, a woman in her mid-thirties rode up jauntily on a bicycle to Kim Shunpei's house. Her hair was parted down the middle and tied up at the back with a tortoiseshell comb. She wasn't particularly beautiful, but she was fair-skinned and had a cultured air about her. Her white blouse and black skirt expressed a refined simplicity. The women at the water pump stared at her in wonder and asked among themselves, "Who could this be?"

"Kim Shunpei's new mistress, I bet," said Mrs. Kinkai as she adjusted the baby on her back.

"Seriously? She's coming here in broad daylight, right under the wife's nose?" said Mrs. Kuremoto as she washed the vegetables in her basin.

"She better watch out. If the wife finds out, it ain't gonna be pretty," said Mrs. Tomimura, rolling up her *chima* and squatting down.

"Well, I know a sixty-year-old man with four mistresses. They all get along fine," said Mrs. Kinkai.

"By the looks of it, this one's gone to a girl's school. Why would an educated Japanese woman sleep with that mean old drunkard? I see nothing but trouble," said Mrs. Kanemura.

"So true!" said the other women in unison.

After about an hour, the cultured-looking woman came out of the house and rode away jauntily. The women at the pump watched in envy at how her black skirt fluttered in the breeze. It was rare to see a woman ride a bicycle at all. This one came around every two or three days. Her outfit changed each time, and the neighborhood women speculated that she was a rich widow. But they still couldn't figure out why a rich widow would ever want to visit a man like Kim Shunpei. They could only conclude that Japanese women were desperate for anybody since so many men had died during the war.

"I can lend her my husband if she wants," said Mrs. Tomimura half-jokingly. Everyone laughed. But the mistress blithely ignored all the chatter, visiting Kim Shunpei daily and then, finally, moving in.

Lee Young-hee wasn't happy. Whenever this woman came around, Kim Shunpei shut the front door and windows even in the mid-afternoon heat. Lee Young-hee could nonetheless hear the woman's choked moans, as could the women at the water pump.

Thirty-five-year-old Yamanashi Kiyoko loved how the muscular Kim Shunpei could take her to the heights of pleasure again and again. He lifted her with ease, and when he penetrated her, it felt like falling backward into a dark abyss. Kim Shunpei's appendage felt like a part of her own body, while his large, hot hands moved back and forth from her vagina to her anus to her nipples. Feeling like all her orifices were filled with his flesh, she would scream in a fit, "Let me die!" As enormous amounts of energy passed through her body, she really did wonder if she was about to die. "You'll kill me if we do this every day," she told him, but she wanted him so much that there was nothing else to do but move in.

The one who had introduced Yamanashi Kiyoko to Kim Shunpei was Manada Aira, the owner of the Manada-*ya* wholesale store. Kim Shunpei had been complaining to Manada about his sexless life with his wife Lee Young-hee. Yamanashi Kiyoko was the wife of one of Manada's distant cousins, a tailor in Teradachō who had been drafted in 1942 and killed in the Philippines the following year. They'd been married for only three years. Luckily their house escaped the air raids, but Kiyoko wasn't able to continue her husband's business on her own. She could sew skirts and kids' pants, but she didn't have the skills of a full-fledged tailor.

She tried being a supplier for the black market, but her goods were confiscated twice by the police. She also tried renting out the second floor of her house, but her tenant only paid her for the first month and absconded nearly a year later with twenty yen of her mattress money. Kiyoko was a stereotypical case of the extreme difficulties a woman faced living on her own. Next, she lied about her age to work at Minami Cabaret. Her income there wasn't substantial enough to support her, so she moonlighted as an escort. She lived a precarious existence. Eventually she went to Manada Airi for loans. Her debts piled up, and she became Manada's mistress. Over the course of three years, she visited him once or twice a week for hours at a time. She stopped seeing Manada when his wife found out about their arrangement. The wife marched into her home, dragged her around by the hair, and used scissors to cut all her clothing into shreds.

One day, Manada showed up unexpectedly at Kiyoko's door. "I need to talk with you about something," he said, grinning. "I know a *kamaboko* factory owner who's filthy rich, worth thirty million yen. He has a wife, but they live in separate houses—and he told me he's about to divorce her. He's a little over fifty, but he won't look at any woman over forty. He's pretty buff, and even the thugs are scared of him. But you know how people are when they get older. He's lonely by himself. He asked me to introduce him to a nice girl. What do you think?"

In other words, Manada was Kim Shunpei's hunting dog.

In a world overflowing with starving people, a thirty-five-year-old widow had few choices when it came to survival. Becoming a second wife or mistress to an old man was a comparative blessing. She took Manada's words with a grain of salt, but when a nice house could be bought for half a million yen, a man with thirty million yen was nothing to laugh at.

"What's his wife like?" asked Kiyoko.

"Never met her. But she shouldn't be a problem, since they're separated. She has two grown-up kids. It's up to you. You can be her replacement if you want. There's no question he'd die before you, and half the assets would be yours. If the guy likes you enough, he'll be generous. You still have a good body, and he's good in bed."

Manada leered at Kiyoko, lapping her up with his eyes. Then he took Kiyoko's hands and sidled up to her. "He gave me a deposit of fifty thousand yen. That'll tide you over for a while."

He put the roll of cash in Kiyoko's hand and slipped a hand under her skirt. Kiyoko moved away from him but couldn't ignore the feeling of the fifty thousand yen in her hand. Manada pushed her onto her back and removed her panties while fingering her between her thighs. "To be honest, I don't want you to go. Nothing I can do 'bout that, but you get how I feel?"

Kiyoko was disgusted by the opportunistic Manada. She lay there waiting for him to finish.

"He's expectin' you tomorrow. Don't try to defy him. He's gone without sex for a long time, understand? I'm telling you this 'cause I care," panted Manada. Soon his elbows crumpled, and he fell onto Kiyoko as if he were a corpse.

The next day, Kiyoko used the map and address Manada gave her to look for Kim Shunpei's house. She turned the corner when she saw the udon shop and entered the alleyways, casting her eyes about for a nameplate. Eventually she found a refurbished house with the name "Kim Shunpei" emblazoned next to the new front door. She was overwhelmed by the seedy-looking chaos of the rowhouses around her. And she quailed a little under the curious stares of the women by the water pump in the empty lot. But she gathered her bearings and ignored them: she couldn't turn back now. She opened Kim Shunpei's front door as if it were the door of fate.

She stood on a cement-paved *genkan* and saw a two-*jo* room, as well as a kitchen and bathroom further in. If one went out the back door by way of the kitchen, the neighbor's house—Lee Young-hee's—wasn't even ten meters away.

Kim Shunpei was waiting in the two-*jo* room. He smiled faintly when he saw Kiyoko. Manada had told her Kim Shunpei was a large man, but the man in front of her was even larger than she'd expected. He had sharp eyes and thick lips. His fat neck supported a stout jaw. A long scar ran from the top of his crew cut down to his eyebrows, and lesions swarmed the area between his misshapen right ear and his chin. His nostrils flared with lust. From the look of his thick, sinewy arms and skin, one wouldn't have guessed that he was over fifty. Kiyoko stood there, transfixed.

"Thanks for coming. Come on up," said Kim Shunpei, beckoning her up the stairs. Kiyoko followed him up to the second floor.

There were two four-and-a-half-*jo* rooms on the spacious second floor. Sashimi, boiled vegetables, pickled vegetables, and fruit sat on a low table. Kim Shunpei had never hosted a guest like this before. He sat down and handed Kiyoko a seat cushion. "Make yourself comfortable," he said gently.

Kiyoko sat *seiza*-style on the cushion and looked around. A futon was laid out in the next room. Kiyoko quickly looked down at her lap.

"It's not much, but help yourself," said Kim Shunpei awkwardly as he picked up the bottle of *sake*. Kiyoko took the bottle and poured him a glass. "You drink too," he told her.

Kiyoko nodded. Kim Shunpei poured her a glass, and they drank in lieu of introducing themselves to each other.

Kiyoko could tell from Kim Shunpei's accent—as well as that of the women at the water pump—that she was in a Korean neighborhood. This was her first time interacting with Koreans. She of course bore some prejudice against them, but in reality she knew nothing about them. Her ignorance didn't make her hostile. She just saw Kim Shunpei as she saw any other man. At the same time, he was clearly different from the average man.

He radiated sexual energy that overwhelmed her. She was like a little bird captured in his hand.

"If you take care of me, I'll take care of you. I have a wife somewhere else, but I'll break things off with her soon." He seemed to be implying that he wanted a new wife.

Kiyoko's face was flushed from the alcohol, which she hadn't tasted in a long time. The two of them didn't know how to talk with each other, and their unease also arose from their constitutional ethnic differences. There was nothing to do now but wait for Kim Shunpei to make his move. His desire was written on his face. Kiyoko acted like she was tipsy and put a hand to her forehead. Kim Shunpei reached for that hand and pulled her to him until she was pressed against his chest. Kiyoko buried her face into his shirt. His chest was as hard as steel. Kim Shunpei lifted her up and carried her to the futon in the next room. Then he started taking off Kiyoko's clothes as she lay there with her eyes closed.

"Please be gentle," she whispered. Kim Shunpei pressed his mouth over hers as if to silence her. She could barely breathe from the powerful, spicy musk of him, but his moist tongue awakened her desire. That tongue ran from her lips down to her breasts, and then further down to her navel. Kim Shunpei then adjusted his body and inserted his penis into her. He twisted his thick penis inside her, concentrating all his power in it. Soon Kiyoko felt her desire for Kim Shunpei surge within her, and her vagina started overflowing. His wild strength seemed to break her open. Before Kiyoko knew it, she screamed loudly. She couldn't believe those carnal screams were coming from her. At the same time, an indescribable energy pierced through her whole body and gave her a taste of pure pleasure that escaped her almost immediately. Gasping and clutching onto him, Kiyoko shook violently in a state of catatonic joy.

Everything around her was dark. Kiyoko fell asleep, naked.

When she awoke, Kim Shunpei emerged from the stairs in a different set of clothes. "Want some food?" he asked.

"No, thank you." Kiyoko couldn't remember what her body had done, nor what sounds she'd made, but her body still throbbed with a trace of that former pleasure, and she felt ashamed.

Kim Shunpei walked her to the front door and said, "Come back in two days."

"Okay," said Kiyoko, nodding. She rode off.

A month later she sold her house and moved in.

There was no way Kiyoko could avoid encounters with Lee Young-hee. They would make eye contact as they ran errands, cleaned their entryways, or opened their back doors. Lee Young-hee always looked at her very coldly. Whenever Kiyoko encountered Hanako and Sung-han, they coldly rebuffed her as well. Kiyoko was confused. The workers never stepped foot into Kim Shunpei's house, so she never talked to them either. Sometimes the manager Ko Nobuyoshi came by to discuss work matters or share a drink with Kim Shunpei, but he never stayed long. He was trying to be considerate to Lee Young-hee. His greetings to Kiyoko were short and perfunctory.

Kim Shunpei kept his violence to a minimum after Kiyoko moved in. They were having sex almost every night, and perhaps that appeased him. Sometimes they would ride together to the Tsuruhashi markets to shop for dinner. They acted as if they were newlyweds, much to the surprise of the workers and neighbors.

"Young women are the best ones, huh."

The idle chatter by the water pump all converged on this fact—that men were infatuated with young women.

The workers could attest to this fact as well.

It would be a lie to say that Lee Young-hee didn't feel any jealousy at all. When she saw the fullness of Kim Shunpei's life with this woman, she wondered what all those years of marital discord had been for. Sadness filled her heart. She was the one who had raised all the funds to establish Kim Shunpei's factory, and Han Masahito was the one who had gotten Kim Shunpei the business license. Hanako had quit school to cook the workers their meals, and Sung-han had woken up early every morning to write out Kim Shunpei's bills. Without the help of his family, Kim Shunpei would never have gotten to where he was now. But instead of sharing the fruits of his business with his family, he hoarded everything for himself. The family had a right to Kim Shunpei's enormous assets. But instead those assets were going to a Japanese woman. It was intolerable. If circumstances permitted, this Japanese woman would become his legal wife and inherit everything, and Lee Young-hee couldn't do anything about it. She considered getting someone to intervene on her behalf, but who would agree to face Kim Shunpei? Lee Young-hee surrendered to her fate. All her years of life amounted to this.

She considered it a good thing that she and her family could now live without the constant threat of Kim Shunpei's violence. And she was comforted by the presence of all the people who came to drink her *sake* and talk. She found particular comfort in her late-night consultations with fortune tellers and shamans. Her tears washed away her despair like a purifying river. Only then did she feel like she could endure the pain of living in this world. Soon she would have to prepare for her journey to the next one. She had a black-and-white portrait of herself drawn and framed. Then she prepared a set of Korean-style silk clothes, socks, and shoes to put into a trunk, along with a comb, a gold ring, and a bag with several rolls of cash. A cash offering was required to avoid being sentenced to hell, and an additional offering was required to reach paradise. Lee Young-hee took special care to set aside enough money for her afterlife insurance.

An incident occurred about a month after Kiyoko moved in. Every summer Kim Shunpei would prepare his horrifying pork recipe to stave off summer fatigue, but this year he was a bit late. As autumn approached, Kim Shunpei didn't miss his chance: he brought home a pig from his nephew's hog farm and carried it to the back kitchen, where he held it down and cut its throat. He spent half the day disassembling the pig before cutting the meat into thin slices. The weather was getting cooler, but within three days the house stank of rotting meat. The smell made Kiyoko nauseous, and she shut herself up in a room on the second floor unless she had to go to the bathroom. Kim Shunpei ignored her and sat in the two-*jo* room drinking *shochu* and eating the rotting pork with relish. But two nights later, Kim Shunpei started moaning and clawing at his chest. He writhed on the futon as if he were poisoned. Kiyoko felt as if she were watching a movie. She had no idea what to do.

"Doctor . . . Call a doctor!" choked out Kim Shunpei.

"O-okay. I'll call him now."

Kiyoko put on a *haori* over her nightgown and ran to the nearby clinic. She pounded on the door and shouted, but it was past midnight, and the doctor wasn't answering.

"Please, open the door! There's something wrong with my husband! Please wake up!"

The lights flickered on inside the clinic and in the neighboring house. An old woman pulled open the curtain behind the front door.

"Sorry to bother you, but there's something wrong with my husband. We need a doctor!"

The old woman retreated without a word, and then the old doctor appeared. Kiyoko explained what happened, and he got his bag. He muttered complaints under his breath as they traversed the short distance to Kim Shunpei's house.

When they arrived at the house, the doctor covered his nose and mouth. "What's that smell?"

"It's nothing. Please come up to the second floor," said Kiyoko.

When they saw Kim Shunpei, they stood there in shock. His teeth were falling out, and his mouth was all bloody. This was too much for the doctor to handle. He had no explanation for what was causing these symptoms. But Kim Shunpei's pain had subsided for the time being.

The next day, Kim Shunpei had a full examination done at the university hospital. It was unclear why his teeth had all fallen out. The doctor did discover that it had to do with damage to the cranial nerves. It was possible, according to him, that the bacteria that caused Kim Shunpei's teeth to fall out had attacked his cranial nerves. But Kim Shunpei didn't *look* like he was suffering from a neural disorder.

"For now, we'll keep him here for observation," said the doctor.

Kiyoko was certain the bizarre symptoms had to do with the meat he ate.

Kim Shunpei was ill for half a year and was forced to stay in the hospital the entire time. Two months into his hospitalization, Kim Shunpei lost his workers and clients. Osaka had dozens of *kamaboko* factories at this point, and competition was fierce. Asahi Industries was a lost cause.

Ko Nobuyoshi visited Kim Shunpei in the neurosurgical unit from time to time, and he blamed himself for his powerlessness. "It's just me and Kimura left. And Kimura told me he's done. Sorry," he said timidly.

By appearance alone, Kim Shunpei didn't seem terribly sick. The only thing was that he couldn't sleep properly. He took sleeping pills, but he was having waking dreams. He never remembered what he dreamt. The doctor said this was a symptom of his neural disorder. The patient couldn't distinguish between hallucinations and reality as he slept.

Kim Shunpei opened his toothless mouth and muttered, "I'll close the factory."

The muscles around his mouth had shrunk, which made him look twenty years older. A dentist was working on getting him dentures.

Ko Nobuyoshi kept blaming himself. "I had no guts. I couldn't do anything to help," he said.

"Don't worry about it. I was gonna close the factory anyway,"

Indeed, the closure of the factory was unlikely to cause Kim Shunpei any trouble. He'd earned enough to be comfortable for the rest of his life, and perhaps it was high time for him to retire. There had been no time to relax when he was going to the fishing boats at dawn, making sure his employees showed up for work on time, and keeping those damn ruffians in line. Ever since he was hospitalized, he'd realized how truly annoying other humans were. They always avoided him and talked behind his back. Who cared whether he lived or died? And what would he care if someone else died? Even the death of a parent or child wouldn't be worth remembering for more than three days.

"Death is the end. For everyone. People will forget

about you after three days. That's how humans are."

Ko Nobuyoshi listened glumly to Kim Shunpei's pet theory of humankind. "That's not true. My children will hold a *jesa** for me."

"Huh! Well, my children were a mistake. They're spoiled rotten by their mother, and Sung-han's got no backbone. I expect nothing from him. I'm raisin' a son of my own."

Ko Nobuyoshi didn't hide his surprise. Kim Shunpei was apparently serious about raising "a son of his own." His sexual prowess was unrivalled, so he could likely have a younger woman bear him one. But Kim Shunpei didn't understand how difficult it was to raise a child. Kiyoko sat on the other side of Kim Shunpei's bed and smiled wanly. She'd never told Kim Shunpei that she was infertile.

His symptoms weren't clear-cut, so it was an open question whether he was recovering or not. Kim Shunpei wanted to be discharged, but the anxious doctor convinced him to stay. He didn't take well to the dentures: they made him cough, and they would fly out of his mouth in the middle of his meals or when he talked. They

---

* A Korean memorial service conducted for one's ancestors

were the bane of his existence.

"You'll get used to it," the dentist told him.

He couldn't chew up chicken bones and tougher meats, and he couldn't eat his favorite foods. He couldn't even clench his teeth when he was angry. Clenching his teeth allowed him to channel his energy into his jaw and abs, but now he had no outlet for his anger. This greatly affected his fighting spirit.

When Kim Shunpei was finally discharged, he went straight to his defunct factory. The factory was dark and cool, and the smell of fish hung in the air. The machines had rusted, and there were cracks in the wooden steamers. The second floor of the factory where the live-in workers slept was scrubbed clean, and the closets were empty. Kim Shunpei looked over the factory as if he'd gained a newfound understanding of something. Meanwhile, the neighbors greeted him with condolences for the factory's closure. The Kunimoto family's new stubby-legged bulldog mix barked at the sight of him.

Lee Young-hee watched Kim Shunpei carefully from a second-floor window. She hadn't visited him once at the hospital, and she feared that he would take revenge on her later that night. She'd asked Ko Nobuyoshi whether she should visit or not, but he advised her not to go, since Kim Shunpei already had Kiyoko at his beck and call. But Lee Young-hee now regretted not doing anything. She could have at least made her children go see him, but they'd staunchly refused.

After six months in the hospital, Kim Shunpei's body had atrophied. To recover his strength, he biked ten kilometers every day. He also went to a construction site and came back with a trailer truck full of scrap wood. He piled the wood along the sides of his house until it spilled out onto the empty lot next to him. He chopped the wood with his axe every morning at six. The neighbors awoke to the *thump, thump* of Kim Shunpei's axe and knew it was time to get out of bed and prepare breakfast.

The sweating Kim Shunpei replenished himself by drinking from a bottle full of algae-green liquid—his special extract of daikon radish leaves, which he collected from the Benten Market dumpsters. He drank this extract as if it were water. He made all sorts of concoctions from the ingredients he bought at the Chinese herbal medicine shop. His strange alchemical diet was back in full swing. The shelves in his kitchen were lined with exotic medicines and spices, which made Kiyoko feel queasy.

Kim Shunpei regained his enormous appetite. In spite of his dentures, he dumped food into his mouth willy-nilly. He cut up his meat into tiny pieces and swallowed them. He was like a wild animal, snarling and snapping at his prey.

Kiyoko started to find her nights with Kim Shunpei disagreeable. It was painful for her to satisfy his insatiable desire. She could barely get up in the mornings, feeling like her body had been ground to dust. Her sex drive was decreasing, and she felt like her life force was being sucked away. Three months after Kim Shunpei was discharged, his strength had returned to normal. He would stand in front of the full-length mirror in the bathhouse and inspect every nook and cranny of his body. The other men at the bathhouse were intimidated by his countless scars. Even the thugs with their back tattoos paled in comparison to him.

"What a freakish build!" a thug said enviously as he poked one of Kim Shunpei's scars.

"Don't touch me!" barked Kim Shunpei, and the thug pulled his hand back as if he'd been shocked.

Kim Shunpei turned back to alcohol after a six-month hiatus. With the help of *sake,* his built-up resentments could finally find their release. His target was Lee Young-hee and her brood. His existence meant nothing to them, and he needed to teach them a lesson.

They dare disrespect me . . .

Drunk, Kim Shunpei stood at Lee Young-hee's front door. The Kunimoto family's short-legged, fierce-tempered dog barked at him. Kim Shunpei lunged at the dog. When he picked it up, it bit deep into his arm. Kim Shunpei casually twisted the dog's neck. The dog lay on the ground with its tongue lolling out, still breathing. Kim Shunpei crushed the dog's head under his boot and then turned around and kicked Lee Young-hee's door until it smashed apart. When he marched up to the second floor, he saw that Lee Young-hee and Hanako had already escaped. But Sung-han was sitting at his desk, reading a book. His eyes burned with hostility.

Taken aback, Kim Shunpei shouted, "You little shit! You think you can fight me?"

In the next moment, Sung-han went through the open window and leapt lightly off the balcony. Kim Shunpei was shocked by Sung-han's agility and audacity. Sung-han had grown a lot since he'd last seen him. Kim Shunpei felt as if he'd just seen a younger version of himself.

Something seemed to pop within him. It was the sound of the eruptive encounter between a man who was coming of age and a man who was just aging.

Chapter 21

Sung-han entered Takatsu High School as a part-time student. He'd wanted to take engineering courses at Miyakojima Industrial High School, but he'd failed the school's qualifying exam. He barely passed the make-up exam to enter a part-time school. While attending Takatsu High, he worked at a small, cramped shoe store behind the Tsuruhashi black market. Hanako graduated from her two-year sewing course and started a side hustle as a seamstress. Lee Young-hee kept up her *sake* business while activists and other acquaintances continued to stream through her house.

Kim Shunpei, on the other hand, rarely hosted visitors. Any visitors he did have were there to borrow money. At this point, Kim Shunpei was a well-known moneylender. One time, a company president who oversaw over a hundred workers came to kowtow in front of him.

He also lent to gangs. Kiyoko managed the contracts and promissory notes, but the illiterate Kim Shunpei committed all the numbers and deadlines to memory. His ability to remember things was astonishing. Like a woman, he could recall the most trivial details from the past. His vengeful personality only added to his power of recall.

No one could get away without paying Kim Shunpei back, gangs included. Three days before a deadline, Kim Shunpei always circled around the debtor's house on his bicycle. This kind of intimidation lasted all three days, and the unlucky debtor could only quake in fear. Kim Shunpei used the same tactic for gang members. But for them, he lent only the amount of money he would place on a bet.

Lending money was a natural fit for Kim Shunpei's disposition. Hapless men besieged by their finances knew how merciless Kim Shunpei was, but even so, they knelt before him and begged for a loan. If they couldn't repay him in time, they knelt down again and begged him to push the deadline back. People were helpless when it came to money. Money was power, and it was a window into one's soul. People lied, begged for compassion, and sometimes took the offensive. Ever since Kim Shunpei became a moneylender, he grew more and more distrustful of others.

Only one person was the exception: Ko Nobuyoshi. After Kim Shunpei closed his *kamaboko* factory, Ko Nobuyoshi couldn't find another job, and he was back at his barrack-like house near Miyukimori Shrine helping his wife. Selling magazines wasn't enough for a five-person family to get by. At a loss for what to do, Ko Nobuyoshi asked Kim Shunpei for a loan.

"I'm in no place to ask you this. But we've damn run outta luck with our little back-alley shop. My wife and I've been talkin' about how much we'd like a store along a main street. Turns out a space is up for sale in Korea Market—the sixth unit from where Korea Market meets Ichijo Street. I could go back into construction like I used to, but at this age my body can't take it. My kids are getting bigger and costlier, too. If something doesn't change now, we'll have no place to live. We'd love to try our hand at a store along that street, but by gosh, we don't have the means to purchase the space. Could you give us a hand? If I can't pay you back right away, I'll make sure my children do."

This was the first time Kim Shunpei had heard Ko Nobuyoshi make such an impassioned speech. Kim Shunpei tossed back his drink and stood up. "Let's take a look at that store," he said.

They had no time to lose. Ko Nobuyoshi got on his bike and led Kim Shunpei there.

The Korean market by Miyukimori Shrine was about two kilometers away from Kim Shunpei's house. The area around Ichijo Street was full of Koreans. The shops increased in number as they approached Korea Market, and soon they could catch a whiff of something characteristically Korean. The strong smell of spices filled the air, and Korean was being spoken everywhere. Most of the people on this street were their compatriots. The market was a transplant of Korea itself. It had been a while since Kim Shunpei's last visit, and he suddenly felt nostalgic. Many of the storefronts looked recently renovated. The unit for sale was a fairly large two-story tiled house with a width of two *jo* and a length of six *jo*. On the first floor was a kitchen and six-*jo* room, and on the second floor were three rooms with a narrow hallway. It was an ideal space for a five-person family to live and work in.

"Looks pretty good to me," said Kim Shunpei.

"Seems kinda like a pipe dream for us to live here, but we think we'd do alright if we could," said Ko Nobuyoshi, trying not to appear too forthcoming about the future.

"Gotcha. How much do you need?"

Ko Nobuyoshi gulped. "450,000 yen."

"Four hundred and fifty . . . That's just for the title? What about the land rights?"

"Land is separate. That's just for the title."

"Huh, not bad. Seems about right for a property like this," said Kim Shunpei approvingly as he looked around. "Right. I'll lend you the money tomorrow. I won't charge you any interest. We'll just have the contract. Return the money whenever you like."

Where did such generosity come from? Ko Nobuyoshi thought he was dreaming. The notorious miser Kim Shunpei—the same Kim Shunpei who refused to give a cent to his own family—was lending him 450,000 yen with no interest and no timeline for repayment. This was the one time Ko Nobuyoshi saw a halo around Kim Shunpei.

"Come over for dinner. You'll see how happy you've

made us," said Ko Nobuyoshi, beaming with gratitude.

"No, I'm heading home." With that, Kim Shunpei rode away. As Ko Nobuyoshi stared after him, he felt an ache in his chest. It pained him to see Kim Shunpei drag along that lonely shadow of his. Ko Nobuyoshi was—and likely would be—Kim Shunpei's only friend. In the name of friendship, Kim Shunpei was loaning him a huge sum of money without any strings attached, but there was something sad and forlorn about the whole thing. A man like Kim Shunpei was supposed to lead a happy life with his family, but why did he so resolutely refuse to love and be loved? Did Kim Shunpei even know how to love? This incurable loneliness was what turned into violence, and it was destroying him. Ko Nobuyoshi suddenly wondered if he should even borrow the money or not. He asked himself if this transaction would only deepen Kim Shunpei's isolation. But he couldn't think of any other way to get the money he and his family needed.

After the Korean War's ceasefire agreement was drawn up, Japan's economic boom from wartime procurements suddenly contracted, and companies went bankrupt one after another. The ones that got hit first were the small and mid-sized businesses. That included Kim Shunpei's borrowers, who kept postponing their principal and interest payments. Kim Shunpei had to resort to stricter measures.

It was the middle of typhoon season, and a typhoon was closing in on the Kansai area. In Osaka Harbor, wind speeds were recorded at thirty meters a second. The roadside trees swayed to and fro, and leaves danced in the night air. Wooden planks covered up the tenement house windows. Gusts of wind cut through the air with eerie shrieks.

A small man in his fifties was at Kim Shunpei's house, his nose pressed to the tatami floor in supplication. Kim Shunpei poured himself a cup of *shochu* and gulped it down. In the other room, Kiyoko held her breath, her body tense. As the wind moaned outside, she listened through the gap in the door to what the men were saying. Kim Shunpei had turned into a demon. As he drank, his face turned more and more savage.

"So what are you gonna do?" yelled Kim Shunpei in a hoarse voice.

"Please wait four or five more days. I've been talking to my clients and drawing up the agreements." The man's voice shook. He kept his face to the floor to avoid seeing the look on Kim Shunpei's face.

"Wait four or five days? Last time and the time before that, you told me to wait three days. Today it's four or five days, huh. Four or five days from now, it'll be another four or five days. How long do you think you can keep this going? Stop fucking around!"

Kim Shunpei bit the rim of his glass until it cracked apart. Then he rolled up his left sleeve and used the sharp edge of the cracked cup to draw a straight line down his arm. Blood gushed out. Kim Shunpei let his blood trickle into the cup and said, "You'll be drinking this. You take my money, you take my blood. Drink it!" He thrust the cup out.

The man was so frightened his teeth chattered, and he could barely get himself to speak. "I-I understand. I-I'll settle my accounts."

Kim Shunpei wrapped his arm with a towel, drank straight from the *shochu* bottle, and exhaled. He seemed to be breathing out all the horrible things that existed in the world. Kiyoko felt as if she were going to faint.

After the man left, Kim Shunpei started groaning in pain from the long cut on his arm. The blood wasn't stopping, and he had to call the doctor. The seventy-year-old neighborhood physician braved the storm to come see him. He took one look at the gaping wound and said, "I can't help you with this. You have to get this stitched up, or else."

The old doctor gave him a shot to ease the pain, applied disinfectant to the wound, and wrapped it up in gauze. Kim Shunpei decided to wait until the morning, but his wound burned, and soon his whole body was hot with fever. He wondered wildly if the nerves in his brain were being attacked again.

"Stop losing your temper. What'll you do if your brain gets all wonky again? Think about your health." Kiyoko replaced the gauze, which had turned red with blood very quickly.

"I won't forgive those bastards who take my money," cursed Kim Shunpei. "Lee Dal-mun owes me tomorrow. Show me the contract."

Even in a fever, Kim Shunpei was obsessed with collecting his debts. Kiyoko checked the contract and reported that Lee Dal-mun's repayment deadline was indeed tomorrow.

"His interest is a month overdue. That little fucker. He won't get away with this. I'll break his arm."

Kiyoko believed that Kim Shunpei really would go to such lengths, and she tensed up again in anxiety.

Once the typhoon made landfall in Osaka, it quickly slackened, and from Ise Bay it disappeared into the Pacific Ocean. Kim Shunpei couldn't sleep a wink the whole night, and when morning broke, he went to the police hospital where he'd gotten his surgery for his previous knife wound. The surgeon at that hospital was a rude man, but Kim Shunpei apparently took a liking to him. It would be the same kind of operation this time around. After Kiyoko told the surgeon what had happened, he looked at Kim Shunpei's long, open cut and said carelessly, "You really don't act your age, do you? Something wrong with your head?" He stitched the wound up.

Kim Shunpei returned home from the hospital and waited for Lee Dal-mun. He kept looking at the clock and acting as if he were ready at any moment to go raid the man's house. The forty-year-old Lee Dal-mun finally came a little after two. He bowed low and smiled an ingratiating smile.

"I'm sorry for being late. I know I should be punished. Please forgive me." He inched closer as he looked up at

Kim Shunpei.

"You bring the money or not?" The sour-faced Kim Shunpei waited for Lee Dal-mun to play his hand.

"I only brought the interest today."

"You're a month late. And no word from you at all! You think you can play games with me?"

"I'm sorry. I messed up. I brought two months' worth of interest. I hope this will be enough for you to forgive me."

The obsequious Lee Dal-mun was bowing too low for Kim Shunpei to even bother punching him. Kim Shunpei scowled and took the interest payment. "And the principal?"

"Please wait three months."

"Three months? And what about the interest for those three months? We'll subtract the interest from your bill and draw up a separate contract for it."

As Kim Shunpei commanded, Lee Dal-mun wrote down the amount for three months' interest on a new contract. This meant he would have to pay interest on the interest.

"If you're late, at least let me know. That's the honorable thing to do. If you mess up again, I'll break your arm. Understand?" threatened Kim Shunpei.

Lee Dal-mun nodded and said, "Yes, sir."

After he left, Kim Shunpei waited for Jo Nagao to show up. Jo Nagao was the man from last night who had begged Kim Shunpei to let him settle his bill today. Evening approached and he still hadn't come, much to Kim Shunpei's chagrin. Kiyoko was reading the evening newspaper and said, "Hey, take a look at this. Isn't this Jo-*san*?" She pointed at the picture. It was unmistakably Jo Nagao.

"What happened?" asked Kim Shunpei.

"He killed himself."

"What?" Kim Shunpei took the newspaper from Kiyoko and stared at Jo Nagao's picture as if he wanted to suck it up with his eyes. "How dare he take my money and kill himself? That fucker."

Jo Nagao's suicide was just the beginning. One day, two neighborhood children were playing cops and robbers when they slipped inside Kim Shunpei's defunct *kamaboko* factory through the back. They wandered through the dim factory floor and went up to the mezzanine floor out of curiosity. The light streaming through one of the factory's small windows lit up the low-ceilinged mezzanine floor like a stage. The two children thought it would make a good hiding place. That was when they heard a pained moan from the dark corner of a room. The children jumped in shock and turned to run, but when they squinted into the darkness to look more closely, they noticed something wriggling. They ran away at full speed.

They told their friends what they'd encountered, and then a bunch of them went into the dark factory to discover what the mysterious thing was. One of the boys held a flashlight, and five or six others timidly followed him up the stairs. When they cast the light into the dark corner, they saw a woman on the floor, gagged with a towel and bound with wire. One of the children ran down the stairs to tell his mother. Soon Mrs. Kunimoto arrived. She removed the gag and wire, and the woman cried out in Korean. She had welts on her wrists from where the wire had bitten into her. She looked about forty, and she was haggard and exhausted. She'd been confined in this room for five days. Mrs. Kunimoto took her to her house and fed her a simple meal of rice, kimchi, and miso soup. After the woman calmed down a little, she told her story.

She'd been smuggled in from Jeju Island. Kim Shunpei

had paid for her passage at her parents' request, but her parents couldn't meet the repayment deadline. She begged Kim Shunpei to wait another month, but Kim Shunpei locked her up on the mezzanine floor and told her parents he wouldn't let her out until they paid him. Her parents could have reported this to the police, but then their daughter would have been caught as an illegal stowaway and sent to the Omura Detention Center.*

"*Aigo, aigo,* that man isn't even human. How could he treat a fellow Jeju Islander this way? We won't stand for this," exclaimed Mrs. Kunimoto. But the woman didn't want a confrontation. She couldn't predict what Kim Shunpei was capable of doing to her. Rather, she needed her parents to pay Kim Shunpei as soon as possible. Mrs. Kunimoto hid the woman at her house for the time being while she contacted the woman's parents. Two days later, the payment was received, and the matter was resolved. But Kim Shunpei still wasn't satisfied. Even though he'd gotten his money, he was upset about what

---

* The Omura Detention Center (in Omura City, Nagasaki Prefecture) detained Koreans under the terms of the Migrant Control Law and Alien Registration Law. Many of those detained and deported were Korean War refugees.

265

Mrs. Kunimoto was telling the neighbors. One day he got drunk and stood outside Mrs. Kunimoto's door, shouting curses and looking like he wanted to break in. Mrs. Kunimoto cursed back. Her husband couldn't sit there and let his wife take Kim Shunpei's abuse, and he shouted insults at Kim Shunpei from the second-floor window.

"If you had any guts, you'd come down and fight me! Hidin' behind your wife's fat ass, huh!"

There were few languages that could match Korean for its amount of curse words. These words had the power to make Koreans want to rip each other apart. Kunimoto rushed down the stairs holding a knife, but he missed the last step, fell, and accidentally stabbed his own thigh. But rumors spread that it was Kim Shunpei who had stabbed Kunimoto in the thigh. Soon that was what everyone came to believe.

There was no end to Kim Shunpei's trails of money. The head of a small ten-person gang in Tsuruhashi would borrow from Kim Shunpei and then lend the money out at an interest rate of ten percent a day. Those who borrowed at such high interest rates tended to be older men whose small businesses were on the verge of bankruptcy, or gangsters who had gotten themselves into a hellish amount of debt. The lender would set his interest rate so high assuming that the borrower couldn't pay it back and then wage a merciless debt-collecting campaign. Armed with blank checks, he and his gang would go around to the debtor's parents, siblings, relatives, friends, and even in-laws to extort payment. If the man couldn't settle his debt, he might eventually be killed and buried deep in the mountains.

Kim Shunpei lent freely to gangs who engaged in such lending practices. One of the most notorious of these gangs, the so-called "murderous Motoyama-*gumi*" of Imazato-Shinbashi, was led by none other than Won Yoshio. Won Yoshio had stabbed his boss Kim Shunpei on that misty morning four years ago and then spent the next two-and-a-half years in prison. When he got out, he cut off his pinky finger to beg for Kim Shunpei's forgiveness. Then Kim Shunpei introduced Won Yoshio to Kim Shosuke, the leader of the Kanemoto-*gumi* in Umeda. The Kanemoto-*gumi* was a storm-trooper unit for the Kaneshiro-*gumi* in Kobe, an organization that was seeking nationwide domination. Won Yoshio's twenty-man Motoyama-*gumi* became a branch syndicate of the Kanemoto-*gumi* and was responsible for three of the year's big incidents.

The first incident was the decapitation at Manadayama Park. The Motoyama-*gumi* faced off against the Minami Watanabe-*gumi* in a brawl, which led to the Watanabe-*gumi* leader getting his head chopped off with a katana, as well as the death of two of his henchmen. The Motoyama-*gumi* lost one man, and three others sustained serious injuries. The second incident was an attack at dawn. The Motoyama-*gumi* raided the Tanigawa-*gumi* base near Tsutenkaku and shot the leader and his right-hand man in their homes. The third incident was an attack on the Arai-*gumi* base in Fuse and the murder of two of its members. All three incidents were under orders from the Kanemoto-*gumi*. That was how Motoyama-*gumi* gained its reputation for being "murderous." But even the leader of that gang, Won Yoshio, was docile and obedient in front of Kim Shunpei.

"Hearin' the boss's voice still gives me the creeps," insisted Won Yoshio. Indeed, a single blow to the flesh could leave an imprint of fear that lasted for the rest of one's life.

Kim Shunpei treated Won Yoshio like his own son. Sung-han and Takeshi, on the other hand, were tossed aside like defective goods.

"He'll be a big kingpin one day," Kim Shunpei told
Ko Nobuyoshi proudly. It was as if Kim Shunpei were a
parent transferring his own unrealized dreams onto his
child.

Time lost could not be regained. Kim Shunpei and
Sung-han were heading toward two completely different
worlds, even though the progression of time was the same
for them both. Kim Shunpei got up early every morning
to chop the wood he used to cook breakfast. After his
afternoon nap, he went on his bike to circle the homes
of his debtors, and on his way back home he shopped
for dinner. At night he drank and had sex with Kiyoko,
and then he slept. But even Kim Shunpei's tireless energy
began to flag. Sometimes he couldn't keep up his erection
during sex. He suspected that his body was going into
decline. His ejaculations weren't as strong as they used to
be either. The human body had its limitations.

On the other hand, he was watching Sung-han grow
and grow, and he couldn't guess what was going through
the boy's mind. Sung-han was still somewhat slight of
build, but he was shooting up in height and could be

seen swaggering around with his judo uniform over
his shoulder. He was cool and composed when they
met on the street. He showed absolutely no respect. In
fact, his attitude seemed to be one of provocation. Kim
Shunpei was fifty-five, but he hadn't yet given up on the
idea of raising a son of his own. He didn't think it was
too late. But that one thread of hope wasn't being borne
out by Kiyoko, who was approaching forty. One day
Kim Shunpei ran into Manada Aira at an *izakaya* and
unleashed some complaints.

"She's flat as a cracker. I want a son, dammit."

Kim Shunpei had paid Manada a handsome sum
to find him a woman like Kiyoko. It was his right to
complain.

The drunk Manada retorted, "You're kidding me,
right? You two with a baby? At your age? You already
have two kids, and Kiyoko can't have any. Give it up."

"What? Kiyoko can't have any?" Kim Shunpei grabbed
Manada's collar.

"I mean, it's obvious after five years of doin' it with her,
right?" said Manada quickly, trying to cover up the fact
that he'd known all along.

But Manada's words single-handedly crushed Kim

Shunpei's hopes. It was indeed unnatural that Kiyoko had never gotten pregnant after five years of living with him. If she was on menopause that would have been a different story, but Kiyoko was thirty-five when he met her. Not to mention that the Kunimoto bitch who was ruining his reputation just had another baby at forty-nine years old. He envied that bitch's fertile womb.

Kim Shunpei shook Manada off, got on his bike, and rode home, not knowing what to do with his anger. Kiyoko was on the second floor drinking tea and reading a book. The sight of her reading filled Kim Shunpei with revulsion, and he kicked over the low table, sending her teapot and cake flying.

"How dare you read! How 'bout givin' me a child instead? You barren bitch!"

Kiyoko's shameful secret was discovered. She could say nothing to defend herself. Not to mention that Kim Shunpei looked so terrifying she thought she was going to die.

Kim Shunpei flipped over the furniture and rammed himself against the closet. Kiyoko rushed down the stairs and out the door in her bare feet. As she weaved her way through the alleyways, Kim Shunpei followed her, howling like a werewolf in the moonlight. Kiyoko hid in the shadow of a tenement house and covered her mouth to silence her ragged breathing.

That night triggered a new round of violence from Kim Shunpei. He refrained from hitting Kiyoko, but when he got drunk, he threw furniture from the second-story window, cracked the pillars with his axe, raised his voice, and ruled by intimidation and fear. Every time Kim Shunpei came home drunk, Kiyoko fled outside and hid in a dark corner of an alleyway. She wasn't close to any of the neighbors, so no one opened their doors for her. Lee Young-hee witnessed her fleeing a few times. Eventually, she felt compelled to hide Kiyoko in her house. For the past two or three years, Kim Shunpei hadn't broken into Lee Young-hee's house even when he got drunk. He might have been self-conscious about doing such a thing with Kiyoko around. He and Kiyoko had been getting along very well.

While it was of course bizarre for a wife to shelter her husband's mistress, misery loves company, as the saying goes.

"He scares me so much. I don't know what to do!" wept Kiyoko, her body shaking. Lee Young-hee felt as if she were seeing a past version of herself. Kiyoko probably had nowhere to run to, either. But the current situation couldn't go on. Lee Young-hee considered Kiyoko her replacement of sorts. Filling that role meant enduring an everyday suffering worse than death.

Hanako opposed Lee Young-hee's decision to let Kiyoko stay with them. "Why are you defending her? She's been shamelessly living right there! She doesn't get how embarrassing she is for us. This is her punishment." As far as Hanako was concerned, Kiyoko was getting her just desserts.

Sung-han acted as if this had nothing to do with him. He was fed up with all the drama between his father and mother, his father and children, his father and his mistresses. He didn't want to deal with his father anymore. Sung-han saw Kim Shunpei less as his father and more as some enigmatic chimera living off the roots of the Korean spiritual landscape. He had a monkey's head, a raccoon dog's chest, a tiger's limbs, a reptile's tail, and a thrush's voice. In other words, he was an impossible creature—one who couldn't hope to overcome oneself, tormented by the endless births he had to give himself. Who was this man? He was a father and husband, a manifestation of patriarchal power. He enacted his will on the world in the only way he knew how—violence. What other way was there?

Kiyoko took to hiding at Lee Young-hee's house before Kim Shunpei came home. But it was only a matter of time before Kim Shunpei, on the prowl for Kiyoko's scent, broke into Lee Young-hee's house. Lee Young-hee and Hanako were prepared for this moment and kept the second-story window open for a quick escape through the balcony. Of course, Kiyoko was to accompany them. Hanako hated Kiyoko, but she had to admit that Kiyoko was the reason she'd been spared her father's violence these past few years. The outcome was undeniable, regardless of the circumstances. As long as Kim Shunpei existed, his violence had a way of coming back to haunt them.

And finally, Kim Shunpei struck. Lee Young-hee, Hanako, and Kiyoko promptly left through the balcony and went along the roof toward the neighbor's house, but this time something unusual happened. Sung-han stayed behind to confront his father. Kim Shunpei tore through the front door but stopped short at the sight of Sung-han standing in front of him. The person standing there was no longer a small, frightened child. Sung-han had resolved to vanquish his fear and face his father head-on. These past few years, Kim Shunpei had only passed by Sung-han on the street or seen him from afar, but standing so close to him now, he sensed that Sung-han was burning with murderous hatred.

"You little shit! You think you can fight me?"

Kim Shunpei shot out his arm and grabbed Sung-han by the collar. Sung-han flung his head down and grabbed at Kim Shunpei's trunk-like body with all his might. Sung-han's nose was assailed by Kim Shunpei's miasmic scent. It was the first time they'd touched each other since either could remember, and the weird sensation of Kim Shunpei's flesh threw Sung-han into confusion. Flesh thudded against flesh and bone against bone. As they grappled each other without letting go, an undefinable emotion seemed to lock them in a tight embrace. Sung-han pushed at Kim Shunpei wildly, but Kim Shunpei didn't budge an inch. In the next moment, Sung-han was pummeled in the rib by Kim Shunpei's knee, and he crouched in agonizing pain. Kim Shunpei was unforgiving in his follow-through. He dragged Sung-han by the hair and hurled him outside. Sung-han spun two or three times and collided with the wall of the opposing house. "Ugh . . ." he groaned. But he stood back up dizzily to challenge Kim Shunpei again.

"So you'd kill your own father," said Kim Shunpei.

"It's 'cause I'm descended from you," spat Sung-han.

"Speaking out of turn again! I'll make you regret that you ever defied me!" Kim Shunpei headbutted Sung-han violently. Sung-han's vision went black, and he lost consciousness.

Mrs. Takamura and Mrs. Ishihara poked their heads out of their windows to watch the duel. Sung-han could get killed at this rate. They had to intervene.

"Please stop. There's no reason whatsoever for a parent to kill his child."

The two women rushed outside. Mrs. Ishihara stooped over Sung-han, while Mrs. Takamura stood to block Kim Shunpei's way.

"The fucker wants to kill me!" yelled Kim Shunpei.

"We just want this horrible fighting to stop," said Mrs. Ishihara, her voice full of loathing.

The neighbors gathered in droves. They averted their faces from the bloody, unconscious Sung-han while gasping and murmuring in sympathy. Kim Shunpei tasted something bad in his mouth. He returned to his house to avoid the neighbors' stares. Sung-han woke up and cried in vexation.

The next day, Sung-han complained of chest pain, and Lee Young-hee and Hanako brought him to a Korean general hospital in Ikuno. After the examination, the doctor said that Sung-han's nose and two of his ribs were broken and that he had acute pleurisy. Lee Young-hee and Hanako were horrified by the merciless brutality Kim Shunpei was still capable of inflicting on his own son.

"Are you an idiot or what? Just because you know a little judo doesn't mean you should fight Father. Even the yakuza are afraid of him," scolded Hanako.

"I'll kill him next time," said Sung-han, though it was clear even to him that he was outmatched.

"Stupid! What would you do if you killed your own father?"

"He's not my father. He's a monster. Hana-*chan*, you really think he's your father?"

Hanako's face clouded over, and her voice trembled with memories of suffering. "No matter what kind of person he is, a father is a father. We can't choose who our parents are," she said.

"Why can't we? I reject him. I'll fight him whether I die from it or not." Sung-han bit his lips in frustration. If he bit his lips hard enough, he could distract himself from the pain he felt all over his body.

As they sat talking on the waiting room bench, a nurse came by to take Sung-han to his hospital bed. The room had six beds, and Sung-han's was the closest to the door on the right. The nurse showed Lee Young-hee and Hanako how to use the tea stand and warned them about this and that.

"Hey, we'll be back with your clothes and teapot and other things," said Hanako.

"How much does it cost for me to stay here?" asked Sung-han.

"We'll figure it out, so don't worry about it," said Lee Young-hee, smiling.

That very day, the news spread through the neighborhood that Sung-han was in the hospital with broken ribs and a lung inflammation. Upon hearing the news himself, Kim Shunpei shut himself inside for a few days, perhaps as a way of showing remorse. During this time, Kiyoko had no reason to run away. But every single thing Kim Shunpei did frayed her nerves.

Sung-han was discharged from the hospital a month later. His epithelial tissues were adhering, and his chest felt stiff and sore. After a month away from his job, the shoe store fired him. Fortunately, a nearby factory was looking for someone to work their lathes, and they hired Sung-han as an apprentice. It was a small factory on the first floor of a tenement house, with only four lathes. The four operators rotated the long, thin axles to turn metal pieces into small screws. Sung-han was kept busy with supply runs and shipments.

Hanako, having procured the necessary sewing skills from her two-year course at the dressmaking school, made skirts and dresses for local women and, after some self-training, began making suits. Lee Young-hee's *sake* business wasn't very profitable, since so many of her customers were deferring their payments. But she wanted to keep her house bustling with people. Kim Shunpei did what he always did: he chopped wood at six in the morning, traveled around on his bicycle to collect his debts, shopped for dinner, drank, and went to sleep. Sometimes Ko Nobuyoshi came by to chat. His new store was doing well. As upright as ever, he made sure to repay Kim Shunpei a small but steady sum each month. His competent wife was left to manage the business, while Ko Nobuyoshi became a district council member. At his request, Kim Shunpei contributed to his fundraising campaigns.

Sung-han was invited by an upperclassman to join some protests. He threw himself into politics. As he grew older, he grew more distant from his childhood friends in the neighborhood. Everyone was starting to walk their own paths. Sung-han was arrested twice in a year, but the judge acquitted him because he was underage. Han Masahito served as his personal guarantor. Han Masahito had moved to the Ikaino neighborhood in Ikuno, which was far from the heart of council activities. He kept dreaming of making it big as a broker, but he never seemed to succeed. He was proud of his way with words, but his pride was his undoing. He was too confident in his own wits and turned his nose up at work that required physical labor. Han Masahito viewed poverty as a fleeting phase in life. He believed that one day, his long-awaited windfall would surely roll down and land at his feet. There were few things as problematic as the overconfidence of someone who expected money to well up from the ground or fall from the sky.

The world roared on, but the Koreans in the tenement house neighborhoods stayed in the same old rut for years on end until they seemed to be growing stale. One could see this from their clothes. For men and women alike, their summer clothes and winter clothes remained the same for ten years. Sung-han reused the same school uniform year after year, and even the wealthy Kim Shunpei took out his age-old leather coat when winter came around. Sakamoto nailed scrap wood onto his *geta* sandals when they got worn down, while Kunimoto still wore the sweater that had been issued to garrison troops at the end of the war.

Sung-han graduated from his part-time high school and gave up on the thought of going to university. There were no decent jobs for Zainichi Koreans who graduated from even the elite universities. He had friends who had gone to top-rate universities, but the best they could manage after graduation was to stay on as a researcher, go back to work at their parents' butcher shop, or own a café. Most Zainichi Koreans had no steady form of employment. The small factory that employed Sung-han went bankrupt a year after he graduated high school. Once a Korean lost a job, it was hard to find another. If he had no other choice, he could work for pennies as a construction worker, but even that was not guaranteed.

When Hanako was twenty-two, she received a proposal for marriage. Korean parents wanted to marry their daughters off as soon as possible, and Lee Young-hee was no exception. She arranged the marriage interview, and after a single meeting, the marriage was decided. Hanako, for one, wanted to distance herself from her father as soon as possible.

On the day of her wedding ceremony, Kim Shunpei shut himself up in a small room and drank alone. Kiyoko worked on her knitting in a state of suspense. Kim Shunpei, after all, wasn't invited to the wedding. It was a complete loss of face for him as a father. Lee Young-hee's house was full of guests, and the sounds of laughter, singing, and the Korean *janggu** reached them. Kim Shunpei was undoubtedly incensed. In fact, Lee Young-hee was anxious herself about a possible outburst from Kim Shunpei during the banquet. When the groom finally took Hanako away, Lee Young-hee breathed a sigh of relief. The ceremony and banquet had lasted from noon

---

* A Korean two-headed drum

until late at night, but there were no disturbances.

Kim Shunpei wasn't at all sorry about not being able to show his face at his daughter's wedding. The neighborhood gossip was of no interest to him. As the days passed, he adhered ever more to the philosophy that one's own survival was the only purpose of life. Questions about life's meaning were useless. Humans lived until they died, and that was that. What other meaning was there? People sold their bodies and killed each other in order to live. They were entitled to do so. No one else would save them, or him. His children existed in some other world and couldn't save him. Sung-han's unexpected rebellion was proof of that. When Sung-han had gripped his arms and pushed at his chest, it was as if their bloodlines had diverged into completely unrelated bodies, unrelated in sensibility, sentiment, personality, or personhood. But if Kim Shunpei were to lift the lid off his relationship with Sung-han, all he could find there was a son, and if he lifted more and more lids all the way down, like a nest of boxes, he only found a son. On the flip side of that, he could peel away layer after layer as if he were peeling an onion, only to find that nothing was there.

Sometimes he encountered Sung-han on the street.

Sung-han's face and body were filling out, and his eyes had a hungry look to them. And lately, his attitude was becoming more threatening. He barreled ahead without moving out of the way for Kim Shunpei, as if he were trying to collide with him. Sung-han looked as if he were ready to fight at any moment. Who knew what he was thinking? Kim Shunpei wanted to break free from this incomprehensible nest of boxes, which was of his own making and had expanded into something large and heavy. *It's 'cause I'm descended from you!* From the moment Sung-han said that, it was as if their relationship had been flipped on its head.

Kim Shunpei rode his bike slowly to the front of a pachinko parlor along the main thoroughfare. Pachinko machines were getting popular, mostly among children. Pachinko parlors were like arcades. For that reason, profits from the pachinko industry didn't amount to much. The owner of this parlor was a middle-aged Chinese man named Liu. He used to run a Chinese restaurant here, but he remodeled the place after someone had planted the idea in his head that pachinko would be more profitable. Liu had borrowed a huge sum from Kim Shunpei, and he hadn't paid his interest for the past three months. Kim Shunpei would settle the score with him now.

When Kim Shunpei went inside, Mrs. Liu, standing at the cash register, turned pale. Among the thirty pachinko machines were scattered a few children and a single old man. The machines clanged while the song "Otomisan"[*] played from the radio. Mrs. Liu smiled and put her hands together. "He's out but he'll be back soon," she said.

"He promised he'd see me. Why'd he go out?"

"He had an emergency."

"Did a family member die or what?"

"Y-yes, his elder cousin died."

"Where's his elder cousin's house? I'll speak with him there."

"I don't know . . . ."

Clearly, she was faking it. "Don't fuck with me," said Kim Shunpei. He opened the back door and climbed the stairs.

"Excuse me! That isn't allowed!"

But Kim Shunpei was already on the second floor. He opened the screen door to one of the rooms and found Liu

---

[*] A song by Kasuga Hachiro that became a big hit in 1954

drinking beer and watching Rikidōzan* on the television. Liu scrambled back with his legs. Kim Shunpei switched off the television, sat down in front of Liu, and crossed his legs.

"Hey, fucker. You dare try to trick me? How long do you think you can run from me?" Kim Shunpei took Liu's beer bottle and brought it down on his own head, cracking it. At the same moment, Kim Shunpei's dentures fell out. His face looked unnatural without them.

Liu gulped and said, "I'm sorry. Forgive me." He bent down until his forehead touched the tatami floor. He always did this on debt-collection day.

Kim Shunpei took out two sheets of paper from his breast pocket and laid them out. "Put your seal on these documents."

"What are these for?"

"To change the name of the deed on this house."

"Now wait just a moment," said Liu in a panicked voice.

"Shut up. Always telling me to wait, huh. Nothing ever happens when you tell me to wait!"

---

* A former Zainichi Korean wrestler, touted as the "father of pro wrestling" in Japan

"Yes, yes, but this is too sudden. Please let me think things through."

"You've had plenty of time to think. Once you put your seal here, you have to do what I tell you. Quit this pachinko bullshit and turn this place back into a restaurant. I'll pay for the remodeling costs. But you have to pay me rent each month. If you make enough down the line, you can buy this place back from me. You can't beat this offer."

For someone who had run out of options like Liu, Kim Shunpei's proposal seemed logical, but Liu resisted the prospect of having his property taken from him. Liu broke out in a sweat as he struggled to come to a decision.

Mrs. Liu had been watching the whole thing from the door. She stepped inside and said with a serious look on her face, "Honey, let's do what Kim-*san* says. Otherwise we'll lose our entire business."

"You're decent at cooking, aren't you? If your restaurant does well, you can buy the place back."

With that, Liu put his seal on the contract.

In similar fashion, Kim Shunpei bought out eleven other family-owned shops.

As autumn advanced toward winter, everyone's

uniforms changed, from the students to the police. It was October, and any lingering heat from the year's blazing hot summer had disappeared. The sky turned pale, and the air grew cold. When Kiyoko went up to the balcony to hang the laundry out to dry, the view before her looked different than it used to. The Korean tenement houses were like a mirage. Kiyoko blinked and rubbed her eyes a few times. Her legs felt like they were floating. *What's happening . . . ?* Her consciousness flew away from her, and everything went black. The next thing she knew, she found herself laid out on a futon.

"What happened? You fell." Kim Shunpei was sitting next to her.

"Could be anemia. I blacked out all of a sudden."

"Anemia? God, women are such a pain."

But from that day on, Kiyoko started to forget things. She would go to the market and suddenly forget what she was there for. She would forget people's names. She would answer the phone and get up to tell Kim Shunpei, only to forget about the call along the way.

"Something's up with you. You leave the phone off the hook. You leave things boiling until the pot turns black. You're neglecting the contracts too, and I bet you have no idea where you put 'em."

Kiyoko's memory was being cut into shreds. When she spoke, her sentences didn't connect from one thing to the next. Sometimes she couldn't think of the words she needed. She strained to recall what she meant to say, and as soon as the words came back to her, she lost them again. Her body lost its sense of equilibrium and felt like it was about to float up into space. The harder she tried to concentrate on something, the more her head hurt. Was it a psychological disease, or a neural one? Her vertigo was one thing, but her memory loss was too serious to ignore. It was clear something was wrong with her head. That was what Kiyoko kept insisting, and Kim Shunpei agreed to let her see a doctor. She needed to make an appointment, but there were no open slots at the hospital until the beginning of the next year.

Kiyoko's appointment was scheduled for the sixth of January at the university hospital where Kim Shunpei had previously spent half a year. She and Kim Shunpei went to Tennoji by taxi. The hospital was busy and crowded, and Kiyoko was shuttled from the neurology unit to internal medicine, radiology, and brain surgery. She was gone for over two hours. Kim Shunpei was in the waiting area, getting more and more anxious as time went on. The morning visitation period was over, and the waiting area cleared out. Kim Shunpei was the only person left. Eventually a nurse escorted Kiyoko from the brain surgery unit to the waiting area. Kiyoko's eyes looked hollow, as if she were gazing far into the distance.

"The doctor would like to have a word," the nurse told Kim Shunpei.

He followed the nurse down the hallway while looking back at Kiyoko, who was sitting on the bench, her eyes glazed over like a marionette's.

The nurse led Kim Shunpei to a middle-aged doctor, who invited him to sit down. "You wife has a brain tumor," said the doctor.

"Brain tumor?" It was the first time Kim Shunpei had heard the word "tumor."

"Basically, there's a lump inside her head."

Kim Shunpei mulled over the doctor's words and then asked, "You gonna cure her?"

The doctor adjusted his glasses and glanced down at his chart. "She can't be cured with treatment. She'll need to undergo surgery so we can take the lump out."

So Kiyoko's head would have to be cut open and her

brain exposed. Kim Shunpei couldn't imagine such a thing. "And after that she'll be cured?"

"Well, we can't say for sure. But if she doesn't get the surgery, she'll have two months to live, at most."

What was the meaning of this? Two months to live at most?

"We'll move forward quickly, but we shouldn't dally for even a day."

So the surgery would be all or nothing, realized Kim Shunpei. If the doctor was correct, he had no choice about what to do next.

"We need the husband's approval to move forward with the surgery," said the doctor.

"Okay. I approve."

"We'll take her in tomorrow. She'll go through a thorough checkup, and then we'll decide on the date of the surgery."

When the meeting was over, Kim Shunpei went back to the waiting area, where Kiyoko sat as dazed as ever. Her body looked smaller than he ever remembered.

Chapter 22

Kiyoko spent three days at the hospital undergoing examinations before her surgery. The surgery took over seven hours. When it was over, the comatose Kiyoko was carted out with her shaved head wrapped in a bandage. Her mouth was hanging open, and her face was a bloodless white. One of the nurses was preparing Kiyoko's articles for daily use and told Kim Shunpei, "I'll take care of her clothes." Kim Shunpei could only stand by and watch.

He was then called into the doctor's office.

"The lump was lodged deep, so she really went through the ringer. But we managed to get it out."

"She's better now?"

"There will be aftereffects."

Kim Shunpei didn't bother asking any more questions.

He figured it would all be the same in the end.

It was no use just staring at Kiyoko's prone body, so Kim Shunpei left everything to the nurses and decided to go home. On the way out, he was told to prepare a deposit of two hundred thousand yen. He found the amount truly absurd.

When he got home, he drank by himself and called his two nephews, as well as Ko Nobuyoshi, to let them know about Kiyoko's surgery.

It was a long night to spend alone. The rooms felt cold without Kiyoko's presence, and Kim Shunpei was unable to fall asleep. Even after drinking a whole bottle of *sake,* his head felt clear. It was possible that Kiyoko wouldn't recover. Her white, bloated face flashed up in his mind. Kim Shunpei sat in the cold room and drank until he could no longer hold his head up.

The next day, he left for the hospital on his bicycle. After paying the registrar two hundred thousand yen, he went up to Kiyoko's private room, where he found Ko Nobuyoshi.

"Bad luck, huh," quipped Ko Nobuyoshi.

"Can't be helped. No one wants to get sick."

The nurse invited them to sit down and served them

tea. Kiyoko was awake, but her face was twisted in pain. The nurse changed her IV bag. Then her supervising doctor came in for her checkup. He looked over the chart where the nurse had recorded the progress of her fever, and then he took her pulse. After a moment's thought, he said, "I expect she'll settle down in four or five days." He left the room.

"Are you doing okay, missus?" ventured Ko Nobuyoshi, but Kiyoko just looked at him with her hollow eyes. She didn't seem to recognize him or Kim Shunpei.

"She won't recognize anyone now, I reckon," said Kim Shunpei.

"She'll remember you soon enough," said Ko Nobuyoshi reassuringly.

Soon Kim Shunpei's two nephews came in with baskets of fruit. They entered the room nervously, as if they were afraid to be seen. They took a quick look at Kiyoko and retreated to a corner of the room. At this stage, there was nothing anyone could say about Kiyoko's condition.

"How is she?" asked Kim Tae-su.

"No idea," replied Kim Shunpei curtly as he smoked a cigarette.

"Must be hard on you, Uncle, to take care of Aunt Kiyoko like this," said Kim Yong-su.

"It's fine. How's work, anyways?"

"It puts food on the table."

Except for two ancestral rites, the nephews hadn't laid eyes on Kim Shunpei in the past year. He hardly even attended the rites, since it was such a bother for him to interact with people. The four men had nothing to talk about, and they left Kiyoko's room within thirty minutes. The nephews had come by train, so they parted ways with Kim Shunpei and Ko Nobuyoshi in front of the hospital.

"Wanna come over for a drink?" Ko Nobuyoshi asked Kim Shunpei.

Kim Shunpei had nothing to do by himself in his empty house, so he agreed to stop by.

Korea Market was bustling with activity. Freshly boiled pig heads sat on either side of the door to the meat shop. Diving women sat on the bare earth selling mollusks and abalone they'd caught from the coastal waters that very morning. Kim Shunpei stopped and searched through their haul, until he remembered his dentures and quickly moved on.

Ko Nobuyoshi's shop sold a wide range of items, from

Korean silk to dried foods. Akemi was busy attending
to the customers. She was assisted by her older daughter,
who was now of marriageable age. When Akemi noticed
Kim Shunpei, she hurriedly led him up to the second
floor, saying, "*Aigo,* you finally came! Welcome!" The
second floor had three six-*jo* rooms. When they entered
one of the rooms, the younger son, a pimply-faced third-
year student at the Korean high school, greeted Kim
Shunpei with an "*Annyeong-hashimnikka?*"* and retired to
another room.

Kim Shunpei found himself smiling—it was refreshing
to hear the Korean language.

Akemi brought over a bottle of rice wine and a tray
full of Korean food. As she poured Kim Shunpei a bowl of
the rice wine, she asked, "How is your wife?"

"Not clear at this point. Whatever happens, happens."

Kim Shunpei didn't look as if he wanted to talk about
Kiyoko. Akemi had met Kiyoko only once, when she
and her husband went to visit Kim Shunpei some time
ago. Akemi didn't know how to feel at the time, as she
was a close friend of Lee Young-hee's. Even now, she

---

* A formal Korean greeting

was a bit ambivalent about Kiyoko, what with all the rumors she was hearing. Of course, it would be taboo to mention Lee Young-hee and her children. Akemi and Ko Nobuyoshi had attended Hanako's wedding, but they felt awkward about visiting Lee Young-hee's house apart from occasions like that. Akemi poured the men another round of drinks and excused herself.

When Akemi was out of earshot, Kim Shunpei spoke again. "There's something I want to discuss."

"What?"

Kim Shunpei hesitantly tipped back his bowl to his lips. "I didn't think her disease would get this bad. I'm not sure I can stay by her side and care for her all the time. And her personal nurse's doing a good job."

"Well, why don't you ask that nurse's employer about it? The hospital's borrowing her services, too."

Kim Shunpei twisted his lips. "Not someone like that, but a regular woman. A Korean woman if possible. She'd be a live-in nurse," he said reluctantly.

"A live-in Korean woman . . . That doesn't sound possible," said Ko Nobuyoshi, realizing what Kim Shunpei's intentions were. Kim Shunpei was looking for Kiyoko's successor. And it would have to be a young woman who could bear children. This was no matter to treat carelessly. "I have no leads for a woman like that," said Ko Nobuyoshi, making sure to keep his face blank.

"Is that so? Well, don't worry about it." Kim Shunpei stood up.

"Leaving already?"

"We've finished the bottle, so yeah."

Ko Nobuyoshi followed Kim Shunpei down the stairs. Akemi called out, "Leaving so soon? It's been such a long time, so I thought you'd stay for dinner." She glanced at her husband.

"Thanks for the drinks," said Kim Shunpei. He strode out slowly, and as the sunlight hit him his face turned a reddish color.

"Did I say something wrong?" Akemi asked her husband as the two of them stared after Kim Shunpei.

"No, nothing like that." But Ko Nobuyoshi was left with an unpleasant feeling.

About a month into Kiyoko's hospitalization, the women at the water pump started spreading more rumors and speculations—that Kiyoko had run away with Kim Shunpei's money, that she'd broken up with him, and other such specious claims. Mrs. Kunimoto's information was the most accurate. She stealthily went to Lee Young-hee's house and spoke to her in a low whisper outside the kitchen.

"That woman got surgery done because there were lumps inside her head. Her brain got like that 'cause Shunpei's so terrifying. Korean women are used to men's violence, but Japanese women have weak nerves, so they get affected up there in no time. And with Shunpei around, it's no wonder."

What Mrs. Kunimoto said about Japanese wives was little more than an inference, but Lee Young-hee would have expected anyone to get lumps inside their head after living with Kim Shunpei. She'd once thought Kim Shunpei would drive her insane with his aggression and violence. That kind of fear wasn't something people could understand unless they'd experienced it for themselves. Lee Young-hee sympathized with Kiyoko for that reason.

Kim Shunpei visited Kiyoko once every three or four days, and eventually Kiyoko was able to recognize him. But she still couldn't speak. She would move her lips fretfully and force out "ah, ah, ah" sounds from her throat, but no one could grasp what she wanted to say. And then one day Kim Shunpei saw the nurse replace

Kiyoko's bandage. Kiyoko closed her eyes, and as the bandage came off her head, what lay underneath amazed him. Her skull had been cut in half, and the incision line extended from her forehead down past her right ear to the back of her head. The jagged scar from the patched-up incision resembled the footprints of a bird. Her forehead was swollen, while her cheeks were so sunken they appeared to be sliding down her face. Kim Shunpei thought he was looking at a misshapen rock.

The doctor took Kiyoko's chart from the nurse and wrote something down. "Her left side is paralyzed. Her ability to speak is damaged. I think she'll be able to use her right hand soon, which means she can use the toilet by herself. You'll have to be patient with her, regardless," he said drily, before he left the room.

Kiyoko lay down.

"You hungry?" asked Kim Shunpei. Kiyoko shook her head. Kim Shunpei stood there for ten minutes watching Kiyoko silently, and then he left.

On his way back home, he wandered through the streets of Abeno on his bike. The Abeno area in Tennoji had a lot of meaning for him. The flaming blue memory of Yae still remained deep in his heart. As he made his way through the red-light district and the surrounding streets, he saw that the shop he'd once wrecked was still in business, and he went inside to indulge in the memory. Four naked lightbulbs hung from the ceiling, and the walls and tables were a shabby brown. No customers were inside. The hunched, silver-haired shopkeeper was wiping his hands on his dirty apron. "Whaddya want?" he asked curtly.

"A glass of *shochu*," said Kim Shunpei.

The shopkeeper went to the galley and brought back a cup of *shochu*. He was the same man from all those years ago, but he didn't seem to remember Kim Shunpei at all. Kim Shunpei wondered how it could be that he'd aged right alongside this shopkeeper. He downed the *shochu* in one go. As he left the shop, the *shochu* burned in his chest and tightened his throat.

He returned home and was taking off his leather jacket when a button fell off. He got out the sewing kit from the closet and tried to sew the button back on. But the needle kept missing the thread. He brought the needle up and tried to focus on the eye, but it kept escaping from him. He tried over and over to fit the thread through the eye of the needle, but his eyes got tired, and he gave up. He'd never before felt as if his body were actually declining. But his failure with the needle and thread brought home the fact that he was just as old as that shopkeeper in Abeno.

Kim Shunpei went to the eyeglasses store and had lenses done for farsightedness. When he tried on the glasses and looked at a newspaper, he was shocked. The print stood out more clearly to him than he thought possible, even though he couldn't read any of it. He bought the glasses and went back home, where he tried to sew the button on again. The thread went through easily this time. With his thick, knotted fingers, he worked the button back into his jacket. He then stashed the glasses inside a drawer to use only when he had to, finding them rather humiliating.

He had nothing to do all day. He sat down in the two-*jo* room and stared at the people passing by on the street. He noticed different kinds of people with different kinds of expressions on their faces. His son Sung-han passed by and glanced into Kim Shunpei's house. Sung-han didn't acknowledge Kim Shunpei sitting in the shadows. He may have been deliberately ignoring his father to assert his own existence. Sometimes Kim Shunpei drank and drank until the anger within him was on the cusp of boiling over. When that happened, he paced back and forth in front of Lee Young-hee's house. He used to have no problem kicking her door down, but ever since his awful fight with Sung-han, his former methods now gave him pause. He felt that from now on, Sung-han would always be waiting on the other side of that door, ready to challenge him. Of course, it would be easy for him to beat Sung-han into submission. But that would be like beating down his own shadow. Every time he saw Sung-han, his stress rose, and he fell into a lingering depression.

Then a car pulled up to Kim Shunpei's house, and a man got out. He was the president of Hashimoto Precision Instruments, a company that employed more than three hundred people. He combed back his thinning hair and redid his top button, and then he bowed toward the window of the two-*jo* room where Kim Shunpei was sitting. Yi Soman brought Kim Shunpei three bottles of specialty *sake* whenever he visited.

"My apologies for keeping you waiting." Yi Soman had the bearing of someone who employed over three hundred workers. Kim Shunpei made a sour face, but he allowed him up to the room. Yi Soman's interest payment was three days late. He'd called Kim Shunpei before the deadline to let him know, but once three days passed, Kim Shunpei knew this was going to be a troublesome case.

"I have this month's interest on hand," said Yi Soman, pulling out an envelope with his advance payment.

Kim Shunpei took the envelope and asked, "How are your profits?"

"They're okay. We're doing well, and we're not doing well."

What did that mean? It sounded like a Zen koan. Kim Shunpei became more suspicious. "You're doing well, and you're not doing well. Explain so I understand."

Yi Soman had borrowed thirty million yen, and his interest each month was nine hundred thousand yen. Yi Soman had the largest debt among Kim Shunpei's clients. For that reason, Hashimoto Precision Instruments' profits were of great interest to Kim Shunpei.

"The products are selling well and creating revenue. But the more products we sell, the more financial trouble I fall into. My products cost hundreds of thousands of yen to make, so I have to take out loans. But the banks don't want to arrange any loans for a Korean like me. Which is why I have to handle loans through my own personal funds. Who has that kind of money? The more products I sell, the more debt I'm in. Which means that ultimately, I'm at a deficit."

"Then don't sell anything."

Yi Soman sighed. "If I did that, I'd have to stop production, and I'd go bankrupt."

Kim Shunpei had no idea what Yi Soman was talking about.

Hashimoto Precision Instruments was the second largest manufacturer of barber stools in the nation. Since business was going well, Yi Soman wouldn't have needed to borrow from Kim Shunpei at such high interest rates, if only a bank had agreed to a loan. But the banks didn't give out loans to Koreans.

"I'm trying to decide if I should naturalize as a Japanese citizen," said Yi Soman.

Kim Shunpei wasn't expecting Yi Soman to say this. He knew about the complications that arose for Koreans who wanted to naturalize.

"The bank would agree to a loan if you naturalize?" Kim Shunpei opened one of the bottles Yi Soman brought and poured out two cups.

"I don't know. But I'll no longer be a Korean if that

happens. Maybe the banks will deal with me then." Yi Soman took a sip of the *sake* Kim Shunpei offered him.

"People have to figure out how to live whether they're Japanese or Korean. Obviously, naturalizing is better than going bankrupt. If you went bankrupt, who'd help you? No one."

"You're completely right," said Yi Soman submissively.

"I just have one thing to say. You'll return my money before you go bankrupt. Otherwise I'll kill you."

Yi Soman's face turned white.

A honk was heard outside. A large truck was on the narrow street, unable to get past the car parked in front of Kim Shunpei's house. Yi Soman stood up and bowed several times on his way out. Kim Shunpei, once again alone, considered how he could get his money back from Yi Soman. He would have to see it returned in installments, instead of all at once. But Yi Soman was at a dead end. He had likely already taken out a second or third mortgage on his house. It was beyond Kim Shunpei's singular capacity to collect thirty million yen in debt. He had to force the money out as soon as possible—perhaps with the help of the Motoyama-*gumi*. If he did enlist the Motoyama-*gumi*, he would get only half or a third of the total share. But there was no other way. When it came to collecting debt, victory went to the swiftest. If he dawdled, Yi Soman's office equipment and manufacturing tools would be requisitioned.

That night, Kim Shunpei finished the opened bottle of specialty *sake* and took the two other bottles with him to the Motoyama-*gumi* base on Imazato-Shinbashi Street. It took Kim Shunpei ten minutes to bike there. He was drunk, but he biked with purpose. He passed through the commercial district on Shinbashi Street, which was crowded with shoppers and moviegoers.

When he reached the base, he called up to the second story, "Hey, Yoshio! Ya there?"

Three young henchmen flew out of the building at the sound of Kim Shunpei's voice. "Whaddya want?" one of them barked, bending backward to look up at this large, grizzled man.

"Tell Yoshio it's me." Kim Shunpei spoke as if Won Yoshio were a child.

"What for?" asked another henchman coldly.

At that moment the leader Won Yoshio came out. He looked more impressive than ever with his crew cut, rugged face, and thick chest. As soon as he saw Kim

Shunpei, he said respectfully, "Ah, it's you, Boss. Come in."

The others gaped at Kim Shunpei. The leader of the so-called "murderous Motoyama-*gumi*" was treating this man with astonishing deference.

Kim Shunpei was led into the inner drawing room, where he sat on the sofa and spread his legs out. He put the two bottles of specialty *sake* on the table.

"Thank you for thinking of us," said Won Yoshio. He turned to one of his young bodyguards. "Hey, bring us two cups. And go get us some drinks and food."

"Yes, sir," said the bodyguard.

"I'm goin' to Tokyo tomorrow to take care of some business. You came just in time."

"Tokyo? What for?" asked Kim Shunpei.

"To put out some fires."

"Fires, huh. Actually, I'd like you to do something for me too. Right after you come back from Tokyo."

It was rare for Kim Shunpei to ask for anyone's help, let alone in this reserved way. "Shoot," said Won Yoshio, interested.

Kim Shunpei explained the problem concerning Yi Soman.

"I know about the Hashimoto company. It'd be a pain in the ass if some other gang got involved. I'll look into it right away."

A henchman brought in *sake* and some store-bought grilled fish. Won Yoshio was a bachelor, so he didn't have a girlfriend to serve him. The ten young men gathered here had more than a few idiosyncrasies about them.

"I'll be fine with ten million if you succeed. The rest's yours," said Kim Shunpei shortly.

So Kim Shunpei was settling for a third of the share. Considering how much of a miser he was, his terms were quite generous. Won Yoshio found no reason not to accept.

"Understood. Once I come back from Tokyo, you'll get your ten million. Leave the rest to us."

Kim Shunpei, never one to converse for long, stood up. "I'm countin' on you. Come see me at my place. I'm there every night." Kim Shunpei didn't give Won Yoshio so much as a glance as he was ushered back outside. He mounted his bicycle and rode away down Shinbashi Street.

"Hey, Boss, who *was* that dude?" asked one of Won Yoshio's right-hand men.

"A monster by the name of Kim Shunpei. No one's as scary as him, far as I know."

"Seriously? He just looks like any other old stinker."

"Quiet, fool. Even ten of ya couldn't take on a guy like him." As Won Yoshio watched Kim Shunpei recede into the distance, he gripped the handle of his knife and thought back to the time Kim Shunpei had hit his head with a club. The image of that towering titan was seared deep into Won Yoshio's mind.

The Motoyama-*gumi* acted quickly. Six members stormed into the Hashimoto Precision Instruments factory with Yi Soman's contract and told him that his bill would be dishonored if he didn't pay up within a month. A dishonored bill would lead to the seizure of Yi Soman's accounts receivable from his barber stool sales. Not only was President Yi Soman forced to sign a pledge acknowledging these conditions, but two Motoyama-*gumi* members occupied a room in his mansion. Motoyama-*gumi* asserted the right to occupy the house of any debtor with a revolving mortgage.

Yi Soman came crying to Kim Shunpei the following day. "Haven't you gone too far, Kim-*san*? I paid the interest on time, didn't I? But your thugs threatened me with conditions I can't possibly fulfill. I'm begging you, have mercy! For ten years, I've poured my blood and sweat into building this factory. I can't let it go bankrupt. Otherwise, three hundred workers will be turned out into the streets. If you count their families, that'd be twelve hundred people at least. Please, think of these people! Thousands of them!"

Yi Soman put his head to the floor and sobbed. But Kim Shunpei felt no compassion.

"Human beings change their minds any number of times in a day. I thought about your case, and I changed my mind. I told you, didn't I? Pay me before you go bankrupt, or I'll kill you."

"You're jumping to conclusions. I haven't gone bankrupt yet, but you're already trying to kill me!"

"Jumping to conclusions? Your company's as good as gone. You don't think I know that? I've lost twenty million yen from having to deal with you. You're finished."

"You're joking . . . If you want ten million yen, I can take care of that tomorrow. Please think this over. I'll give you ten million yen tomorrow."

But Kim Shunpei was unmoved by any pleading or kneeling or crying. "Shut up. The gangsters and I've come to an agreement, and we're not backin' out. I'd need twice the money to negotiate with them again. Just give up and pay 'em the thirty million. You have no other choice."

"But you've broken your agreement with me. You sold them my contract and promissory note, which were supposed to be kept between us!" This time, Yi Soman was shaking in anger.

"Shut up. You're the one who fucked up. Now get outta my sight!" Kim Shunpei threw his glass of *shochu* toward the kitchen, where it shattered into tiny pieces.

In three months' time, Hashimoto Precision Instruments declared bankruptcy. Motoyama-*gumi* took over Yi Soman's mansion and arranged for a fifth of the credit to go to one bank, and a tenth of the credit to go to another. Then Motoyama-*gumi* sold the mansion to a real estate company for sixty million yen. The gang ended up with a balance of forty million yen.

Kiyoko was discharged from the hospital on a clear autumn day, five months after her surgery. To avoid prying eyes, Kim Shunpei wrapped Kiyoko up in a blanket and carried her out of the taxi into the house. Her body was as light as cotton. After being laid out

on the futon, she stared at the ceiling vacantly, unable
to say a word. She took an interminably long time to
open her mouth, only to let out slurred speech that Kim
Shunpei found incomprehensible. He could only infer
what Kiyoko was feeling or communicating through the
tone of her voice or the expression in her eyes. The doctor
had optimistically predicted that Kiyoko would be able
to use her right hand and walk on her own before long.
But Kiyoko's right hand refused to work. Unable to use
chopsticks or a spoon, she couldn't eat anything without
assistance. Kim Shunpei had to find a caregiver for her
immediately.

In the meantime, he made Kiyoko soft foods like
boiled fish, miso soup, and *tamagoyaki*. He made separate
meals for himself with the heavily seasoned beef, pork,
and organ dishes he liked. Kim Shunpei was a skilled
cook from his experience as a *kamaboko* worker, so
cooking twice for each meal wasn't much of a problem.
Even when Kiyoko had been healthy, Kim Shunpei had
often cooked his own meals; he couldn't expect a Japanese
woman to know how to make his favorite Korean foods.
Not even a Korean woman could be expected to prepare
food that conformed to his singular tastes. He no longer

ate those monstrous raw pork filets, but he hadn't given up on his other medicinal staples.

After twiddling his thumbs for five months, his hands were now full of tasks. During meals, he forced chopsticks into Kiyoko's hands to try to get her to eat by herself, but she could never pick anything up. So he had to feed her himself. Even then, Kiyoko couldn't chew properly, and the food would dribble down her chin along with her drool.

"Swallow. Why can't you swallow, dammit?" urged Kim Shunpei, as if he were scolding a child. Whenever he spoke like that, Kiyoko's eyes tightened in fear. She was able to sit up with help and could stay seated with her back against the wall, but when Kim Shunpei scared her, she lost her balance and fell over. Kim Shunpei was appalled at what her body had become.

Kim Shunpei also had to take Kiyoko to the bathroom several times a day. At first, he carried her there and held her over the squat toilet as if he were potty training her. But it was impossible for two adults to squat at the same time in that tiny bathroom. He bought a brass pan so that Kiyoko could pee while laying down. Taking care of her was mentally exhausting.

He had to wash Kiyoko once a week. He poured boiling water into a large aluminum basin and adjusted the temperature with water from the pump. When he set Kiyoko down in the water, her face expressed her pleasure. Her once springy white body was reduced to skin and bones, as if she'd aged thirty years. Her thin hair would only grow to a length of five or six centimeters. As Kim Shunpei washed her bony body, he asked himself how long they could go on like this.

One day, Kim Shunpei came back home to find a bad odor on the second floor. Kiyoko was laying on the futon, staring up at the ceiling as always. Kim Shunpei turned back her covers, and the stench filled the room. He rolled up Kiyoko's soiled clothes in the sheets, carried the futon down the stairs, and threw the futon onto the cement floor of the *genkan*. He used the gas stove to boil water in a large pot. It had been two or three years since he'd last used the gas stove, as he wanted to avoid any unnecessary bills. He mixed the boiling water with pump water in the aluminum basin, washed Kiyoko, and set her down on a clean futon. After much inner debate, he decided to throw the dirty futon away instead of cleaning it. That night, he stuffed the futon into his bicycle rack and disposed of it in a canal.

He couldn't even unload his frustrations onto Kiyoko, who was completely helpless. But now he hesitated to leave her alone at all. He drank *sake* by himself in the room next to her. He felt like the two of them were clinging onto a plank from a wrecked ship and floating above the great deep. But she was losing the strength to hold onto the plank. Kim Shunpei was using all his strength to hold her up while the waves buffeted them. What else was he to do? He wandered through the darkness of his own heart. He was enveloped in layers of darkness that became a hellish furnace, making his blood boil and seethe. All humans died in the end. No one could choose the time of their death, whether it came early or late. Only the power of a terrible god could release others from the pain of death. The drunk Kim Shunpei wished that he could become that kind of terrible god.

Kim Shunpei made calls to his nephews Kim Yong-su in Nishinari and Kim Tae-su in Nara. The nephews were surprised to hear from their uncle so late at night.

"After work tomorrow, come straight to my place. Understood?"

It was an order. Had something happened? What did

Kim Shunpei want? The two nephews couldn't remember doing anything wrong, but they kept themselves awake that night chasing shadows.

The next day Kim Shunpei was drinking *sake* in the two-*jo* room when his nephews arrived. "Sorry to keep you waiting," said the elder nephew Kim Yong-su. Beside him, Kim Tae-su bowed his head.

"Sit," said Kim Shunpei. The two nephews sank to the floor.

Kim Shunpei poured out two cups of *sake* and informed his nephews about Kiyoko's condition. The two men's faces stiffened. Was their uncle going to conscript them into taking care of her? They wouldn't be able to refuse him if he did.

"Find me a woman. Any woman. She'll live here and look after Kiyoko. She needs to be strong, so a young woman's best."

The nephews half comprehended what Kim Shunpei meant. They knew that Kim Shunpei could barely leave the house with Kiyoko confined to bed, so hiring a caretaker for her made sense. But his requirement that she be a young, live-in woman was more perplexing. Where would they find such a woman? The nephews struggled to respond. If they told their uncle that no young woman could be expected to move in, he could force *them* to be Kiyoko's caretakers. They grimaced, unable to say yes or no.

"Well, spit it out!" The sight of his dithering nephews provoked Kim Shunpei to no end, and he raised the two *sake* glasses threateningly. The nephews shrunk back.

"Uncle, we understand your struggle, but I can't imagine any woman who'd do that," said Kim Yong-su, keeping his eyes fixed on the tatami floor.

"That's why I'm tellin' you to go find me one! Are you tellin' me no woman like that exists? Not even gonna look, huh. You think it's such a hassle? Or are you just deaf?"

"No, we'll look. But I don't think it'll be that easy to find someone . . . ."

Kim Yong-su's answers were vague and evasive, which exasperated Kim Shunpei further. "I see. Then both of you will come here tomorrow and nurse her yourselves. I have a whole 'nother tenement building to myself. I'll live there."

It would be one thing for Kim Shunpei to make his nephews Kiyoko's personal nurses, but it was beyond the pale for him to leave Kiyoko behind and escape for his own comfort. He would be abdicating his responsibility. Compromise was impossible: the nephews had no choice but to find a young woman willing to be a live-in worker for Kim Shunpei. Strangely, they felt compelled to do this not just because of Kim Shunpei's outrageous conditions, but because they felt bad that Kim Shunpei had to do care work.

Last summer, Kim Yong-su had lost fifteen of his twenty hogs to an epidemic, and he'd borrowed money from Kim Shunpei to purchase new piglets. Kim Tae-su, too, had borrowed money from Kim Shunpei to start a grape orchard in Nara after he quit his job at the slaughterhouse. Of course, both of them were paying their uncle an interest rate of three percent each month. Kim Shunpei's motto was that a three percent monthly interest rate was lower than the interest rates one could find on the stock market.

"Who'd lend money to the likes of you? Go to the stock exchange and see, you'd have to pay five percent or ten percent interest there. And only if they give you a loan in the first place. I'm generous with you 'cause you're my nephews. I normally charge five or six percent interest, so

I'm lendin' to you at a loss. Get it?"

Kim Shunpei wasn't in fact exaggerating. That was why the nephews had reason to see their relationship with their uncle as a critical leverage point.

Any vague answers were unacceptable. They had to clearly promise to find a woman who met Kim Shunpei's requirements.

"We'll make sure to find someone," said Kim Yong-su weakly.

"Within a month," demanded Kim Shunpei.

"Yes, sir," said both nephews. There was nothing else they could say.

But they had no idea where to begin their search for this hypothetical woman. They sighed heavily as they left Kim Shunpei's house.

"*Aniki*, do you have any clue what to do?" asked Kim Tae-su.

"'Course I don't. But unless we tell him what he wants to hear, he'll make one of us take care of that Japanese broad. You think we could let that happen? And if we didn't do *that*, he'd want his money back, and I'd have to kill my pigs. You'd be fucked, too."

"So what do we do?"

"We search. He said any woman would do, as long as she's young and available. We could pick up a beggar from the streets." As he said this, Kim Yong-su suddenly thought of someone.

Kim Yong-su parted from his younger brother in Tsuruhachi and headed toward Nishinari. His hog farm and house faced a watery ditch with several barrack-style huts on the other side. The huts had been built illegally, and the authorities had cut off electricity, running water, and gas. At night they looked like black mounds of trash. Most of the residents simply went to bed when night fell, but a gas lamp or two could sometimes be seen flickering inside. About thirty meters away from this cluster of huts sat a small shack. Every morning Kim Yong-su casually scanned the other side of the ditch and occasionally saw a woman and child come out of the shack, though he never paid them much attention. The woman looked to be just under five feet tall and had dark, rough skin. Her teeth and cheeks jutted out, and thick eyebrows sheltered her starved, sunken eyes. Her child was a mentally slow seven-year-old girl who followed her around with her nose dripping constantly. No one knew how the woman made a living. Rumor had it that she was a hooker in the

321

Tennoji area. Kim Yong-su wondered if this woman could be a potential candidate for Kim Shunpei. He resolved to talk with her the next day.

Work at the hog farm started early in the morning when the hogs started squealing loudly for their food. After feeding the hogs, Kim Yong-su cleaned their pens and boiled their next meal, all while keeping an eye on the woman's shack. At eight in the morning, the woman finally came out to fire up her earthenware brazier. Kim Yong-su took off his apron, washed his hands, and crossed over the ditch in his rubber work boots. The woman was crouching by the brazier smoking a cigarette and fanning the brazier's flames. As Kim Yong-su approached her, she turned to look at him as she kept waving the fan.

"Hey there, I'd like to talk with you about somethin'. Could you spare a moment?" called out Kim Yong-su.

The woman dropped her arms to her sides and stood up wearily. "What's this about?"

Kim Yong-su had thought the woman would be about forty based on the darkness of her skin, but in the sunlight, she looked hardly over thirty. Her short, stout body indeed looked strong.

"There's no need to be suspicious. I'm Kanemoto, the

owner of the hog farm 'cross the river." He pointed across the ditch.

The woman seemed to know who he was already, and she didn't seem particularly threatened by him.

"We don't have to stand here and talk. Wanna meet at the café next to the cigarette stand? At ten?"

"What do you wanna talk about? Is this gonna be complicated? Keep it simple."

"It's not complicated. It'll be a pleasant conversation."

"What do you mean, a pleasant conversation?"

"Let's talk at the café. Or inside your room."

The woman didn't want this man entering her shack. Kim Yong-su looked over her shoulder into the shack, which consisted of nothing more than a three-*jo* room with a wooden floor.

"Ten at the café, you said? I dunno what you want from me, but I'll go, I guess."

"Ah, thanks, thanks. I'll be there at ten." He turned around.

Kim Yong-su changed out of his work clothes and arrived at the café at ten sharp, taking a seat at a table in the back. Five minutes later the woman arrived with her daughter. No other customers were there. They ordered coffee, toast, and boiled eggs. Kim Yong-su took a nervous sip of his coffee and drew from his cigarette before he spoke.

"So my uncle in Higashinari's in a bit of a pinch. He has hundreds of millions of yen in assets, but his partner's ill and can't get out of bed. He's too busy to take care of her and asked me to look for someone who could. You came to mind. I see you around every mornin'."

The woman hadn't been expecting to hear anything interesting, but her face fell as Kim Yong-su talked. Leaning back in her chair and crossing her legs, she said, "You lookin' for a personal nurse, then? Ain't there an agency for that?"

"He could hire a personal nurse, yeah. But this is different. How do I put this? Basically . . . he has an eye out for a second wife."

Kim Shunpei hadn't said a word about wanting a second wife. But there was no other way of framing it, since he was adamant that she live in the house with him.

"Wait, but the first wife's still alive. I never heard of a man having two wives at once."

Beside her, the young girl was chomping on a piece of toast that glistened with phlegm. Her mother looked

324

at her coolly as she blew out smoke. Kim Yong-su wasn't impressed with this woman's carelessness. But he figured that such a woman would be most likely to go along with his proposal.

"The woman he's with now has only two or three months left. You could marry into his wealth. If you bear him a child, his assets are yours."

Kim Yong-su was coaxing this woman in the same way Manada Airi had coaxed Kiyoko. And this woman's desperate living situation was a step down from what Kiyoko's had been. A prostitute—or a woman rumored to be one—had few choices left to her. Hesitancy flashed across this woman's face. She inhaled her cigarette fitfully, as if she were very aware of her compromised situation. She was calculating the chances that this opportunity would turn her bad luck around. Kim Yong-su took out an envelope from his breast pocket and placed it on the table.

"There's fifty thousand yen in here. If you go meet my uncle tomorrow, you can use this cash to buy yourself and your daughter new clothes."

The woman looked around the cafe to make sure no one was watching them. The waitress was at the counter watching television. Right at that moment, two men came in. "Hey, miss, morning sets for both of us, please," one of them said. As they sat down at the counter, the woman quickly hid the envelope away.

"Fine. I'll go see this uncle of yours. But that don't mean I'm livin' with him," she said defensively.

"I get it. I'm not tellin' you what to do. If you're up for it, you can live with him, that's all."

Accepting the cash meant she was agreeing to the basic conditions. Above all, it meant she wanted to escape from her current life.

"So just to make sure, how old are ya? I'll tell my uncle about you to let him know you're comin'."

"I'm thirty-one."

Kim Yong-su studied her face.

"If you don't believe me, I can show you my commuter pass." The woman pulled out a seasonal bus pass from her drawstring purse. The illiterate Kim Yong-su held the bus pass at arm's length and stared at it.

"I'm farsighted so I can't read it. What's your name?" he said, squinting.

"Toritani Sadako."

"Place of birth?"

"Kagoshima." Sadako smoked her cigarette unhappily as she crossed her legs again.

Kim Yong-su could sense her displeasure. "I'm not interviewing you! I just needed your name and age. Sorry 'bout that. Right, I'll come over at noon to take you to my uncle's." He stood up.

As Kim Yong-su paid the bill, Sadako took her daughter's hand and exited the cafe. Kim Yong-su waited for the derelict-looking mother and daughter to gain a bit of distance from him before he walked out slowly.

Chapter 23

Kim Yong-su woke up earlier than usual to take care of his morning tasks at the farm. He then called his brother Kim Tae-su and told him to come to Kim Shunpei's house a little after noon.

After breakfast, Kim Yong-su's wife Yeong-ja burst out, "You're really gonna bring *her*?"

"I have no choice! I only have a month, and it's not like he's picky. Anyone better come to mind?" Kim Yong-su understood his wife's agitation, but for him, the end justified the means.

"What if he hates her? Never mind that she'd probably hate him."

"I'll deal with that when the time comes. First, they have to meet."

"You should've just told your uncle no. But you don't

have the guts, do you? That's why we're in this mess."

"Why don't *you* say no to his face, then?"

Of course, she didn't think she could. Husband and wife could join forces and be none the better off in front of Kim Shunpei.

"Plus, he'll fuck us over if I don't do what he says. He's gonna force us to live with that Japanese woman and clean up her shit and whatever. Sound like something you'd wanna do?"

"Why should *we* do any of that? Who does he think we are? We're repaying him with interest every month like we're supposed to. Are we his slaves or what?" The more Yeong-ja thought about it, the angrier she got. She stopped cleaning the kitchen and sat down at the table in a huff. The smell of the boiling pig feed wafted through the house, as it did every morning. This morning, the noxious stench pissed her off. She and her husband didn't have any children, and their arguments could turn dark very quickly.

Kim Yong-su didn't have the energy to deal with his sullen wife, and he got up from the table to change out of his work clothes. "Don't overcook the feed," he reminded her as he left the house.

He crossed over the ditch and found Sadako and her daughter outside the shack in brand-new clothes. They didn't look so bad, considering how seedy they'd looked the day before. But Sadako's face was too heavily made up—the white powder on her face looked like smeared soap, and her dark eyes gleamed like a bird of prey. Her bright red lipstick had rubbed onto her front teeth. Kim Yong-su thought about telling her to redo her makeup, but he didn't want to hurt her pride. All humans wanted some level of self-respect. It looked like Sadako had tried her best, and Kim Yong-su held himself back from encroaching on sensitive female territory.

In any case, she looked different from yesterday, and she was carrying a cloth bag. "Here's the leftover cash," she said.

"No, keep it. The money belongs to my uncle." Trying to appear as generous as possible to put Sadako at ease, Kim Yong-su took her to the main thoroughfare and flagged down a taxi.

"It's been so long since I rode in one of these things," said Sadako.

Her daughter looked out the window in fascination as she wiped her nose on her sleeve, which was already shiny with snot.

"You taught her to blow her nose yet?" said Kim Yong-su in distaste.

"Yeah, but she doesn't get it." Sadako wiped her daughter's nose with the end of her cloth bag.

Once the taxi reached Sennichimae it was a straight line to Imazato.

"How long have you lived in Osaka?" asked Kim Yong-su. He could pick out Sadako's Kagoshima accent.

"Eight years."

"Eight years . . . So your kid was born here?"

"Yep."

"And her father?"

"He ran off when I was still in the hospital with her."

"A cruel man." Kim Yong-su glanced at Sadako, wondering how much he could believe her.

The taxi pulled right up to Kim Shunpei's front door, and Kim Yong-su shielded Sadako and her child from view as they went into the *genkan*. Kim Shunpei and Kim Tae-su were in the front two-*jo* room drinking *sake*.

"Ah, you're here, Tae-su?" called out Kim Yong-su, but Kim Tae-su was too busy looking at Sadako and her runny-nosed daughter to reply. Kim Shunpei was also appraising the mother and daughter silently. Sadako kept her eyes on the floor.

"Uncle, I brought her," announced Kim Yong-su. To Sadako he said, "Hey, don't just stand there. Go in."

Sadako reluctantly stepped up from the *genkan* and sat down in a corner of the two-*jo* room. Everyone's knees almost touched in the packed room.

"This is Toritani Sadako and her daughter," said Kim Yong-su formally. He had called Kim Shunpei the night before to give him the basic details about Sadako.

"Nice to meet you," said Sadako in a small voice, while her daughter hid behind her in the corner.

"How old's the kid?" asked Kim Shunpei.

"Seven," replied Sadako.

Kim Shunpei addressed her like she was his indentured servant, which wasn't far from the actual case. "And you'll live here, yeah?" Kim Shunpei's eyes bore into her menacingly.

Sadako paused for a moment and then nodded.

"Great," Kim Tae-su broke in, smiling.

Kim Yong-su was very pleased with his work. "Wonderful, wonderful! You won't regret it!" he cried.

"Uncle, shall I order some sushi?" asked Kim Tae-su

brightly, while Kim Yong-su went to the phone to tell his wife Yeong-ja the news.

"Turn right on the main street and go straight for a bit. You'll see the sushi place soon enough," said Kim Shunpei.

Kim Tae-su bounded out and got on his bicycle, uncharacteristically buoyant. He came back with the sushi shop's delivery boy. It was a strange sight for this group of people to be sitting around the low circular table for a meal. Sadako ate while covering her mouth with her hand.

"How 'bout a drink?" suggested Kim Tae-su. Sadako shyly took two sips from her glass. Her daughter, unable to use chopsticks, ate the sushi with her hands. Rice grains stuck to her chin and nose and dropped to the floor in clumps.

"Yuki-*chan*, eat properly."

But little Yukiko kept stuffing sushi into her open mouth as if she hadn't heard.

"She's a kid. Can't be helped," said Kim Shunpei. The two nephews were surprised to hear their uncle say something so generous.

"Sorry about that," said Sadako sweetly.

For the rest of the meal, the two nephews tried to deflect attention away from Sadako as much as possible. They didn't want to learn more about her past or her way of life. An unsavory detail could sour Kim Shunpei's opinion of her and spoil Kim Yong-su's hard work. Instead, the nephews spent the next two hours gossiping about this and that.

After the nephews left, Sadako cleared the dishes and gave a bow, saying, "I hope I can help in any way I can."

"Yeah, well, just look after the woman. She'll take up all your time," said Kim Shunpei. "Let the kid play outside for now," he added.

Sadako sensed what he meant. "Yuki-*chan*, here's some spare change. Go treat yourself to some *okonomiyaki*. It's your favorite, right?"

"I'm full. I'll eat *okonomiyaki* later." Yukiko had indeed gobbled up a large portion of the fancy sushi.

"Just do it. Can't you listen to your mother? And don't wander off. Eat a lot and come straight back." Sadako sent Yukiko out and locked the door behind her. Then she folded up the table, stowed it away in the closet, and laid out the futon. She lay down on her side and curled her knees in. Her stomach pooched out and her large breasts sagged. Kim Shunpei gripped a breast and sucked on the nipple. "Ah!" cried Sadako. He silenced her by pushing his tongue into her mouth as he brought a hand to her crotch. He reached into her thick pubic hair, which felt like wet, sticky marshland. Sadako broke into a sweat, and her dark, rough skin gave off the smell of something like rotting fruit. Her whole body was priming itself for sex.

When Kim Shunpei entered her, Sadako let out a groan. She knew Kiyoko was upstairs and was clenching her jaw to stay quiet, but she could no longer hold herself back. The pleasure she was feeling was too powerful to contain. Kim Shunpei's lust for Sadako's young body was insatiable. She didn't have to be beautiful. All he needed was a woman's flesh. What else was there but the rawness of flesh that bled when it was cut open? Kiyoko was ill in both body and mind. Kim Shunpei wanted flesh that reacted to his touch.

Yukiko was pounding on the front door and calling for her mother. When no one answered her, she started crying. Sadako came to her senses when she heard her daughter's sobs. But Kim Shunpei had her in an octopus hold, and she was too numb to move. Eventually Kim Shunpei let her go, and she put on her clothes as she rushed to the door. When she opened it, Yukiko was standing there with tears and snot dripping down her face.

"Why are you snivelin' like that? Stop it right now," said Sadako. Worried that the neighbors were watching, she roughly pulled Yukiko inside and closed the door.

Kim Shunpei was smoking a cigarette back in the room. He told Sadako, "We'll sleep here. Have your kid sleep upstairs."

"Okay," said Sadako, nodding. She didn't want to displease Kim Shunpei.

Kim Shunpei led Sadako to the second floor and showed her into the room that opened out onto the balcony. Kiyoko was in bed, and her eyes settled on Kim Shunpei and Sadako. A craggy ridge of skin ran from her right ear to the back of her head like a split seam. Sadako looked down at Kiyoko triumphantly, a smile playing on her lips.

"There's a button here on the pillar. When she presses it, you'll hear the buzzer downstairs. Come up to check on Kiyoko when you hear it. She just moans and babbles and you won't understand her, but you'll get the hang of her soon. Use this brass pan for her pee and her shit.

She pees twice or three times a day, and she takes a shit once a day. She can't eat on her own, so let her sit up against the wall." Then he turned to Kiyoko. "Hey, this woman's gonna take care of you now. Do what she says. Understand?" Kim Shunpei tried to read Kiyoko's face for a response, but Kiyoko just kept her eyes fixed on Sadako.

"Won't she dislike me?" asked Sadako in a snide sort of way.

"Doesn't matter." Kim Shunpei only wanted Sadako to do what he told her, not to make unnecessary observations or read too much into other people's feelings.

Just when Sadako was wondering what to do about dinner, Kim Shunpei ordered her to put firewood under the stove and prepare some rice.

"Can't I use the gas stove?" asked Sadako.

"You have firewood and the hearth right here. Stop with your stupid questions. Fire up the brazier. I'm goin' to the market for dinner."

Kim Shunpei hung his shopping basket on the bicycle handle and set off for Tsuruhashi.

Sadako was unpleasantly surprised at the prohibition on using the gas stove. She would have to cook the same way she did while living in the shack. This man was

337

supposed to be rich, but he didn't have a refrigerator, nor a laundry machine, nor a television. He didn't have anything. The hallway from the *genkan* to the back kitchen was piled with stoves. The kitchen shelves were lined with herbal medicines and jars; when Sadako peered inside, she could see charred monkey heads and snakes. She decided to get over her initial shock. She'd come here to escape having to beg on the streets. No matter what happened, she couldn't return to that shack by the ditch. She was determined to make Kim Shunpei's money her own. She was young and hardy. She could rely on the strength of her body.

Kim Shunpei came back in about forty minutes. His shopping basket was laden with fish, pork legs, and vegetables. He told Sadako to make Kiyoko's customary meal of miso soup, *tamagoyaki,* boiled fish, and pickles. Kim Shunpei would make his own meal. Sadako watched him throw fish heads, beef tendons, and chicken bones into a large pot, along with daikon, carrots, garlic, ginger, chives, red peppers, and other spices. He skimmed off the foam as the soup boiled. Sadako preferred to eat what she was making for Kiyoko. But Kim Shunpei had other plans. He set down the hodgepodge stew on the low table and said, "Eat this. It's good." Sadako couldn't refuse, and she ladled a small bowl for herself. She was surprised by how good it tasted. The spiciness of it burned her mouth, but the flavor was well-rounded and mellow.

"It's my first time tasting something like this!"

In fact, all the food Sadako had eaten up to that point was paupers' fare compared to Kim Shunpei's soup. Yukiko also ate without any complaints. Their foreheads glistened with sweat, and the spices warmed their stomachs, which stimulated their appetites further. Sadako was astonished at how Kim Shunpei could dump all that food into his wide-open mouth. She didn't think it possible that a fifty-eight-year-old man could eat so much. He looked like a wild lion feasting on a fresh kill.

"The truly good stuff's not at the high-class restaurants. It's the stuff I make." Kim Shunpei's personal opinion was that his cooking was drawn from the fountain of life itself.

After their meal, Sadako cleared the table and brought Kiyoko her meal on a tray table. Kiyoko was staring up at the ceiling vacantly, but as soon as Sadako came in, she turned her head away in a show of absolute rejection. Sadako raised her up, set her against the wall, and put on her bib. When Sadako drew up some rice with chopsticks, Kiyoko refused to open her mouth.

"Why don't you eat? I came here to take care of you. It was the boss's idea, and his nephews begged me to come. I couldn't say no. Who'd *want* to come here and do this for you? You should be thanking me, stupid. And stop glaring at me. Stubborn, aren't you? Eat, eat!"

Sadako pried open Kiyoko's mouth with the spoon and forced rice and miso soup into it. Kiyoko choked and coughed, and the food flew out.

"You're harder to deal with than Yukiko. Bitch." Sadako slapped Kiyoko on the cheek. "Stop lookin' at me like that! It's your fault. You don't appreciate the kindness of other people. Don't eat, then. I'll tell the boss what you did." Sadako's black, bird-like eyes flashed menacingly.

Kiyoko's eyes filled with tears.

"Stop it. You're fakin' it anyway. The boss trusts me with this job. If you don't do as I say, you'll rot in your own shit and piss."

Kiyoko collapsed, battered by Sadako's verbal abuse.

"Guess you're not hungry. You'll eat soon enough. You don't know what it's like to go hungry, do you? If you were really hungry, you'd be okay with cockroaches for dinner. Going hungry is worse than death." Sadako was speaking from her own experience. She stared in disgust at the lopsided, struggling Kiyoko and went down the stairs with the tray table. Kim Shunpei was in the kitchen handling the membrane of a cow's stomach.

"I've tried and tried to get her to eat, but she won't. What should I do?"

Kim Shunpei looked at Sadako over his glasses and stood up. "I'll take it to her."

"Please speak with her. She won't listen to me."

Kim Shunpei took the tray table back up to the second floor. Sadako followed him up and stood by the screen door to Kiyoko's room.

"Why aren't you eating? Sadako is here to take care of you, understand?"

Kiyoko looked at Kim Shunpei bitterly, and tears flowed from her eyes.

"Sadako, try again."

Sadako once again held up some rice to Kiyoko's mouth. Kiyoko, mindful of the fearsome Kim Shunpei, opened her mouth slightly and accepted the rice.

When Kiyoko finished her meal, Sadako went downstairs and sank to the tatami floor. "I'm so tired," she whined.

"Stop complaining. Get out of my house if you have a problem."

Sadako's face went rigid. "I'm sorry," she said quietly.

Within half a day's time, Sadako realized she was living with a short-tempered man who couldn't be crossed.

Within two or three days, Sadako's existence was made known to the neighbors. A few of them noticed a brown-skinned, large-eyed, short and stout woman cleaning the *genkan*. They eventually figured out that the woman was living in the house. They were appalled by Kim Shunpei's shamelessness, keeping two mistresses under the same roof. When Ko Nobuyoshi came to visit and saw Sadako at the door, he assumed at first that he was at the wrong house. Afterward, he went to Lee Young-hee's house and asked her what was going on.

"I don't know any more than you. Why don't you ask *him*?" said Lee Young-hee drily.

"Like I could do that! How do you feel about it?"

"It has nothing to do with me. I don't care how many women he's living with," said Lee Young-hee. At this point, she was thinking of putting a full stop to this ugly situation and moving somewhere else.

"That Japanese woman's an invalid, so it makes sense for someone to take care of her. But isn't there a better way that this?"

In Ko Nobuyoshi's eyes, the new woman's presence wasn't a total scandal. No one could deny that Kim Shunpei was at his wit's end after half a year of caring for Kiyoko himself. His methods flew in the face of societal common sense, but common sense didn't apply to a man who was known to rhetorically ask "Who's going to help you?" Kim Shunpei's life choices couldn't be measured by ordinary means. He didn't subscribe to the half-baked, inconsistent ethics and ideologies—in other words, the common sense—of societies that could sometimes agree to go to war.

Sung-han shrugged at the news. *At it again? How about living with someone a little better than the last one?* he thought. When Hanako came to visit with her newborn baby, she scowled and said, "Such a disgrace. We can't even show our faces around here. And I can't face my own in-laws." Han Masahito thought the same. "It really is a disgrace. Two mistresses in the same house? He has some nerve."

Kim Shunpei was on everyone's lips for a little while. But all hot topics cool off in the end, and people stopped regarding the situation as unnatural. In fact, many of the neighbors sympathized with Sadako for having to be Kiyoko's full-time caretaker. They remained interested in how these two women would get along with each other.

Times were changing, and the economy was on the rise—but only the Koreans were left behind. The neighborhood women of old were as energetic as ever, but their children started leaving one by one. Former childhood friends no longer talked. Everyone was just whiling away their days. The con artist Hong Byeong-saeng and the petty gangster Yi Takane disappeared without a trace. The various activists coming and going through Lee Young-hee's house were beginning to lose their shine. Everyone was aging. Only Kim Shunpei stood out from the pack. He didn't know the meaning of decline.

Two years after Sadako moved in, she gave birth to a girl. A boy would have been preferable, but the sixty-year-old Kim Shunpei still saw the girl's birth as a kind of fresh start. Sadako was particularly conscious of what Lee Young-hee would think. She used to hide in the house if she saw Lee Young-hee out and about, but now she strutted around the neighborhood showing off her newborn. While eating *okonomiyaki* at the nearby snack bar, she loudly proclaimed, "The boss told me all his money is gonna go to my children."

"Well, good for you. He's definitely the richest person here," said the woman shop owner enviously.

"And the boss can't read or write, so I'm in charge of all his loans," bragged Sadako, as if Kim Shunpei's assets already belonged to her. But in reality, Sadako wasn't allowed to have a single sen of her own. Ever since she first met Kim Shunpei, she never got to buy a single article of clothing. Kim Shunpei did all the grocery shopping too. He eliminated any wasteful spending, and it was impossible to ask him for anything.

One time Sadako casually said, "It'd be nice to have a kimono." Kim Shunpei immediately shouted back, "Like hell you will! Where do you think you're goin' in a kimono? You gonna date other men or what?" Sadako was at a loss for words.

Kim Shunpei drank later that night and became violent, much to Sadako's horror. She tried to redirect Kim Shunpei's rage toward Kiyoko. She dumped miso soup all over Kiyoko's lap and threw the contents of her brass pan onto the floor, asserting, "How long do you think you can put me through this hell?" Kim Shunpei's reaction was instantaneous. He remembered his mental exhaustion when he had to take care of Kiyoko, and Sadako's outburst gave him pause. For both of them, Kiyoko's existence was nothing but a burden. She was a living corpse who had turned into a bargaining chip between them. But ever since Sadako gave birth to her daughter, that delicate balance had been destroyed.

About a year after the birth of her daughter, the neighborhood women at the water pump started whispering amongst themselves, "She about to have another one or what?"

Sadako's belly had always protruded enough to be mistaken for a pregnant woman, but lately her belly looked like it was about to split open. It was obvious to everyone that she was in her final month of pregnancy. Kim Shunpei couldn't wait to see if the baby was a boy. He was uncharacteristically considerate toward Sadako and took over some of her responsibilities, including disposing of Kiyoko's waste. Sadako hoped for a boy if only to draw Kim Shunpei closer to her.

It was raining from morning till night, and around midnight the rain gained strength. The old drainage ditch overflowed with water until the water seeped into the house. Kim Shunpei woke up when he felt a cold dampness on his back. He turned on the lights and saw that rainwater had soaked the tatami floor. Sadako woke up too and helplessly stared at the water around them. Kim Shunpei went outside and saw that his neighbors were in a furor. It was no use salvaging the tatami matting. "Let's go upstairs," said Kim Shunpei.

Just then, Sadako clutched her belly and moaned. Her labor pains were starting. Kim Shunpei cursed his luck and padded over to the phone to call the midwife. Then he went to the hearth to boil some water. The hearth was slightly elevated, and the wood hadn't gotten soaked yet, but if the water kept rising, Kim Shunpei wouldn't be able to keep the fire going. Kim Shunpei reluctantly moved the water to the gas stove.

The rainwater rose and rose. Human refuse flowed out from the toilet. The normally prompt midwife wasn't coming. She was likely stuck in the knee-deep water, trying to make her way through the trackless paths. Sadako was moaning on the second floor. Yukiko stood in the middle of the stairs in a daze, her nose dripping as usual.

"Go watch your mom," ordered Kim Shunpei.

"I have to pee," said Yukiko.

"Just pee there," yelled Kim Shunpei in frustration.

Yukiko squatted and did as she was told.

It would be the first time Kim Shunpei oversaw a childbirth. He never thought he would find himself in this position at sixty-two years old. He really was getting old. In the past, it was none of his business whether a woman bore a child or not. The fact that he had to deliver a baby now was proof of his emasculation.

Thirty minutes later, the midwife arrived. "I could barely make it here! The water was up to my knees, and it was so dark I couldn't see." The short-haired, sixty-year-old woman kept grumbling under her breath.

"Thank you for coming at a time like this," said Kim Shunpei, leading her up to the second floor. Three hours later, the baby was delivered. Kim Shunpei was sitting on the steps as he heard the baby's cries. He waited for the verdict. The midwife lifted the baby up. "What a beautiful baby girl!"

Kim Shunpei went down the stairs without bothering

to look at his child. He sat on the hearth and drank straight from a bottle of *shochu*. He didn't say another word to the midwife as she took her leave.

Sadako, meanwhile, could only stare in chagrin at the baby girl sleeping beside her.

Kiyoko was babbling in the next room. She probably needed to empty her bowels. Sadako hated Kiyoko for wanting to take a shit when she was suffering like this. She left her baby on the bed and went to Kiyoko's room. "You waste of space. You should die in your own shit." Sadako grabbed Kiyoko's hair and gave it a yank. Kiyoko peed her pants in response.

The rain eased into a drizzle at dawn and stopped later that morning. The sky shook off its gloom and assumed a bright, transparent blue. A few households had salvaged their tatami mats from the flood, but most had to hang their mats out to dry on their balconies and roofs. Kim Shunpei brought out Kiyoko's soiled bedding in addition to his wet tatami mats.

By that afternoon, the water had largely receded into the gutters, leaving behind trash, wreckage, and the corpses of cats. Insurance agents came by to spray the houses with disinfectant.

Sadako's second baby daughter was born in the middle of a flood, but because she was a girl, she couldn't hope to earn the patronage of her father Kim Shunpei.

Sadako had given birth in the room next to Kiyoko's, and she continued to nurse her baby there. Kim Shunpei also took to sleeping in that room. When Sadako first moved in, she and Kim Shunpei had stayed in the cramped two-*jo* room on the first floor out of consideration for Kiyoko, but at this point, they treated Kiyoko as if she were barely there. The mentally slow Yukiko was a heavy sleeper and didn't interrupt Kim Shunpei and Sadako during their nightly intercourse. Sadako became bolder than ever, writhing and moaning with abandon. But the bedridden Kiyoko wasn't a vegetable, and she made sure to respond when she heard Sadako and Kim Shunpei having sex. As Sadako's moans got louder and louder, Kiyoko would start screaming— which in her case sounded like guttural barks. Whenever that happened, Sadako would lose her enthusiasm and push Kim Shunpei away.

"She's supposed to stay quiet in bed. What a jealous bitch."

Sadako wasn't the only one to get turned off. Kim

Shunpei's penis wilted in embarrassment at the noise Kiyoko made. His arousal would coil up in his belly, refusing to go away, but resuming intercourse was like trying to light a wet match. After this happened several times, Sadako and Kim Shunpei moved back to their original two-*jo* room with the two infants, while Yukiko stayed in the room upstairs. The two-*jo* room could barely accommodate the second futon. And though sex could be managed no matter how tight the space was, Sadako and Kim Shunpei were extremely uncomfortable doing it.

The new year was approaching. The neighbors cleaned their houses, hung *shimenawa* and *kadomatsu* from their doors, and pounded *mochi*. More people than usual showed up at Kim Shunpei's house bearing gifts of *sake,* fruit, tobacco, and ham, hopeful about their various financial plans. Sadako busily inspected the gifts and prepared contracts and promissory notes.

Snow typically accompanied Osaka into the new year, but the first day of this year was like a mild autumn day. The tenement houses looked cleaner and fresher than they'd been in a long time. The New Year's decorations and the sight of children in new clothes added some color to the normally shabby neighborhood.

Kim Shunpei, Sadako, and her children were in the two-*jo* room tasting the New Year's meal Sadako had made. Yukiko ate greedily. The three-year-old Sunako scolded Yukiko as if Yukiko were the younger child. Kim Shunpei looked upon the clever Sunako with some affection. They were like a happy family. Sadako was lifting the crying infant Yuko to her breast when something rolled down from the second floor and violently hit the wall. It was Kiyoko, still conscious. Her body was contorted into a V-shape, and she glared up at Sadako, who stared down at her with Yuko in her arms. Kiyoko's eyes were filled with hatred.

"What's this? You tryin' to kill yourself just to spite us?" said Kim Shunpei, appalled.

How had Kiyoko crawled all the way to the stairwell? And why had she thrown herself down it? Whether purposeful or accidental, it was clear she'd exerted a massive amount of will.

Kim Shunpei carried Kiyoko up the stairs as if she were a heavy piece of luggage and put her back to bed. But Kiyoko wouldn't let go of Kim Shunpei's sleeve. He checked to see how bruised Kiyoko was from her fall, but she appeared mysteriously unhurt. Whenever children fell down the stairs, they could often avoid getting injured if they didn't put up any resistance. The same must have happened to Kiyoko.

"How'd she move all that way by herself?" asked the horrified Sadako.

"She needed to go to the bathroom, I reckon," said Kim Shunpei.

"There's no way she could do that. And it can't be that simple. I'm not leaving my baby upstairs anymore," said Sadako warily. She often kept the children upstairs while she was dealing with Kim Shunpei's guests.

"You're over-thinking it," said Kim Shunpei dismissively. But a trace of uneasiness could be heard in his voice.

Kim Shunpei kept drinking. His eyes had hardened, as if he could break out into violence at any moment. Sadako remained with him in the two-*jo* room, hugging her baby to her chest and drawing her two other daughters around her. Her children were like her shields. She took it for granted that Kim Shunpei would never lay a hand on her daughters. The rest of that day passed by quietly.

The first day of the year was spent paying respects to the ancestors. On the second day, Kim Shunpei's nephews came by to pay their respects. Kim Shunpei had been drinking since morning. He offered his nephews some *sake* and New Year's leftovers.

"Thank you very much," said the nephews, holding up their *sake* cups with both hands. They sat there for almost two hours drinking and trying to fill the silence with haltering chatter. Finally they went up to the second floor to pay their respects to Kiyoko.

"How are you feeling?" they asked her.

The shriveled-up, cadaverous Kiyoko simply opened her eyes and stared at them. Then Kim Shunpei drunkenly walked in. His eyes moved from the nephews to Kiyoko. "It's about time we made this one comfortable," he said.

The nephews stayed silent, unsure what Kim Shunpei meant. He swayed on his feet, moving his dentures around with his tongue. His reddish face looked ominous. Suddenly he covered Kiyoko's face with a newspaper and sat on top of her. There was a loud crack and then a muffled scream and a death rattle. The nephews stood there, with their faces drawn tight, not understanding what had just happened. Even after Kim Shunpei went back downstairs, the nephews stood rooted to the spot in shock.

Blood blotted the newspaper that covered Kiyoko's face. When Kim Yong-su removed the newspaper with trembling fingers, he saw blood running from her nose and mouth. She was still alive. Her eyes were wide open, and she was breathing in and out through her mouth. She gasped as though air were leaking out from the back of her throat. Kim Tae-su wiped up the blood with a handkerchief and shook her shoulder. "*Obasan, obasan,*"* he said in a low voice.

But Kiyoko didn't respond. The stitched seam along her head was also leaking blood.

"This is bad. What do we do?" said Kim Tae-su, his voice quaking.

"We can't tell anyone. That would only make it worse," said Kim Yong-su.

The nephews had gotten wrapped up in something both tragic and ridiculous. They couldn't go home; they couldn't even move. They could only stand by and watch.

Kim Shunpei wasn't coming back upstairs. Neither was Sadako. What was happening? Kim Yong-su went

---

* The formal term for "aunt" in Japanese

355

downstairs and saw Kim Shunpei still drinking *sake,* while Sadako was working on her sewing. Sunako was playing with marbles beside the sleeping baby. *Why is Sadako just sitting there sewing as if nothing happened?* thought Kim Yong-su suspiciously.

Kim Tae-su crept down the stairs and reported, "*Obasan* is dead."

Kim Shunpei didn't move an inch.

Sadako put down her sewing and went to the second floor to check. She then left to call on the old neighborhood doctor. Sadako's calm, prompt response starkly contrasted with the nephews' panic. The clinic was only a five-minute walk away, and Sadako came back shortly with the doctor in tow. The seventy-eight-year-old doctor climbed up the stairs with tottering steps. He examined the bug-eyed, open-mouthed Kiyoko.

"She was breathin' just now," said Sadako, elbowing Kim Tae-su beside her.

"Y-yes, she was," Kim Tae-su confirmed.

"Not much life left in her, eh? Incredible that she's lived this long," said the doctor, as if he knew what he was talking about. "I'll bring the autopsy report," he added carelessly.

Sadako followed the doctor back to his clinic for the autopsy report, leaving the two nephews alone. Kim Tae-su asked Kim Yong-su submissively, "Are we good to go?"

"Yeah," replied Kim Yong-su.

"But this was a murder."

"Nonsense. You want your only uncle to go to prison? Our family name could be ruined," said Kim Yong-su sharply. The confused Kim Tae-su had to accept his older brother's version of things.

The next day, Sadako submitted the doctor's autopsy report to the police and arranged a short funeral. After setting up a simple altar in the two-*jo* room, she put up a sign of mourning on the front door and hung a lantern. The funeral was a dreary affair. The neighbors considered Kiyoko's death a fitting end to her long, drawn-out sickness. Lee Young-hee and Sung-han felt no emotion at the news. Ko Nobuyoshi and Akemi were shocked to hear about the death when they came to visit.

"When did it happen?" asked Ko Nobuyoshi.

"Yesterday," said Sadako.

Meanwhile, Kim Shunpei's eyes were red from the alcohol he kept guzzling.

"I don't know what to say. For this to happen during

New Year's . . ." said Ko Nobuyoshi. He looked at the small picture of Kiyoko on the altar and thought back to the easy intimacy Kim Shunpei and Kiyoko had shared when they first started living together. *No one can predict how people will end up,* thought Ko Nobuyoshi. This was also the first time he'd laid eyes on Sadako's second baby. He sent Akemi home early, intending to keep vigil over Kiyoko's body.

Akemi went over to Lee Young-hee's house, where a few customers were making merry over rice wine.

"We thought we were coming for a celebration, but we came to a funeral," Akemi said as she threw salt on herself for purification.

"Poor woman," said Lee Young-hee briefly.

Only Ko Nobuyoshi, the two nephews, and a few others attended the wake. After the young monk finished chanting the sutras, Kiyoko's corpse was carried out and loaded into a hearse. Kim Shunpei, Ko Nobuyoshi, and the two nephews followed the hearse to the crematorium.

Chapter 24

An itinerant monk in a straw hat was chanting sutras
while holding out an alms bowl. His shadow flitted across
the frosted glass of the front door. Kim Shunpei was in
the two-*jo* room listening to the monk's low, melancholy
voice. *Did I kill Kiyoko?* he pondered. He told himself
that he'd simply rescued her from her suffering—she had
been a living corpse, after all. But when he'd carried her
up to her room after she fell down the stairs, her grip
on his sleeve was tight and unrelenting. His arm still
remembered how her grip felt. Kim Shunpei rubbed his
arms to get rid of the feeling. It was perhaps the ill will
with which she'd gripped him that provoked him to kill
her. The more he tried to deny that he'd meant to murder
her, the more his arm tingled with Kiyoko's phantom
grip—a sensation that held Kiyoko's resentment of him

and her fear of death.

Humans advanced closer to death with each passing day, closer to the moment of their complete end. Kiyoko's death had cut her off from Kim Shunpei with the absoluteness that only death could bring. That was what he believed. But at the same time, the faces of the dead crowded the darkness of his heart and wandered there, still alive.

The monk's chanting reached deep into Kim Shunpei's ears and echoed there, getting louder and angrier.

"Shut up!" screamed Kim Shunpei.

Sadako rushed out from the kitchen and threw a few coins into the monk's bowl. The monk left without another word.

Sadako hated living in the house. Even though the second floor was now cleared of Kiyoko's presence, she avoided going upstairs as much as she could.

"Stop gettin' upset for no reason," said Kim Shunpei. But inwardly he didn't want to live in the house either. He decided to buy a two-story house nearby that had been on the market for some time. The house was close to the main thoroughfare, right behind an udon shop and an apartment building. It was constructed the same way as the other tenement houses in the neighborhood. Osaka's tenement houses were built right along the city's drainage ditches. In general, Osakans thought of yards as wasteful luxuries.

Except for the upper-class neighborhoods in Ashiya and Tezukayama, Osaka largely lacked green spaces. And only the rich had baths inside their own homes. Kim Shunpei's current house was already considered luxurious compared to his neighbors, so his upgrades to the newly purchased house were all the more impressive. He had the walls and ceilings cleaned, the tatami mats replaced, and the *genkan* expanded into a six-*jo* room with a wooden floor. As far as Kim Shunpei was concerned, a luxury only deserved the name if it was within one's means; otherwise it was just wasteful spending. He sneered at his peers who rode in cars, saying, "They don't even have the money. Idiots."

Kim Shunpei set up a desk with chairs and a phone in the newly annexed six-*jo* room. This room would serve as both his office and his bedroom. Sleeping on a hard floor with thin bedding was part of his health regimen.

Kim Shunpei put up his former house for lease. Since it was on the corner, it was suitable for a little extra business. Four or five days after putting up the notice on the front door, he had an equal number of prospective tenants come calling. His nephew Kim Yong-su considered renting the house for some business of his own, but decided against it when he thought about having to live so close to his uncle.

The person who ended up renting the house was a bald, round-faced, jolly man named Kang Touma. He lived with five children and a diligent, reliable wife. Mr. and Mrs. Kang hoped all five of their children, starting with their fifteen-year-old daughter, would attend university. "I have no education myself, so I want my children to study and learn important skills," said Kang. This was why he and his wife worked so hard.

The Kangs used the house to sell all things pork: steamed pork belly, pig's heads, pig's feet, and offal, along with various spices. Koreans in Osaka typically had to go to Morimachi or Korea Market for their favorite pork dishes, so it was a huge boon for steamed pork belly to be sold right in the middle of a Korean neighborhood. After the Kangs opened for business, Lee Young-hee's *sake* shop flourished as well. Everyone knew that Korean men hankered after rice wine whenever they were about to eat steamed pork. In this way, Lee Young-hee and the Kangs enjoyed a symbiotic relationship.

But around this time, Lee Young-hee's body started breaking down. She would complain of headaches and fatigue and then fall into a deep sleep. It was as if her body had finally realized how overexerted it was. Then one day, she started bleeding. Lee Young-hee wasn't very knowledgeable about medicine and thought the blood was a sign that her menopause had reversed itself. Her aches, pains, and general listlessness also reminded her of her periods. But could this be a symptom of something else? She was too embarrassed to consult with a friend. But the phenomenon was too strange to ignore, and she was feeling worse by the day. She decided to go visit a famous women's clinic in Tsuruhashi. The elderly doctor there didn't say much. He just told her he needed to speak with her son. Lee Young-hee went back home and told Sung-han what the doctor said. Sung-han immediately went to the clinic. He had the feeling his mother had a serious disease. What else could the doctor want to talk about?

The doctor told him, "Your mother has uterine cancer."

"Cancer?" It was the first time Sung-han had heard of such a disease. It didn't sound like any ordinary illness.

"She has about two or three months left to live. Get her examined by the Red Cross Society."

Sung-han was aghast. A disease he'd never heard of before was about to kill his mother in a matter of months. "Can she be cured? Can she?" he pressed.

"No, she can't. It's too late for surgery."

The doctor spoke without mercy. He could have given Sung-han a thin thread of hope to cling onto, but instead he passed down a death verdict with the cold, hard expression of a judge.

After Sung-han received the referral slip from the doctor, he tottered out of the clinic thinking about how he would break this news to his mother. Two or three months was no time at all. And she would no longer be in the world after that. Sung-han couldn't hold back his tears. He made his way from Tsuruhashi to Ueroku and climbed the hill to the Red Cross Hospital. The Red Cross Society's enormous, chalky-white building was visible from the clinic he'd just left. Until a few years ago, the American military had used this building as its hospital. Sung-han always felt intimidated by the sheer hugeness of it, too lofty and splendid for a poor person like him.

A week later, Sung-han brought his mother into the

building for her follow-up examination and gave the front desk the referral slip.

Patients waited on the long bench along the hallway, their bloodless faces looking tired, or angry, or worried. Lee Young-hee didn't dare ask Sung-han for an explanation. When one was inside a hospital, it seemed like all the people of the world were sick.

Sung-han was called into the doctor's office when Lee Young-hee's examination was over. The young, bespectacled doctor was writing on Lee Young-hee's medical chart. "It's terminal uterine cancer. She has two or three months left to live. Nothing else can be done. Just make her comfortable—let her do what she wants and eat what she wants," he said. It was the exact same diagnosis as the doctor at the Tsuruhashi clinic.

With a second doctor's confirmation of her condition, Lee Young-hee could do nothing else but accept her reality.

"We don't have room in our ward, but I'll refer you to Ogata Women's Clinic in Umeda. She'll get radiation therapy done there. Ogata's a good clinic."

But whatever the doctor said, Lee Young-hee would still die in two or three months.

Sung-han went to the Ogata clinic and arranged for
Lee Young-hee's hospitalization. The clinic was in an old
gothic-style building and was respected for its medical
tradition, which extended back to the final years of the
Edo period. The cost of hospitalization and treatment
was high: a month's stay was over two hundred thousand
yen. Sung-han brought in less than fifteen thousand yen
a month from his job as an errand boy at a chemical-
resistant shoe factory. There was no way he or his mother
could afford it. Sung-han considered going on public
assistance, but the thought of that depressed him. Also,
the government would notice that the rich Kim Shunpei
was Lee Young-hee's husband. After pondering the
problem for a few days, Sung-han decided that he had to
negotiate directly with his father. They hadn't talked for
several years after their vicious fight, and they had barely
even seen each other. Asking Kim Shunpei to help pay
for Lee Young-hee's hospitalization was an exceedingly
risky move. Chances were that they would fight again. But
Sung-han had to grit his teeth and face him. Regardless of
how stubborn either of them were at this point, Sung-han
expected his father to feel some measure of pity for his
dying wife. He assumed that humans became generous

when it came to death.

Sung-han took a deep breath and walked to his father's house. He entered the *genkan* and saw his father in the six-*jo* office eating fruit with Sadako. Kim Shunpei and Sadako froze, their mouths hanging open. Sung-han's visit was entirely unexpected.

"I need to talk to you," said Sung-han. He removed his shoes and stepped onto the wooden floor. Back when he'd fought with his father, he was a high school student. Now he looked like a full-fledged adult. The tone of his voice had also mellowed out.

"What about?" Kim Shunpei drew his metal ashtray closer to him and lit a cigarette. He adjusted his legs and turned to face Sung-han.

Sung-han could feel Kim Shunpei's energy radiate off him. Even now, Kim Shunpei looked as if he were on the verge of standing up and attacking Sung-han right then and there. Sadako scooped her baby up and evacuated to the second floor.

Left alone with his father, Sung-han told him why he was there and how much money he needed.

"She has only two or three months left to live. We should take care of her before she dies." Sung-han had so much more to say, but he wanted to keep the conversation dispassionate. As he spoke, Kim Shunpei's face turned dark.

"And what do you want from me?" he interrupted. "What's *she* got to do with me? I don't care if she lives or dies, do I?"

Sung-han lost his temper in spite of himself. "She's your wife! All these years, how many times did you nearly kill her? You've never given us a single sen. Now of all times, you could at least pay for her treatment, and you'd be none the worse off."

"Shut up! You wanna pick a fight with me?" Kim Shunpei picked up the metal ashtray and hurled it at Sung-han.

Sung-han was prepared for such an attack and dodged the ashtray as he got to his feet. Kim Shunpei also rose and grabbed at Sung-han's shoulder to headbutt him. But Sung-han dodged that too. The two men grappled each other as they broke their way through the front door. The glass on the front door shattered thunderously. They tackled each other, falling to the ground, and then scrambled back to their feet and charged toward the electric pole. Sung-han moved out of the way at the last second, and Kim Shunpei's head slammed against the pole. He fell. Onlookers surrounded the scene, and neighbors watched from their windows. Sung-han made his way through the onlookers and limped back to his house, his clothes tattered to his waist. He washed his face, changed his clothes, and left for Kanemonocho in Nipponbashi. He knew Kim Shunpei would come for his revenge. He bought a grappling hook. *Let's go ahead and kill each other!* he thought wildly.

Kim Shunpei was taken to the hospital, and three hours later he returned. He'd been beaten. He keenly felt his body's age, and his head swam from his concussion. Sung-han loomed in his mind's eye as if he were twice his actual size. The boy had attacked him like someone hell-bent on death, and he would perhaps stop at nothing to achieve that end. Kim Shunpei couldn't calm down. He drank and drank even though his head swam. Soon his eyes were burning with hatred.

He dare defy me? I'll kill him!

Upstairs, Sadako took hold of her youngest daughter and told her two other daughters, "I'm outta here. You two stay. Dad won't do anything to you 'cause you're kids. And no crying!"

Evening advanced into night. The moon peeked through the clouds as if it were waiting to see what terrible thing was about to happen. Kim Shunpei stumbled onto his feet drunkenly, hooked his cherry tree club onto his belt, and left the house. The thudding of his feet echoed through the dark. He reached Lee Young-hee's house and kicked down the front door.

"Come out! I'll snap your neck!" He proceeded to break the furniture from one end of the house to the other.

When Sung-han heard his father kick through the front door, he slipped out the back and ran to his father's house. He broke in and went up to the second floor and swung his bat onto any piece of furniture he could find, while Sadako's two girls watched from the corner. Sung-han then threw the futons out onto the street. The two men were destroying each other's houses. No one could stop them. The police also kept a careful distance. For the next half month, the conflict continued, and both houses became battered war zones. Whatever Kim Shunpei did, he couldn't catch the fleet-footed Sung-han, and he was unable to sleep at night for fear of what Sung-han would do next. Whenever he nodded off to sleep, a rock would break through one of his windows. Meanwhile, Lee Young-hee's house was an empty shell. Lee Young-hee had moved to a friend's house. Sung-han made sure to keep his location hidden as he broke Kim Shunpei's windows at irregular hours. His guerilla warfare was relentless. Eventually Kim Shunpei stopped his attacks, which prompted Sung-han to stop too. Kim Shunpei had never imagined that Sung-han would go so far as to wreck his property. Their hatred of each other was at an all-time high.

It was clearly a mistake for Sung-han to have thought that Kim Shunpei would have enough humanity left to aid the dying Lee Young-hee. Sung-han decided to sell his mother's house in order to scrounge up the funds for her palliative care. He moved into a cheap house in Ikaino with the remainder from the sale. A canal ran through the back, while the view from the front was dominated by the towering chimneys of a brick crematorium. Sung-han spent all day going back and forth from this small, seedy tenement unit to the hospital. Any and all luxuries had to be eliminated. His former neighbor Mrs. Kinkai was the one who bought Lee Young-hee's house. She had a large family and wanted a house with two floors. The arrangements had gone quickly. Sung-han figured that with the move, he would never have to see his father Kim Shunpei again.

Kim Shunpei stopped his early morning ritual of chopping wood. And since he no longer had firewood on hand, he started using the gas stove. He bought a television, too, now that Sunako was entering kindergarten: she said the other kids would bully her for not having a television in her home. He also bought a refrigerator. At last, he was moving along with the times. He had to admit that those electric appliances did make his life more convenient. He watched television with his family after dinner and even laughed on occasion. Whenever he caught himself laughing, he felt like he was someone else. In any case, the television was just a momentary comfort. Most of what he saw was meaningless to him.

After spending an hour watching television with his family, he moved to the front room and continued drinking there. As he drank, he got lost in thought. Sometimes he mixed up past and present. At one point he called out, "Kiyoko, bring me more *sake*! Kiyoko!"

"She's dead. Stop calling me that, it creeps me out," said Sadako. She set down a bottle in front of him and went back up to the second floor.

Whenever Kim Shunpei drank by himself, he felt like he was being buried deep underground, no matter how bright the room was.

After Lee Young-hee and Sung-han moved out, Kim Shunpei told Mrs. Kinkai that he wanted to buy the house from her.

"May I ask why?" Mrs. Kinkai couldn't see any reason for Kim Shunpei to want a house he was previously bent on destroying.

"I'm bequeathing it to Sung-han," Kim Shunpei said with a serious look on his face.

"But there's no way he'll go back there."

It was a natural assumption to make. But Kim Shunpei offered Mrs. Kinkai twice the amount she'd paid for the house. His single-mindedness mystified the neighbors. "Has he finally lost it?" they whispered amongst themselves. "He's just trying to buy up all the property on the block," others said.

Mrs. Kinkai agreed to Kim Shunpei's terms, which were better than she could have ever hoped for. After Kim

Shunpei bought the house, he refurbished it from the inside out. It looked too new and out-of-place among the grimy tenement houses in the neighborhood. But despite the refurbishments, the house was left empty. Just like any other uninhabited house, it began to decay within two years. It seemed like Kim Shunpei was waiting for something. But whatever he was waiting for, it wasn't coming.

One day in the middle of autumn, Ko Nobuyoshi came with some news. Lee Young-hee had died. She was sixty-seven years old. Ko Nobuyoshi also reported that Hanako had committed suicide. Hanako had recently remarried after divorcing her first husband, but her second husband was a raging alcoholic. People went their separate ways and met different ends, even though time passed the same for them all. Four months before Lee Young-hee died, Sung-han got married. It was apparently his mother's dying wish. Sung-han married his girlfriend, so it wasn't out of pure obligation. In the end, Sung-han was the only child Kim Shunpei and Lee Young-hee left behind in the world. Kim Shunpei and Sung-han were completely cut off from each other. If either of them were to die, neither would show up to the other's funeral. In fact, Kim

Shunpei hadn't shown up to either a wedding or a funeral for any of his children.

Kim Shunpei listened to Ko Nobuyoshi without saying a word. Sadako came in and served the men *sake*. She was pregnant with Kim Shunpei's third child. Ko Nobuyoshi couldn't help but wonder what was going to become of all these young children.

The third child turned out to be a girl once again. Kim Shunpei thought it was his fate to not be blessed with a son.

"My body ain't done yet," Sadako insisted fretfully, even to people outside the family. "We'll keep tryin' 'til I get a boy."

The neighbors marveled at Kim Shunpei's unrelenting vitality. He looked like he was in his early fifties, even though he was sixty-eight. Kim Shunpei's body caused a stir in the bathhouse. His muscles weren't what they used to be, but his skin was still lustrous and smooth like a young person's. For the past ten years, he'd worn the same T-shirt in the summer and the same leather coat in the winter. His neighbors got older around him, but he stayed the same, as if he were drinking a secret potion of everlasting youth. The foundry worker Kunimoto was ten years younger than Kim Shunpei, but he looked ten years older with his stark white hair and stooped back.

Sadako was twenty-eight years younger than Kim Shunpei, but they didn't look unnatural as a couple. In fact, Sadako had always looked older than her age, so at forty years old she could have been mistaken for someone of the same generation as Kim Shunpei. She had a fertile womb that kept bearing children. When she walked to the bathhouse with her four children in tow, she looked like a mother duck with her ducklings. She carried herself with composure in her threadbare, patched-up clothes. Her children weren't much better off and looked like common street urchins.

"See a rich person in rags, and you still know they're rich. But if you're poor and in rags? You're treated like a good-for-nothin' tramp," said Mrs. Kuremoto.

Mrs. Ishihara agreed. "Yeah, if I wore rags, everyone would see through me in a flash. But Mrs. Kim can wear rags all she wants. They have so much money it's rotting in their closet. She knows she's gonna be alright."

The neighbors spoke of the Kim family with a hint of scorn. As for why the miserly Kim Shunpei had bought Lee Young-hee's house and renovated it, the neighbors had no explanation. He wasn't leasing the house out to anyone. The Takamuras, a six-person family living in a small two-room house, would look out at the empty house across from them and grumble, "What a waste."

The tenant Kang Touma wanted to clean up the scrap wood piled around Kim Shunpei's former house. "I'll evict you if you dare do that," Kim Shunpei told him. Kang Touma was speechless. Even now, Kim Shunpei was in the habit of collecting scrap wood and stacking it into tall piles. "He's not doin' anything with it! Makes no sense," said Kang Touma, throwing up his hands in resignation.

At this point, everyone saw Kim Shunpei as an eccentric.

Two years after Sadako had given birth to her third girl with Kim Shunpei, her belly ballooned again.

"She never quits, does she. What's she playing at?" The neighborhood women observed the progress of Sadako's pregnancy with great interest.

"Is it gonna be another girl?"

"If she pops out another girl, she'll be kicked out of the house for sure."

"But they're really trying, aren't they? Hell, my

husband can only get it up for me once a year."

Rumors brought on more rumors. Everyone was paying attention to Sadako's ballooning belly. And everyone was expecting another girl. The birth of another girl was sure to set Kim Shunpei off. But contrary to expectations, Sadako's dreams came true, and she gave birth to a boy.

The midwife lifted the baby up and called Kim Shunpei upstairs. "His face looks just like his father's!" she crooned, even though she couldn't tell who the baby resembled. Kim Shunpei broke into a grin and beamed. Sadako looked up at him triumphantly.

In direct contrast to the times Kim Shunpei had ignored the midwife after she delivered the baby girls, this time he sent the midwife off with an envelope containing ten thousand yen in cash. Then he called Ko Nobuyoshi and his two nephews. The following day, they showed up with *sake*.

"It's such a relief you have an heir now," said Kim Yong-su.

"May you live a long life for your son's sake," said Kim Tae-su obsequiously.

"Damn right. You have to live till a hundred. I can bear

you even more sons," said Sadako, smiling toothily and letting out a coarse laugh.

Everyone was in a celebratory mood, but Ko Nobuyoshi felt like something was missing. The birth of a son was of course worth celebrating, but this baby wasn't supposed to supplant Kim Shunpei's first, more legitimate son Sung-han. Kim Shunpei, of all people, couldn't forget that. But like the others, he was subconsciously repressing Sung-han's existence. Perhaps the only thing Kim Shunpei could do was give Sung-han up for lost, as there was no hope of them reconciling. But it wouldn't be an exaggeration to say that Kim Shunpei's hard-won assets had something to do with Lee Young-hee and her child. Ko Nobuyoshi—and the two nephews, for that matter— were familiar with Kim Shunpei's backstory, and none of them could wholeheartedly embrace this other son begotten by another mother. As for Sung-han, rumor was that he'd started a business after his mother's death but declared bankruptcy three years later and fled to Tokyo. His whereabouts weren't confirmed.

Kim Shunpei was in high spirits on the day of the birth, unlike his normal volatile self. Ko Nobuyoshi wondered if having a son at Kim Shunpei's ripe old age was really something to get so giddy about. They all needed another twenty years to see the son come of age. Ko Nobuyoshi was sixty-nine. Thinking about where he would be in twenty years put him in a daze. Kim Shunpei was probably determined to live out the next twenty years in the best possible health.

Sadako, at the very least, was as proud as a peacock. She wanted to have a formal family picture taken, and Kim Shunpei bought her and the children kimono to wear for the occasion. This was the first time Kim Shunpei had bought Sadako clothes of any kind. With Kim Shunpei wearing his three-piece suit and Sadako and her children following behind him in single file, they marched like ants to the photo studio in the Imazato-Shinbashi commercial district.

Kim Shunpei had his son christened "Yong-il" by a Confucian scholar in Ikuno. The name "Yong-il" was written in calligraphy on a long sheet of *washi* paper and hung on the wall of the alcove. Kim Shunpei stared at the name for a long time as he drank, taking pleasure at how the characters looked.

By the time little Yong-il could hold his head up three months later, Kim Shunpei was taking him on walks around the neighborhood. Sometimes elderly folk who weren't up-to-date on the gossip called out in Korean, "What a cute grandson!" "He's my son," Kim Shunpei replied, both embarrassed and pleased.

Kim Shunpei took Yong-il everywhere he went. Even in the house, he had Yong-il on his lap whenever Sadako wasn't feeding him. He also took Yong-il with him to the bars. The other men commented, "Already drinking buddies, eh?" Kim Shunpei looked pleased and treated the men to drinks. Pleasantly drunk, Kim Shunpei walked back home with tottering steps, enjoying the night breeze with Yong-il in his arms.

It may have seemed like Kim Shunpei had changed with the birth of his son, but he hadn't changed at all. The rest of the family felt constricted by Kim Shunpei's tightfisted ways. When Sunako entered elementary school and needed money for tuition, school meals, and school supplies, Kim Shunpei obliged her with a litany of complaints. Sadako wanted her mentally disabled daughter Yukiko in a special school, but she didn't dare bring it up with him. His stinginess extended to food as well. Specialty hot pots like sukiyaki were a once-a-year affair. His daughters had little knowledge of Japanese food. Even when it came to his beloved son Yong-il, Kim Shunpei dressed him up in old hand-me-downs he'd gotten from who knows where. He was particular when it came to what he allowed his children to wear.

One day Sunako came home from school crying, saying that the other kids were bullying her. The next day, Kim Shunpei accompanied her to the school gate and took hold of her hand. He stood there glaring at the children who passed by. All the children shrunk back in horror at the gigantic Kim Shunpei, and they left Sunako alone after that. Sunako didn't have any friends, of course. Everyone marked their distance from the girl who had a wild and irrational father at her beck and call. None of the daughters had much in the way of friends, so they became close with each other. They supported and cared for each other when they had no one else.

The children grew up in the blink of an eye. The changes were hardly noticeable when a child was one's own, but other people's children grew shockingly fast. A few years back, Kim Shunpei saw one of the Ishihara sons return home for a visit, and he hadn't recognized him at all. The boy from elementary school that he remembered had become a man of thirty before he knew it—which meant that Sung-han was also in his thirties by that point. If Kim Shunpei were to encounter Sung-han somewhere, he probably wouldn't recognize him.

When Sunako entered middle school, Kim Shunpei gave a start at the sight of her in her sailor's uniform. She was now a little adult instead of the child he'd always thought her to be. She'd inherited her father's large frame. She was also at an age where she was acting more distant and rebellious. When she came back from school, she would avoid her father and barely speak to him. When she saw him walking around the neighborhood with Yong-il in his arms, she would say, "Stop doing that. It's embarrassing."

"Why should I be embarrassed to take walks with my son?"

"You look like his grandfather. No one thinks he's your son."

Sunako's temper was also like her father's.

Kim Shunpei hated it when his own daughter called him old, and he slapped her across the face. The other girls started bawling immediately. It was as though Kim Shunpei had poked a hornet's nest. That night, the drunk Kim Shunpei gathered Sadako and the girls into a room and stabbed the tatami floor with a meat carver.

"I'll cook you one by one and chew you up!" he threatened. The children quaked in fear, but the situation was different than it had been in the past. They were now sizing Kim Shunpei up. At over seventy years old, he didn't have the same capacity to get violent as he used to. What hadn't changed was his personality, which relied on the threat of violence to demand submission from others.

At the beginning of every winter, Kim Shunpei went to the animal shelter and picked up hundreds of joints that had once belonged to stray dogs. He let the joints simmer in a large pot for three days and three nights. At first, layers of scum formed on the surface and gave off a sour smell, but after Kim Shunpei patiently removed the scum again and again, the broth turned into a clear and transparent yellow by the third day. He stored the broth in jars and drank a cup a day. It was his way of preventing nerve pain and lower back pain.

This winter was no different. As he boiled the dog joints on the brazier in the front room, he opened the top pane of his front door to circulate air. Lately, he'd been drinking heavily before bed in order to fall asleep. He woke up the next morning and tried to get up to go to the bathroom, but his lower body had lost the ability to move. His face was flushed, and his body felt numb. The numbness reminded him of the time he'd tasted blowfish liver in Kyushu, which had made his tongue tingle. Was it food poisoning? Nothing he'd eaten in the past day had been spoiled. What was it, then? The mystified Kim Shunpei placed both arms on the floor and tried to raise himself up, but it was no use. He wondered if he was dreaming. He tried to lift himself up a number of times, but then his arms sagged downward and refused to move. Kim Shunpei started to panic.

"Sadako! Sadako!" he called. His tongue felt heavy in his mouth. As he kept calling up to Sadako on the second floor, he felt like he was trapped in his dream and calling into the abyss. Finally Sadako came down and said suspiciously, "What's with all the noise?"

"How many times do I have to call you, dammit?" growled Kim Shunpei, angry at Sadako's obliviousness.

"What's wrong? What . . ."

Kim Shunpei was sweating, and his face was rigid. Sadako had never seen him look so grim. His face was a little red. He was surely still drunk, thought Sadako. He sounded like he was drunk too.

"I can't stand up."

"You can't . . . ?" Sadako knitted her eyebrows in confusion.

"My legs are numb and I can't stand up. Call an ambulance. Quick."

Sadako realized the seriousness of the situation. She immediately went to the phone, dialed 119, and requested an ambulance.

"Help me up. I need to use the toilet before the ambulance gets here."

Kim Shunpei clung onto Sadako as she lifted him up. His legs shook and were barely able to hold up his weight, and he clutched to Sadako as she dragged him to the bathroom.

"Can you stand by yourself? I'm lettin' go," said Sadako. Kim Shunpei kept his feet planted on the floor and concentrated on keeping his balance as he peed. By the time they returned to the front room, the ambulance had arrived.

"What's wrong?" asked the paramedic.

"He woke up and his legs were paralyzed. He can't stand up," said Sadako.

"Right, well, let's get him to the hospital and see what the doctor says." The two paramedics lifted Kim Shunpei up and carried him into the ambulance. Sadako changed out of her bedclothes and accompanied them with a bag of extra clothes for Kim Shunpei. Morning commuters glanced at the ambulance as it drove by. The owner of the neighborhood snack bar paused in her sweeping and stared after the ambulance, wondering what had happened.

The ambulance headed for the Red Cross Hospital in Ueroku—the same hospital that had examined Lee Young-hee for her uterine cancer. Two nurses received Kim Shunpei, and they brought him to an examination room in the surgery unit.

"Good thing the surgeon is on duty," said the older nurse reassuringly.

A bespectacled doctor in his fifties showed up. His face looked a little puffy, as if he'd just woken up. He moved his neck left and right, stretched his back, and took a deep breath before he took a look at Kim Shunpei on the bed. Sadako waited in the hallway.

The doctor shined a flashlight onto Kim Shunpei's eyes and checked for a response. He then checked Kim

Shunpei's tongue and took his pulse. As he massaged Kim Shunpei's legs, he said, "Shall we take an X-ray? I'm guessing he has multiple areas of cerebral infarction."

Kim Shunpei was taken to the X-ray room. The doctor must have been speaking out of his ass if he needed a machine to confirm the diagnosis. Kim Shunpei felt just like a fish on a cutting board. He had no choice but to go along with all the doctor's decisions. Was he going to get better? For Kim Shunpei, this question was of paramount importance. What if he wasn't? His anxiety increased at that thought. The paralysis of his lower body wasn't a dream after all. He felt a fear he'd never felt before in his life, and a shiver went up his spine.

Kim Shunpei waited in the X-ray room for the technician to show up. In the meantime, the doctor told Sadako about Kim Shunpei's condition. When a blood vessel in the brain clogged up or burst, it was typical for the right or left side of the body to become paralyzed. But in Kim Shunpei's case, he had minor blockages in several areas of his brain, which would sometimes lead to numbness and paralysis in the lower body.

"It's basically a palsy. Since the blockages are in various places, it would be tough to do surgery, but for now, we'll give him some medicine so it doesn't get worse."

But the doctor's explanations weren't satisfactory.

"Is he gonna be okay?" asked Sadako.

"Not sure. It'll be a tough road. Like I said, the medicine should help, and he should keep using his legs. Practice walking as much as he can."

The doctor's recommendations for rehabilitation didn't come from a place of expertise, and Sadako was left more confused than ever. She didn't bother asking him further questions.

After the X-ray was done, the doctor repeated his explanation to Kim Shunpei.

"This sort of thing happen a lot?" asked Kim Shunpei, still in disbelief that it could be happening to his own body.

"Yes. People die all the time from having strokes in their sleep. You're lucky. You can still speak and use your hands."

As the doctor spoke, Kim Shunpei thought of Kiyoko. His condition was preferable to hers, but the very comparison made him want to disavow his paralysis all the more. He could tell from the doctor's tone of voice that recovery wasn't likely. What was with such indifference? It was as if the doctor had thrown in the towel from the start. Kim Shunpei was being labeled incurable. Were there no other possibilities for treatment? His dog joint broth had turned out to be utterly useless, like his other medicinal concoctions. He was too late in every way. Kim Shunpei felt a depression come over him. Kiyoko's spirit was possessing his body. How else could he explain what was happening to him? He could still hear her death rattle in his ears. He didn't believe in God or Buddha or demons, but he couldn't help but feel that a horrific karma was acting upon him.

Kim Shunpei stayed in the hospital for three days. When he returned home, he kept up his walking exercises, took his medicine, and followed a prescribed diet of unseasoned mountain vegetables. Sadako helped him up whenever he needed to get up, and he walked with great effort. But why did he have to practice walking if he couldn't even get up by himself? Little Yong-il was now able to totter around on his feet. Seeing Yong-il move made Kim Shunpei realize how wonderful it was to be able to walk or run.

Kim Shunpei slept in the front room with a chamber pot next to his futon. In the morning Sadako emptied the contents of the chamber pot into the toilet. Whenever she asked Sunako to do it, Sunako said bluntly, "No way. Dad's pee smells. It makes me wanna throw up." Accordingly, Sunako's younger sisters didn't want to help either.

"You think you can treat your father that way?"

The lack of sympathy from his daughters was humiliating enough, but Sunako added salt to the wound by replying, "You're not my father."

"Who's your father then?"

"I dunno. Stop asking me."

Sunako was now in the habit of drawing close to Kim Shunpei and talking back to him with impunity. Whenever he reached out to grab her, she danced back and forth to trifle with him before leaving the room. She was clearly ridiculing him. Kim Shunpei shook with a humiliation he'd never felt before.

Kim Shunpei asked Sadako to sleep in the front room with him. But Sadako refused, saying she needed to be near her young children. It was as if Sadako and her children were plotting something on the second floor. That was what Kim Shunpei believed. What could they be plotting? The children didn't feel like his own.

Perhaps shared blood ran thin with children begotten by a Japanese mother. Kim Shunpei regretted ever having children with a Japanese woman. But his biggest miscalculation had been to believe that his health would last indefinitely. That belief had crumpled in a single instant. He was in a purgatory of endless endings and beginnings. He was frightened of having to live on and on, flailing helplessly in the face of death. And that was just the beginning.

Chapter 25

Kim Shunpei's disability had a decisive effect on every movement he needed to make in his daily life. It interrupted the simple continuity of getting up and walking around, and it greatly reduced his sphere of daily activities. Going to the bathroom was both physically and mentally painful for him. He gripped Sadako's hand and dragged his feet little by little until he reached the handrails by the toilet, which barely allowed him to balance himself as he stood or crouched down. The physical and mental exertion of getting there was sometimes so great that he couldn't do his business.

"Finished yet?" tutted Sadako impatiently from outside the door. Sometimes she disappeared up the stairs and wouldn't come down no matter how many times Kim Shunpei called her. He had no choice then but to cling to the wall and drag himself back to his room. He reminded himself of the cripples he'd seen at the end of the war who had crawled through the streets in filthy rags. Whenever winter came, their limbs hardened like blocks of frozen tuna, and they died in the cold.

When he reached the front room, he grabbed onto the desk and lowered himself onto his chair. Once he adjusted his posture on the chair, he didn't look like someone with palsy. He had to stay firm and look calm and composed, never showing his weakness to others. That was what Kim Shunpei told himself. Sadako and the children sometimes remembered how terrifying he could be when he cast sharp looks from his chair, but eventually they learned to ignore him. Sadako ate her meals with the children in another room, after which she brought Kim Shunpei leftover rice and a few unseasoned vegetables. "Don't spill anything," she would say over her shoulder as she left for the second floor to watch television. Later, Sunako would come down and jeer at him, "Still not done? Hurry up, or I can't clean up your mess."

Even though Kim Shunpei shook with rage every time this happened, he lost the energy to yell at her. Instead, he called Ko Nobuyoshi and his two nephews on the phone and complained to them about how much his family was abusing him.

"Sorry, but could you come and talk to them? They won't listen to me at all."

Kim Shunpei spoke as if he were about to cry, and the nephews couldn't refuse him. They visited the next day and politely reminded Sadako of her duties. Ko Nobuyoshi also came by and lectured Sadako and the children about human morals. Sadako and the children listened quietly as the men spoke, but when they left, they treated Kim Shunpei even worse.

"So we abuse you now? Stop bad-mouthing us. You don't know how much we suffer, you selfish prick! You think we're your servants, huh? What've you done for me, for your own children? We've just been living in fear this whole time. In sixteen years, the only thing you got me is this shitty kimono. Look how shitty it is!" Sadako took the kimono out from the closet and tore it up as everyone watched.

Ko Nobuyoshi and the nephews couldn't meet Kim Shunpei's demands every time he called. The more he flailed about, the more isolated he became. But there came a point when Sadako went too far. While Kim

Shunpei was in the bathroom, he discovered that the bankbooks were missing. His heart stopped. Sadako had stolen them from the hole in the ceiling where he'd hidden them. The contracts and promissory notes were in a safe in the closet, but Sadako wasn't supposed to know where the bankbooks were. When had she found out? She must have done a deep search of the house at some point in the past, while Kim Shunpei was out. And even after finding the bankbooks, she'd acted all this time as if nothing had happened.

When Kim Shunpei opened the safe in the closet, he saw that the contracts and promissory notes were gone as well.

"Sadako! Sadako! Come down right now!" Kim Shunpei slammed the closet door against its hinges and banged his head against the pillar.

"What the hell are you makin' this ruckus for?!" Sadako looked down at Kim Shunpei from the stair landing.

"You bitch! Where are my bankbooks?" shouted Kim Shunpei as he held onto the pillar.

"Cancelled, all of 'em."

"Cancelled? What about my money?"

"I deposited it into a bank account under my name. That money's mine."

"What the fuck? You thief! I'll call the police! You're dead!" Kim Shunpei crawled up the steps one by one. As he approached the landing, Sadako kicked his head, and he tumbled down the stairs like a rag doll.

"Go ahead and call the cops. I'm the mother of four of your children. I talked with a lawyer. The police won't meddle in family matters. Go ahead and take this to court. I'll fight for ten or twenty years if I have to."

Sadako had gotten help from a lawyer to cancel Kim Shunpei's bank accounts and transfer all his money to her own account. She'd stolen about 130 million yen from him.

"I'm raisin' five children, see? That money belongs to us, so stop complaining."

Sadako's silhouette coagulated into a black lump. The blood vessels in Kim Shunpei's brain were at their breaking point. He couldn't let himself fall for her tricks again.

"You have more bankbooks lying around, right? I'll find 'em, don't worry."

What Sadako stole amounted to about a third of Kim

Shunpei's total assets. He'd entrusted the rest to a Sōren-affiliated* bank, per Ko Nobuyoshi's recommendations. As for the contracts and promissory notes, they were beyond what Sadako could handle. The amount of money Kim Shunpei loaned out far exceeded what Sadako had already taken, and only Kim Shunpei had the constitution to collect what he was owed by a slew of thugs and other men. Now that he couldn't move, Sadako was hardly the one to take his place. Sadako knew this, and she collected whatever small debts she could. However, word of Kim Shunpei's disability had spread far and wide, and people lost their motivation to pay their debts. Most of the debtors Sadako visited didn't answer their doors, or else they drove her away. She had to admit that Kim Shunpei's presence really did strike fear into everyone's hearts.

After Kim Shunpei found out about the bankbooks, Sadako underwent a dramatic transformation. She took her children to department stores, treated them to meals, and bought them clothes, dolls, and toys. The floodgates had burst open, and Sadako threw money at everything

---

* Sōren, or Chongryon, is the North Korean-affiliated General Association of Korean Residents in Japan. The organization provides various services to its members ranging from employment to marriage and legal assistance.

she saw. Her room was full of new clothes. She bought
a new dresser, a large refrigerator, a large TV, a laundry
machine, and all manner of electric appliances. She
even went to driving school to get a driver's license. Kim
Shunpei, meanwhile, was at her mercy.

Sadako's greed knew no bounds. Flush with more cash
than she'd ever dreamed of, she went out night after night
to make up for lost time. She woke up past noon and
ordered take-out from the nearby udon restaurant. She
left at three to soak in the freshly drawn baths, and when
she returned, she spent a good deal of time making up her
face before leaving again at dusk. Her schedule resembled
that of an escort or prostitute. Right before she left, she
handed Sunako some money and told her, "Order some
sushi for dinner."

She went out in a mink coat and high heels, carrying
an imported handbag on her arm. She left through the
back to avoid having to pass Kim Shunpei in the front
room. The neighbors saw the gaudily dressed Sadako
out on the street and mistook her for someone else,
so accustomed were they to seeing her in the same
threadbare sack year after year. She called a taxi on the
main thoroughfare and ordered the driver to take her

to the Minami district, where she absorbed herself in nighttime pleasures.

The neon lights of the red-light district bloomed in the darkness like sterile flowers. Sadako's heart couldn't help but quicken as she saw lust-filled men roaming these streets. Drunk on the sex-charged air, she walked through Shinsaibashi looking at the shop windows bedecked with goods. She entered a café and ordered coffee. The feeling of freedom was beautiful. It was only natural for humans to seek pleasure: pleasure, after all, was the lubricant that kept life moving. Young lovers cuddled with each other out in the open, their fingers interlaced as they talked in low whispers. Did they have that much to talk about, wondered Sadako. She'd never experienced anything like that before. After killing some time at the café, she crushed the rest of her cigarette and stood up. The night was still young. Sadako had come out intending to spend every bit of this long winter night enjoying herself.

Sadako left the café and walked toward Soemoncho. She passed Cabaret Fuji and Cabaret Bijinza to make a full circuit around Soemoncho, which was packed with bars, clubs, and restaurants. Sadako stopped in front of a host club and walked in without a second thought.

"Welcome!" A man in a formal suit bowed politely from the waist. Sadako stepped onto the thick carpet and followed the man to a table. A band was playing some light-hearted tunes on the front stage. Disco lights spun across the ceiling and walls like stardust. Everything in the room felt grand and luxurious. As Sadako settled comfortably into the sofa, she forgot her other life with Kim Shunpei—a life she could barely breathe in.

"Are you waiting for someone, miss?" the man asked.

"No."

"Is this your first time with us?"

"Yes."

"I see. Please wait here."

Three or four minutes later, a host in his mid-twenties came and knelt in front of Sadako. "Nice to meet you. I'm Takeru."

"Nice to meet you," said Sadako awkwardly.

Takeru sat down on the sofa and broke the seal on a bottle of Hennessy he'd brought with him. After diluting the Hennessy with some water, he said, "Cheers."

The slender, tastefully dressed Takeru twirled his dainty fingers around his hair and kept his eyes fixed intensely on Sadako. She was bewitched by his gaze. This entire situation was nothing but an illusion, but she let herself drown in it. Never in her life had a young man looked at her from so close. In fact, never in her life had a young man even come near her like this. His sweet scent set her body aflame with desire. Before she knew it, her hand was in his. His hand felt soft compared to hers, which were old and stale. Sadako felt sexual energy pulse through her.

"Will you dance?" asked Takeru.

"I've never danced before," she said, shrinking back.

"It's okay. I'll lead." Takeru took Sadako's hand and led her into the hall. A few other couples were on the dance floor. Takeru put his hand on Sadako's plump back and stepped around on light feet, swinging his body back and forth. He strengthened his grip on Sadako's back, brought her closer to him, and put his cheek against hers. He pulled away and gazed into Sadako's pupils for a moment before leaning down and sucking on her lips. She clung to him, feeling as if she were about to faint. His tongue pushed deeper and deeper into her mouth. The skillful way he moved his mouth made Sadako forget about the other people on the dance floor.

Two more hosts were waiting at the table when they

returned. The three men plied Sadako with liquor, and she soon lost track of how much time passed. She didn't know what time she left the club. She was charged over ten thousand yen, but she didn't think the price was too high. In fact, the richness and intensity of the experience—something she'd never tasted before in her life—was worth even more than what she paid. The once-crowded streets were now sparse. Half of the bright neon lights were turned off. Sadako stumbled through the dim streets of Soemoncho, not knowing where she was going. She looked at her watch: it was two in the morning. Kim Shunpei's face appeared in her mind's eye, but she didn't care. She bought some *takoyaki* and rode a taxi home.

The tenement houses in the neighborhood were wrapped in darkness and silence. The front and back doors of Kim Shunpei's house were locked. Sadako called up to Sunako repeatedly while trying to keep her voice down. Finally, a window on the second floor opened, and Sunako peeked out.

"Open the door," said Sadako.

Sunako came down and opened the back door. Sadako went inside and gulped down some water from the faucet.

"You stink of *sake*." Sunako made a face and went back

upstairs.

Just then, Sadako heard Kim Shunpei shout angrily from the front room. "What time do you think it is? Where have you been?" His voice was loud enough for the neighbors to hear.

"That's *my* business! I'm doin' what I want from now on."

"What did you say, you bitch? You spendin' all my money?"

"It's my money, not yours. I get to do whatever I please with it." Sadako stomped loudly up to the second floor. Sunako buried her head under the covers and turned toward the wall, as if to show her disapproval.

"Hey, have some *takoyaki.* I got it in Minami. It's good," said Sadako.

"No. I'm sleeping."

"Stop talkin' back and just eat it. You hurt my feelings when you talk back like that. For sixteen years, I've raised all of you while living like a beggar. Everything was for you. You know how much I thought about runnin' away? But I knew we'd starve in the streets, which is why I've had to put up with this till now. I wanna be free for once, you understand? Sunako, you hear me?" Sadako burst into tears and took Sunako in her arms.

Sadako's laxness and self-indulgence began affecting the lifestyles of her children. She would let them go without breakfast and give them money for bread and milk that they could buy at school, but more often than not, they skipped school instead. Sadako continued to sleep until noon or later, not bothering to make sure that her children went to school.

Sluggishness and decadence crept into the family's lives, and everyone lost interest in doing anything. Ever since Sadako started going out at night, she didn't cook a single meal. She and her children either ordered in or went out to eat. They didn't care whether Kim Shunpei had anything to eat. As a result, he had no choice but to have food delivered for himself as well.

If Sadako used to come and go through the back door, now she brazenly entered through the front door when she returned late at night, slipping past the sleeping Kim Shunpei on her way to the kitchen. She always stank of *sake,* and she always guzzled water as soon as she got home. She arrived home later and later with each passing night, sometimes at the break of dawn. She was spending money left and right, clearly entertaining herself with male escorts. Kim Shunpei's bowels churned at the thought of Sadako using up his jealously guarded wealth to be entertained by strangers. But there was nothing he could do. He couldn't think of any way of assuaging the woman's frenzied passions. Instead, his rage and hatred only grew.

The house grew dusty and unclean, and spider webs seemed to hang from every corner.

"Sunako, clean the floors every once in a while, why don't you?"

"Why should I? I hate cleaning," retorted Sunako, suggesting that her mother should be the one cleaning instead. The children spent all day munching on snacks and watching television on the second floor. They kept their eyes glued to the television whether their mother was in the house or not.

The house became a kind of sinister presence, shrouded in gloom and mold. It had once been the cleanest, brightest, newest-looking house in the neighborhood, but now the walls and ceilings were stained black, and the tatami floors were full of holes. The scrupulous Kim Shunpei felt as if the dark house were silently crumbling around him. He felt as if he were rotting from the inside out.

One night, Sadako didn't come back home at all. She always used to come home by dawn at the latest, but she was nowhere to be seen. She came back the following night as if nothing unusual had happened. She went up to the second floor, flung herself down onto her futon, and fell asleep in her clothes. She woke up again nearly twenty-four hours later. She told Sunako to order some sushi and ate heartily on the futon without bothering to wash her face. After getting a perm done at the salon, she changed clothes and went to Minami to soak in the sauna, and then she left for the entertainment district. At this point, Sadako had a wide variety of watering holes to choose from. She hopped from host clubs to bars, from cabarets to gay bars, from sushi stalls to restaurants, as if she were a rich widow. She had three or four sugar babies, including Takeru. When Takeru gave her the attention she wanted, she lavished him with gifts—clothes, shoes, watches, and most recently, a car.

Sadako's absences from the house grew more frequent. Sometimes she wouldn't come home for three days. Kim Shunpei felt an acute sense of crisis. The family was in utter ruins, but he had no power to do anything to Sadako.

The biggest reason for this was the children. Who else was going to look after them? Kim Shunpei was—now of all times—anxious about their future. If Sadako were to abandon the children and leave, and if Kim Shunpei were to die, the children would be turned out into the streets. No matter how much money they were left with, they wouldn't know how to manage it. Others would swoop in like vultures and strip them of all they had. There were already indications of that on the horizon.

As long as Kim Shunpei remained immobile, no one was going to pay back the debts he was owed. It was a waste of effort to hound his debtors over the phone. The same went for his renters. No one on any of his thirteen properties was paying their rent—not even the reliable Kang Touma. A man named Takagi was renting out what remained of Kim Shunpei's former *kamaboko* factory. He'd converted the factory into a printing shop, but it wasn't doing well. The law didn't allow renters to stop paying their rent just because the country was in a recession. Even so, Kim Shunpei's claims were totally ignored.

Kim Shunpei decided he had to consult with his nephews and with Ko Nobuyoshi. He wanted to come to an arrangement with Sadako, and he needed intermediaries to negotiate on his behalf. Ko Nobuyoshi and the nephews showed up at the house the following day. Sadako had been out since the previous night. The men sat around Kim Shunpei's desk and debated how to handle this serious problem. They discussed options for an hour, but they couldn't settle on a specific plan. They all sighed heavily. Would the men let themselves lose so easily to a single woman's insurrection?

"Anyway," said Kim Shunpei, searching for words. "It's about the house and the kids. The kids are barely in school. And no one's using the laundry machine. No one's using the vacuum. Look, the rooms are covered in garbage and dust. It's worse than a pigsty." He let out another heavy sigh. "She's not even here. I bet she won't even come back today."

The two nephews said nothing. They found Sadako's behavior unforgivable, but they'd already talked with Kim Shunpei many times over the phone about his travails.

Ko Nobuyoshi pulled himself out of his thoughts and spoke up. "If she's not gonna come today, we'll draw up a written pledge. Each side presents their terms. We get each side to accept the other side's terms, and I'll be the witness. If someone breaks the pledge, they take the children and leave the house. No money involved. She took *that* already."

No one else could come up with a better idea, and they all set about preparing the pledge. They proposed this and that and racked their brains until they settled on the following terms:

Take care of the children and the house. Make sure the children go to school. Be back at the house by midnight. Let Kim Shunpei know if you're spending the night elsewhere, and tell him where. You get an allowance of up to one hundred thousand yen a month. Take care of Kim Shunpei. For this you will be paid three thousand yen a day.

Though Kim Shunpei and his family weren't registered as such in the Japanese family registry, it was absurd to state these terms for a couple that had four children between them. And Sadako was basically given the green light to cheat on Kim Shunpei with other men. For Kim Shunpei, the pledge was disgraceful, and his pride was severely wounded. But Ko Nobuyoshi and his nephews urged him to agree to the pledge nonetheless.

Kim Yong-su also found the terms humiliating. "We can't show this to anyone else," he said.

"Yeah, well, as long as the house is taken care of and the kids are in school, it can't be worse than now," said Kim Tae-su.

If the situation between Kim Shunpei and Sadako improved, the nephews' burdens would also become a little lighter. But Sadako had to be there for any agreement to take place. Whenever she came back after more than a night away, she slept until the evening of the following day. Ko Nobuyoshi and his nephews would have to be there when she woke up.

After the three men left, Kim Shunpei was left alone to ruminate over the terms of the pledge and bear the unbearable humiliation. Things had been bad enough when he was first struck with palsy, but he never imagined he would be stuck in a swamp like this.

The hearts of human beings were inconstant, but Kim Shunpei knew what frightening things could lurk there. Human life remained incomprehensible until the very end. Who could say what new trials and tribulations awaited him? Anything could happen tomorrow, and it would no longer shock him. Kim Shunpei thought about whether he should kill Sadako and himself. But could he kill Sadako in this body? If he botched the attempt, Sadako could kill him instead. In the face of such a possibility, Kim Shunpei lost the courage to make the attempt.

The weakened, paralyzed Kim Shunpei became nervous and frightened of himself. He was frightened of living on and on day after day, waiting for death to creep up on him and wring his neck. Back when he could fight ten or twenty thugs at a time, he didn't fear death at all. Death didn't even register in his mind. He just thought of death as a single moment in time. Now he realized that the path leading to that single moment was long and full of suffering. At the end of such suffering, a big gaping hole waited for him, ready to envelop him in darkness. It was up to each person to face their own death, but Kim Shunpei was in the habit of saying that death was the end. That last moment looked to him like an overly empty void. *Who's going to bury me?* The passage of time mercilessly cut into Kim Shunpei like a knife.

Sadako rejected the terms of the pledge and continued going out for nights on end as though she were perfectly entitled to do so. She turned her nose up at Ko Nobuyoshi and the nephews and laughed when they remonstrated with her. The three men could hardly countenance Kim Shunpei's complaints. "She left yesterday and still isn't back yet!" "She's fucking who knows how many guys!" "It's 'cause you found that whore that my life's gone to shit!" Kim Shunpei blamed Kim Yong-su for being the one who had introduced Sadako to him in the first place. But he also begged Kim Yong-su to move into one of his nearby properties to take care of him.

Kim Yong-su wouldn't hear of it. He knew his uncle's personality, and he also knew that taking over Sadako's caretaking responsibilities wouldn't solve any of the underlying problems. And things would spiral out of control if his family got involved. Kim Tae-su felt the same way. Everyone wanted to mark their distance from this ugly state of affairs.

Kim Shunpei's stomach churned in discomfort from morning till night. He had to inch his way to the bathroom again and again. With just the strength of his arms, he squatted over the toilet and tried not to tip over even slightly. If he did, he ended up pitching forward or falling backward and flailing around on the dirty floor like a beetle.

He suspected that his diarrhea was due to a nervous breakdown, rather than to any food he'd eaten. None of his days were restful when he had to deal with his palsy. His nightmare continued whether he was awake or asleep. His paralyzed lower body grew thin, and his arm and chest muscles wasted away. It was difficult for him to even hold himself up.

Kim Shunpei felt a fourth bout of diarrhea move through him, and he turned himself over on his futon and crawled desperately toward the bathroom with his arms. But no matter how much he exerted himself, he wasn't getting any closer. He gritted his teeth and concentrated all his energy into clenching his anus. He writhed on the floor, not even sure whether he was crawling forward or holding back his diarrhea. In the next moment, Kim Shunpei let himself fall into a kind of ecstasy. He relaxed his muscles and felt all his energy leave his body. He lay on the floor in stupefaction, bathed in his own shit.

Just then, Sadako returned from one of her overnight escapades. "What's this smell?" she barked out, twisting her face in disgust.

Kim Shunpei looked up at Sadako with hollow eyes

and said, "Help me up." He limply raised one of his arms, looking as if he'd been smashed to pieces with a hammer.

"Don't touch me! Disgusting! I can't even breathe in here." Sadako clamped a hand over her nose and mouth and sidled past Kim Shunpei to go upstairs. He grabbed onto Sadako's leg. She clung to a pillar and tried to free herself from Kim Shunpei's grip.

"The fuck? Let go of me!" Sadako used her other leg to kick at Kim Shunpei, who was using all his strength to pull her down.

"I'll kill you, you dirty whore! How dare you spend my money and make a fool of me! I could kill you over and over!"

Kim Shunpei's body was clammy and greasy.

"Sunako! Sunako!" screamed Sadako. As Sunako came down the stairs, Sadako told her, "Hand me that rod over there."

Sunako went to the front room and retrieved Kim Shunpei's cherry tree club. She handed the club to Sadako, who swung down the club on Kim Shunpei's arm. That was the same club he'd carried around everywhere for self-defense. But Kim Shunpei still didn't let go of Sadako's leg. She hit his arm again and again. His arm

dangled downward, as if she'd broken it. She finally
extricated herself and, blind with fury, started showering
Kim Shunpei with blows. She pummeled his head, his
shoulders, his arms, and his legs. He groaned in pain.

"Mom, stop!" said Sunako, who could no longer
stomach the violence.

Sadako glared down at Kim Shunpei, her chest heaving
and her hair all disheveled. "Nothin' left for you to do
but die. Don't mess with me!" Her voice was low and
threatening, like a man's.

Sadako went upstairs, got out her travel bag, and
stuffed it with clothes. When she finished packing, she
took Yukiko's hand.

"Sunako, I'm leavin' with Yukiko. Wait here for a bit.
Call me if something happens, and don't show this phone
number to anyone else. I'll give you some money too. You
should be fine with this much. Don't be wasteful with it,
you hear? I'll come back for you soon."

"Okay," said Sunako, nodding. The other children
were watching television, unaware that anything had
happened downstairs.

On the first floor, Kim Shunpei had crawled toward
the phone at his desk. Sadako threw him a withering look

and left with Yukiko through the front door.

"Hello? Nobuyoshi?" said Kim Shunpei in a hoarse
voice. "It's me. Come here quick. That bitch hit me. My
arms and legs are broken. Call my nephews too." He hung
up. He started trembling, and then he put his head on his
desk and bayed like a cow. Regret, shame, humiliation,
hatred, powerlessness, resentment—all the tragedy of
the world tore his chest apart. He wanted to die. But how
could he? He didn't even have the energy to die.

It took Ko Nobuyoshi twenty minutes to ride to Kim
Shunpei's house on his bicycle. He half doubted Kim
Shunpei's claims that Sadako had broken his bones,
but he called the nephews as Kim Shunpei had asked.
When he came in, the stench of shit assailed his nose,
and his throat closed up. Kim Shunpei looked up at Ko
Nobuyoshi from the desk. "Ugh, ugh, ugh," he sobbed.

Blood ran down Kim Shunpei's forehead, and bruises
were forming on his left eye and his cheeks. His shit-
drenched pants were halfway down his legs. Snot dripped
from his nose into his open, toothless mouth, and tears
streamed from his eyes. Ko Nobuyoshi had never seen
someone look so pitiful. He felt compassion and at the
same time, anger. He checked Kim Shunpei's arms and

417

legs. They weren't broken, but the bones were likely cracked.

Ko Nobuyoshi helped Kim Shunpei into the washroom, where he removed Kim Shunpei's clothes and scrubbed him with soap and water. He then went up to the second floor to find Kim Shunpei new clothes, and the four children turned their faces from the television to look at him. They stared with cat-like eyes that bore him hostility. The rooms were strewn with clothes. Ko Nobuyoshi found some of Kim Shunpei's T-shirts and pants in the closet and dresser, but the clothes were coming apart. Kim Shunpei should have bought new clothes a long time ago, but he was so stingy that he kept reusing the same shirts and pants over and over as if they could be worn forever. Ko Nobuyoshi wondered what all that stinginess and penny-pinching had been for.

Kim Shunpei calmed down a little after he changed, and he lay down on the futon. Ko Nobuyoshi threw away his soiled clothes and scrubbed the shit-smeared floors. Even then, the smell of shit didn't go away.

Soon the two nephews arrived. They made a face at the smell, but felt relieved when they saw their uncle on the futon in the corner. But when Kim Shunpei turned to face them, the nephews' breath caught in their throats.

"Shunpei's in bad shape. I think the bones in his arms and legs are cracked. And we need to treat his cuts and bruises. Could you two call a doctor? There's an orthopedic doctor in Nakamichi, right? Yong-su, call him. And Tae-su, go to Yoshioka Clinic in Imazato and bring a surgeon over."

The nephews went back outside and did as they were told. Orthopedic surgeons didn't typically make house calls. With some wheedling, the nephews were able to get doctors from both Nakamichi and Imazato to make a special visitation.

The first one to arrive was the orthopedic surgeon from Nakamichi. Once he inspected Kim Shunpei's arms and legs, he said, "Yep, they're cracked. His bones are strong, so it's not a huge concern. Just keep a poultice on 'em and don't move around so much. Be patient, and they'll heal."

Everyone relaxed at the orthopedic surgeon's optimistic diagnosis.

"Come by for the poultice. I'll give you a prescription. Take care." The orthopedic surgeon bustled out. The surgeon from Imazato replaced him.

"So what's the problem? I don't make house visits, you know," said the surgeon self-importantly. When he examined Kim Shunpei's arms and legs, he became more interested in the case. "We don't have to put these in casts. Just wrap them up with poultices and keep them in place. But we should get your head stitched up to hasten recovery. We need anesthetic, so you'll have to come with me to the clinic."

No one could defy the doctor's orders, so Kim Shunpei was set on the luggage rack of a bicycle and taken to the clinic. Along with five stitches for his head, he also got some poultices, which meant that Kim Yong-su had to cancel the prescription at the orthopedic clinic. "What a hassle. You should've just told us to bring the surgeon . . . ."

In any case, now that Kim Shunpei was on track for recovery, the three other men looked at each other questioningly, unsure of what to do about the situation. The fugitive Sadako was one thing, but who was going to take care of Kim Shunpei and his four children? No one had the means to assume such a responsibility. But neither could they just throw their hands up and let the situation sort itself out.

The three men wanted to go home. They waited for

someone to get up from the table, but all of them stayed put, unable to leave Kim Shunpei here to fend for himself. After they sat in silence for a few minutes, Kim Yong-su reluctantly opened his mouth and said, "In this kind of situation . . . the only thing we can do is call Sung-han."

Ko Nobuyoshi slapped his knee as if he'd been zapped by lightning. "I was thinking the same thing. Sung-han is Shunpei's only legitimate son. Sung-han's now thirty-six? Thirty-seven? He's a fine, fully grown adult. He'll know what to do."

The men's faces dawned with realization, as if they'd stumbled upon something important they hadn't even known to look for. Sung-han was the break in the deadlock, the trump card that could let the other men off the hook. But Kim Shunpei made a sour face. He hadn't seen Sung-han in fifteen years. And they'd been in mortal combat with each other. Would this same Sung-han even consider coming back to be Kim Shunpei's caretaker? Their relationship was a kinship forged with violence. Lee Young-hee, Hanako, and Takeshi were dead, which meant that Sung-han was the one bearing their resentment on top of his own. Not only that, but Sung-han would have to deal with the unfinished business of Kiyoko, Sadako, and his half-siblings. It would be intolerable for Kim Shunpei to show Sung-han how decrepit he'd become. But was there any other way?

"It'd be great if Sung-han could come back. But where is he now?" said Kim Tae-su.

"I heard he's a taxi driver in Tokyo," said Kim Yong-su as he breathed into his inhaler.

"The ward office could tell us his address. I can go to the one in Ikuno and ask. They should match up an address to his alien registration card," said Ko Nobuyoshi. The Ikuno ward office was closest to his house.

The three men continued the discussion without considering how Kim Shunpei felt. They debated whether to write Sung-han a letter, talk to him over the phone, or have one of them go meet him in person. They decided on sending a telegram. Telegrams took people by surprise and seemed like the most appropriate method of communication in these circumstances.

"Uncle, you can relax once Sung-han gets here. We're all gettin' old, so it's better for a younger person to handle this. Everything from before is water under the bridge. Be sure to tell him that," said Kim Yong-su.

Kim Shunpei said wearily, "Is he even gonna come?"

"He will. He's your son," said Ko Nobuyoshi, dismissing Kim Shunpei's fears.

But Kim Shunpei worried endlessly. He feared that Sung-han would come and beat him to a pulp. He wanted one of the three men to stay over for a few days, but he didn't tell them that. He was already weak and miserable enough, and he didn't want to expose his humiliation to anyone else.

The three men left Kim Shunpei to while away the interminable night by himself. It was a humid summer night, too oppressive to sleep through. When would this life end? Every ending was the beginning of something else. Kim Shunpei let his mind wander in the dark. Everything seemed vague and hazy. There was no clarity. The four corners of his room shook. Countless small holes opened up along the walls, and insects came crawling out of them. The insects spread in all directions and started closing in on Kim Shunpei. Their buzzing and chattering filled his ears. As he felt them on his arms and legs, his back muscles went rigid. The insects were biting him, and tingling pain shot through his whole body. He desperately batted at the insects entering his ears, his nose, his eyes. *Help . . . me . . .* he screamed, but no sound came out. The insects were invading all his orifices and eating their way through his rotting lower body. His blood spilled out of him like sand. They were going to eat him alive. His inner organs were being chewed up into ribbons. *I'm . . . scared . . .*

Kim Shunpei woke up from his nightmare and shat all over himself.

Chapter 26

When Sung-han stepped off the air-conditioned bullet
train onto the platform, he immediately broke into a
sweat. He'd received a telegram the day before from his
elder cousin Kim Yong-su: "Come now." Sung-han didn't
know what the telegram was about, but he came to Osaka
nonetheless. This was his first time stepping foot in the
city since his business failed seven years ago. Now he was
thirty-seven, and hearing the Osaka accent in the hustle
and bustle of the crowd made him feel more uneasy than
nostalgic. He rode the subway to Nanba and took a taxi to
Kim Yong-su's house.

The water in the ditch by Kim Yong-su's house blazed
in the sunlight and stank of trash. As Sung-han crossed
over the ditch, the nauseating smell of boiling pig feed
wafted over him. Sadako's old shack was still there, and it

looked occupied. A shirtless man came out of the shack, scratching his long, straggly hair, and urinated in the ditch while yawning widely.

As Sung-han approached Kim Yong-su's house, a dog in a cage bared its teeth and started barking at him. Kim Yong-su's wife Yeong-ja came out of the farm and saw Sung-han approaching. She let her surprise show on her face. "Sung-han . . . You came," she said. She called her husband over her shoulder and rushed to the house. Kim Yong-su came out of the farm and cried, "You're here! Come inside." He took the end of a broom and poked the dog with it, which only made the dog bark louder.

How many years had it been since Sung-han had last entered this house? His mother had once brought him here for an ancestral rite when he was a child. That was probably about twenty-five years ago. The house had only two rooms, and a futon was laid out in the inner room.

"Our bodies aren't what they used to be. It's harder to get out of bed these days . . . ."

There was something forlorn about this childless couple. Sung-han sat down, and the thin-looking Yeong-ja brought him some barley tea. The warm air from the fan caressed Sung-han's sweaty skin. He took a sip of the tea.

"So you're a taxi driver, I hear."

"Yeah . . ." answered Sung-han reluctantly.

"Income ain't bad, right?"

"It puts food on the table."

"And how many children?"

"Two."

"Ah . . . Hope they have all they need."

Kim Yong-su kept probing Sung-han with questions. Sung-han, for his part, wanted to know what was behind the telegram. His impatience rose as Kim Yong-su kept skirting the main topic.

"Is something the matter? You called me here," he asked.

"Yes, well, here's the thing . . . ."

Kim Yong-su told Sung-han the whole story, from Kim Shunpei's stroke to his paralysis to his incident with Sadako. Sung-han smoked a cigarette as he listened silently, but his face turned grim.

"Which is why we need you. All his renters and borrowers are pretending like nothing's wrong. You need to clean up this mess. Your father's money is yours. If you just stand there, other people will take it for themselves. I tried to collect the rent and debt from them. They won't fork up. But if *you're* the one they're dealin' with, they won't play any games. No one can solve this problem but you."

It was hard for Sung-han to believe that his monster of a father would end up with palsy and then get beaten by Sadako until his bones cracked. And this business about the written pledge made him feel as if he were peering into new depths of absurdity. Sadako's revengeful, egotistical behavior seemed to exemplify the passions that ran through womankind in general.

Kim Yong-su phoned Kim Tae-su and Ko Nobuyoshi. "Sung-han's here. He'll be on his way to his dad's place soon. Can you come too?" He was determined to dictate the course of action for Sung-han, even though Sung-han himself hadn't expressed his intentions.

Yeong-ja said from the kitchen, "Want anything to eat?"

"We'll eat after we talk to Shunpei."

Yeong-ja acted timid and nervous in everything she did. She felt subconscious guilt about the fact that she didn't have any children. She likely had never seen a doctor about her condition. It was common for people of Kim Yong-su's generation, both men and women, to blame the woman for not bearing children.

The dog barked furiously when Sung-han left the house as well.

Sung-han could barely breathe in the suffocating heat and the stench. Crows were picking through the trash in the ditch. Kim Yong-su threw some stones at the crows, but they ignored him. "They come here all the time, dozens of 'em. Sometimes they go into the pigpens and steal the feed. Shameless little fuckers." Kim Yong-su glared at the crows hatefully as they crossed over the ditch. Sung-han felt conflicted as he followed his cousin. He didn't know how much of the truth Kim Yong-su was telling him.

Kim Yong-su walked with bowlegs and a hunched back, looking older than his actual age. Sung-han watched him with pity. It was only natural that his cousin would look like that after years of hard labor on the hog farm. The relationship Sung-han had with his cousins was nothing but circumstantial, but he couldn't deny the mysterious causes and conditions of this relationship that pulled him back to Kim Shunpei like an invisible thread. Blood is thicker than water, as the saying went. From the back, Kim Yong-su looked just like his uncle Kim

Shunpei. The same could be said for Sung-han himself. He couldn't renounce where he'd come from.

The asphalt shimmered in the heat of the blazing sun. Kim Yong-su found the heat unbearable and hailed a taxi on the main thoroughfare.

"It's great that the taxis have air conditioners now. Let's go to Imazato." Kim Yong-su wiped his neck and armpits with a handkerchief and took a deep breath. He looked out the window as the taxi passed the Takashimaya department store and the kabuki theater. "I hear this main street's gonna turn into a highway," he commented.

Even as the city changed, some areas remained the same. The taxi entered the Tsuruhashi area. Sung-han saw that the streets he was so familiar with hadn't changed at all. When he got off the taxi at Taisei Street, he felt as if he'd traveled back in time. The udon shop from his childhood was still in business. Scenes from the past played in Sung-han's head like a video recording. The alleyways, once lively with romping children, were now deserted, and the houses looked as dilapidated as ever. An old woman came out of a house, saw Sung-han, and quickly hid back inside.

Kim Yong-su opened the door to Kim Shunpei's house

and beckoned Sung-han in. Sung-han slowly went inside. Kim Shunpei was sitting at his desk in the front room. Ko Nobuyoshi was sitting by his feet. The rest of the room was occupied by the four children. Sunako, now fifteen or sixteen years old, was lying belly down on the floor and reading a comic book in a flimsy singlet, which exposed her voluptuous limbs. Her frame was large like her father's. Sung-han was startled to see her. She seemed to feel no shame showing off her bare skin to a stranger. She briefly appraised Sung-han as he stood in the *genkan* and then returned to her comic book. Sunako's two younger sisters and four-year-old brother sat beside her, staring at Sung-han with large, rabbit-like eyes.

As Sung-han sat down on the wooden floor, Ko Nobuyoshi's wrinkled face broke out into a wide grin, and he said, "You came! Now Shunpei can rest easy."

Sung-han saw Kim Shunpei's reddish face and immediately assumed he was drunk. In fact, Kim Shunpei's face had taken on a slightly reddish cast ever since his stroke.

Kim Shunpei looked overcome with emotion as he gazed at Sung-han. "I can move my legs as I like," he asserted, pushing down on the desk and standing up shakily. "The bugs crawl over me, you see."

Kim Shunpei spoke earnestly, as if he wanted Sung-han to feel compassion for him. The circumstances he was in called for such things. The four-year-old Yong-il got up, ran over to his father, and kicked him in the leg. "Die! Die!" he jeered. He threw a look at Ko Nobuyoshi, Kim Yong-su, and Sung-han, as if to challenge them.

"I get it, I get it. Go play with your sisters," said Kim Shunpei as he stroked Yong-il's head.

Sunako pulled herself up from the floor. "Dad, I'm hungry," she complained.

"Go eat at the udon shop," replied Kim Shunpei. He gave her a one thousand-yen bill. Sunako beckoned for her siblings to follow her as she went out the door in her singlet.

The house looked like a dwelling for savages. The tatami floors were tattered, and the rooms were filled with heaps of trash.

"Look at this. It's like a pigsty, or worse. No one cleans." Kim Shunpei grimaced. Everything around him was going to the dogs, but he could only throw up his hands in defeat. Sung-han felt as if he were peering down a deep, dark hole. The muggy heat wrapped itself around his sweaty throat. He felt as if he were wading deep into a swamp.

Kim Tae-su showed up. He looked at Sung-han in surprise and said, "Oh, welcome back," as if Sung-han's mere presence had solved everything with a snap of the finger. "Uncle, now you have nothin' to worry about," he said glibly.

Kim Yong-su spoke next. "Yes, nothin' to worry about at all. Sung-han's gonna take care of everything. Everyone's treated you like dirt, and no one's been paying you back what you lent them. Sung-han won't let 'em get away with it. Hey, Sung-han, your father bought a house and renovated it for you. He was waitin' for you to come back, understand? You can live there. And all his assets are yours. You'll take over the bank account. You won't let Sadako get her hands on it. She ain't welcome here!" Kim Yong-su was just repeating what he'd been saying earlier, but he made sure to emphasize the last part about Sadako.

Kim Shunpei objected. "No way. What's gonna happen to me if Sung-han gets my account books? I'd be stripped blind. Everyone's after my money, that's why they wanna be near me. If I don't have money, I'd . . ."

All the others' promises turned to dust with Kim

Shunpei's words.

"What are you talkin' about, Shunpei? Who can you trust but Sung-han? You're helpless. Sadako did all that horrible stuff to you 'cause you can't move. Just forget the past and let Sung-han take care of you. He's your son! If you can't trust your own son, who else is there? Sung-han has two kids, you know. They're your grandchildren. Don't you care about them? Listen, we're all here for you. We all want to protect you. Just let it go." The normally taciturn Ko Nobuyoshi let himself speak freely at last.

Sung-han had never asked for this problem to land in his lap, and he felt mutinous as everyone around him went their own willful way. He hadn't wanted to answer the telegram in the first place. For the past seven years, he hadn't thought about Kim Shunpei once. He didn't know if that was because he wanted to forget about him, or because he just didn't care. His cousins and Ko Nobuyoshi were trying to manufacture a fait accompli. "You must be joking," Sung-han wanted to tell them.

Kim Shunpei's face darkened as Ko Nobuyoshi lectured him. His eyes turned fierce, as if to show everyone that he would never trust them. The expression in those eyes had always frightened Sung-han when he

434

was a child.

"No way," said Kim Shunpei again. "I won't give up my assets. And you have to collect the debts *my* way. As long as I'm alive, everything's mine."

Ko Nobuyoshi and the two nephews heaved a huge sigh. At that moment, Sung-han spoke for the first time. "What a waste of time. *Nii-san*, you brought me here for this? I don't know how much money we're talking about, but it's not my problem. You think he'd give me something now of all times? He never spent anything on us. Hey, old man, you did things your way all this time. Stop complaining and take your money with you to the afterlife, or throw it down the drain. You make me sick." Sung-han got up in a huff and put on his shoes.

"Wait a minute, Sung-han. Your father's just bein' stubborn. He really is gonna give you all his money. He needs to be taken care of. You get it, don't you? You can't expect a parent to give a kid free rein all at once."

"It doesn't matter to me what he does or doesn't do," said Sung-han coldly. He strode out the door.

"*Jane, jane,*"*called out Kim Shunpei. But Sung-han

---

* The Korean word for "you," typically used by male friends to address each other

.

435

ignored him. Sung-han's insides were boiling. As he turned the corner of the udon shop, he noticed Kim Shunpei's four children coming out of the shop door—his half-siblings. Sung-han felt their stares on his back, but he sped up his pace and kept his eyes in front of him as he headed toward Tsuruhashi Station.

The brief reunion left a bitter taste in Sung-han's mouth. He regretted ever coming back to Osaka. He felt a little guilty, as if he were getting away on a boat while other people were drowning in his wake. But it was an impossible situation to begin with. He couldn't imagine living with his father, he told himself. No one was at fault but his father. Was there any reason for him to take on his father's sins? Those four children weren't at fault either, but they were implicated in Kim Shunpei's fate. The image of the old, doddering Kim Shunpei didn't stir up any compassion in Sung-han. It was pathetic that Kim Shunpei had called after him with the term *janae*, as if they had no history with each other. But Sung-han understood why Kim Shunpei couldn't bring himself to call Sung-han by his own name. There was something unbearably sad about this fact. Surely he would never have to see his father again after this.

Tsuruhashi Station was as Sung-han remembered it, though there were more passengers there than ever. He made his way through the crowd and bought a ticket for Shin-Osaka Station.

The men back at Kim Shunpei's house had failed in their mission. They'd lost their trump card.

"Why'd you tell Sung-han that? You were supposed to persuade him," grumbled Kim Yong-su. His uncle's greed knew no bounds. But it was too late to remedy anything at this point.

"Even if I told him I'd give him everything, he wouldn't come back," said Kim Shunpei, looking resigned.

"How could you say that?" It sounded like Kim Shunpei was just making an excuse for something he'd arbitrarily decided.

"If it were me, I wouldn't come back. So 'course he wouldn't."

In other words, Kim Shunpei had never intended for Sung-han to inherit his money. So this debacle with Sung-han had been much ado about nothing. Ko Nobuyoshi and the nephews were doing their absolute best to help, but their ability to influence things was limited because the problem lay with Kim Shunpei. The three men had their own lives to live. They now understood completely that they couldn't devote their time and energy to Kim Shunpei. They could only let events runs their course, like the wind. If the wind came from the east one day, the next day it would come from the west, and the day after that, a heavy rain would fall. Things didn't improve little by little; time just went on. There was no word from Sadako or Yukiko. Kim Shunpei was better off this way. If Sadako came back, there was no telling what she would do to him.

The children had been out of school for half a year. They spent their days tirelessly watching television, and sometimes Sunako went out. Kim Shunpei suspected that she was going out to meet her mother. When she came back, she treated him with a new kind of impudence that was likely inspired by Sadako. Lately, she'd been rummaging through the house late at night and saying menacingly, "Dad, where the fuck are the account books?" She glared at him as if she were about to attack him at any moment. Kim Shunpei was shocked. At fifteen years old, Sunako already stood at a height of five feet and four inches. She was much bigger than her mother. Kim

Shunpei was convinced that if he didn't do something now, she would take a cue from her mother and physically assault him.

Sunako's behavior was like the beginning of a bad dream Kim Shunpei had seen before. She started perming her hair, wearing red lipstick, and going out in Sadako's club outfits and high heels.

"You're just a kid! Don't walk around looking like that!" scolded Kim Shunpei.

"Leave me alone! I can do what I want!" Sunako snapped back.

Sunako came back later and later each night, sometimes drunk. She was likely meeting men and dating around. Her behavior conformed to her mother's. Kim Shunpei had no time to lose. He had to make a decision now. He calmly stewed in his thoughts for two days. Then he called Ko Nobuyoshi.

"We need to talk. I know you're busy, but could you come now?" Kim Shunpei sounded different than normal, as if he were about to bid farewell to the world. Alarmed, Ko Nobuyoshi flew to Kim Shunpei's house. He found Kim Shunpei sitting at his desk in the dark, looking dazed and defeated.

"Did something else happen . . . ?" Ko Nobuyoshi turned on the light. The large man in front of him looked so exhausted that Ko Nobuyoshi almost had to turn his eyes away. That once virile face was now frail and wasting away, and his left eyelid drooped.

Kim Shunpei told Ko Nobuyoshi the details about Sunako's behavior. "I don't think she'll do what her mother did, but . . ."

Ko Nobuyoshi listened with his arms folded. By the sound of it, Sunako seemed perfectly likely to do what her mother did.

"Anyway, I can't live like this anymore. I'm goin' back to Korea. North Korea."

"North Korea . . . You mean it?" Ko Nobuyoshi was speechless. But as he thought it over, he felt like Kim Shunpei was correct to make that decision. Ko Nobuyoshi had been a regional committee member of the North Korea-affiliated organization Sōren for many years, and he berated himself for not coming up with the idea himself. Admittedly, Kim Shunpei had no connection to North Korea. He'd never mentioned North Korea in conversation, disinterested as he was in society and politics. So it was unimaginable that he would ever want to repatriate there. He probably came to this conclusion because all his other options had run dry. The July 4 North–South Joint Statement in 1972 had suggested that reunification between North and South Korea was possible. In Ko Nobuyoshi's mind, Kim Shunpei's decision to move to North Korea a year after the Joint Statement had political significance.

"Is it true that North Korea takes care of children and sick people?" asked Kim Shunpei.

"It's true. The Democratic Republic is a socialist country. Housing, healthcare, education . . . it's all free. You made the right decision. It never crossed my mind. Ever since the Joint Statement a year ago, I feel like reunification will soon be a reality. North and South will be one. And right now, your children aren't going to school properly. What'll happen to 'em when you die? In the Democratic Republic, Great Leader Kim Il Sung will take you into his arms, and you and your children will be happy. I wish I'd thought of this sooner. I'm an idiot for not seeing what was right under my nose." Ko Nobuyoshi rejoiced from the bottom of his heart.

"I was kinda worried about it, but what you say must be true. I know you're busy, but could you help me with the move? I'll do whatever you say."

"Okay. I'll go to the main office tomorrow and ask."

For the rest of the night, Ko Nobuyoshi told Kim Shunpei all he knew about the Democratic Republic. Kim Shunpei listened in silence.

The next day, Ko Nobuyoshi visited the Sōren headquarters in Osaka to inquire about the repatriation process. Kim Shunpei waited in the house impatiently.

When Ko Nobuyoshi came back, he told Kim Shunpei that the last boat of the year was leaving for North Korea in mid-October. He would have to wait until the spring for the next boat. It was only two months till October, but Kim Shunpei couldn't wait until the spring. Something bad could happen to him if he waited that long. He wanted to expedite the process as much as possible.

"Also . . ." said Ko Nobuyoshi awkwardly. "Everyone who repatriates makes a donation. The Democratic Republic is a socialist country, so it wouldn't make sense for people to bring their assets with them. Housing, healthcare, and education are all free, and you don't need money for things. So from what I hear, you'll get treated better if you make a donation."

"Okay. I'll do whatever you say."

Ko Nobuyoshi was moved by how much Kim Shunpei trusted him. "I've known you for a long time, and I owe you a lot. I'll do everything I can to help, even though it won't be much. You'll be happy there."

Ko Nobuyoshi threw himself into the repatriation process. He busily went around purchasing items outlined in the donations inventory: five German-manufactured two-color printers and platemakers, five automobiles, five freight cars, a hundred Seiko wristwatches, as well as clothes, shoes, and a considerable amount of Japanese yen. Kim Shunpei's two nephews weren't informed; they were sure to raise objections if they knew. Kim Shunpei told his nephews about the repatriation only after all the preparations were complete. They thought their uncle had finally lost his mind, but as far as practicalities went, they let him be.

Kim Shunpei forgave all his loans and relinquished his real estate properties, and he sold off the house he lived in, as well as the house he'd bought for Sung-han. His donations used up nearly all his assets.

Sunako refused to leave with her father and returned to her mother. Kim Shunpei kept the three other children.

The day before Kim Shunpei was to leave for Niigata,

Ko Nobuyoshi, Kim Yong-su, Kim Tae-su, and several Sōren representatives threw Kim Shunpei a farewell banquet. One of the representatives praised Kim Shunpei for his patriotic donation and promised him that he would find happiness among his comrades under the guidance of Great Leader Kim Il-sung. The representatives' stock phrases weren't much to Kim Shunpei's liking, but he listened contentedly, feeling accomplished. Mysteriously, Kim Shunpei seemed to have parted with his money without so much as a second glance—the same Kim Shunpei who had been close-fisted with his money to the point of obsession. Now, he could do nothing but trust in Ko Nobuyoshi and the Democratic Republic. He traded in all his possessions to entrust this nation with his and his children's future.

Early the next morning, the nephews came with their families to bid Kim Shunpei good-bye. Kim Yong-su brought his wife Yeong-ja, and Kim Tae-su brought his wife and his three adult children. Kim Shunpei had only seen his nephew's children once or twice before, a long time ago. Ko Nobuyoshi came with his wife Akemi.

A Sōren representative and two young activists also came. The activists were to keep the disabled Kim

Shunpei company until he boarded the boat in Niigata for North Korea.

Pictures were taken. "Be sure to study hard, you hear?" Ko Nobuyoshi told the older daughter Yuko. Her eyes filled with tears. She didn't want to go to North Korea, but Sunako had left the house without her.

Two taxis arrived. Kim Shunpei and his family got into the first one, while their chaperones got into the second.

"Shunpei, you did it! Your country's gonna take care of you from now on. You don't have to worry. Our nation will be reunited, and we'll see each other again," said Ko Nobuyoshi outside Kim Shunpei's window, while big tears fell down his face.

"Uncle, please write to us." The nephews and their wives were also crying.

Kim Shunpei's face trembled.

Suddenly, the Sōren representative raised his arms and cried out hysterically, "*Manse!*" No one else followed suit. As the taxi left, Kim Yong-su said as if to convince himself, "He'll be fine."

Kim Tae-su looked up at the low-hanging clouds and said, "Looks like rain. Time to get back to work."

"Me too. The pigs need to eat." Kim Yong-su nodded

to Ko Nobuyoshi and left with Kim Tae-su and the others toward Tsuruhashi Station. Ko Nobuyoshi set Akemi on the luggage rack of his bicycle, and they made their way through the main thoroughfare back to Ichijo Street. Their last meeting with Kim Shunpei had been too short.

The car radio announced that it was eleven o'clock at night. It was the final leg of Sung-han's shift. If he chose the wrong kind of passenger at this hour, it would be hard to make his quota for the day.

Sung-han waited for the light to change at the intersection of Shinjuku Ward Office and Yasukuni. About ten people were waiting at the taxi stop and waving for a ride. Most of the taxi drivers ignored them—a lot of the people there only wanted short-distance rides. Sung-han closely observed each pedestrian crossing the intersection. Judging from their age, face, and clothes, Sung-han could guess a salaryman's status or pay grade, and whether they needed to go somewhere near or far. After driving a taxi for over ten years, he could guess right about seventy percent of the time.

A middle-aged man raised his hand. He looked like he was at least a department head. Ever since the oil shock,

Japan was going through a private housing boom, and a lot of middle managers were buying up homes in the suburbs. There was a fifty-fifty chance that a passenger at this intersection would ask Sung-han to drive him home to Funabashi or Makuhari, which meant taking the highway. Without a moment's delay, Sung-han pulled up to the man on the curb. The man got into the back seat. "Take me to Akasaka, please."

Sung-han had miscalculated. This passenger wanted to drink some more in the city instead of going back to Chiba or wherever he lived. Sung-han couldn't kick the passenger out, so he set off without a word. Surely there were people in Akasaka who wanted to go home. After dropping the passenger off at Sanno Street, Sung-han collected himself and drove along the road slowly, hoping to land a long-distance ride this time.

Another middle-aged man boarded Sung-han's taxi outside the charred building of the New Japan Hotel. He wanted to go to Komagome. Sung-han was in luck. The midnight rush would soon be at its peak. Sung-han dropped the passenger off at a quiet neighborhood in Komagome and went back toward Shinjuku by way of Ikebukuro. Ikebukuro had some unsavory people milling about. Sung-han approached his usual waiting spot in Shinjuku but found it occupied by other cars. He redirected himself toward Kabukicho. The streets there were crowded, and he tried to make a detour, but sure enough, he got caught in a traffic jam that brought him to a standstill. Time inched along. All the taxis in front of him were scooping up passengers before he could. Sung-han's timing was off. The million blinking lights of the city seemed to be swallowing everyone up and spitting them out at the same time. Drunk middle-aged men roamed the streets with swinging arms, eyeing the hostesses trying to get home. Pimps catcalled women as they passed by.

Sung-han completed the Kabukicho circuit and stopped at the light by the Furin Kaikan Corporation. He picked up two women and a man who had just come out of a sushi restaurant. The man had his arms around both women, and he was in a buoyant mood. "Head toward Atsugi," he slurred. Sung-han calculated the fare in his head as he set off. He dropped one woman off at Nakano. As he approached Asagaya, the other woman started arguing with the man.

"No, my mother's sick," she told him.

"Just stay an hour." There was a hard edge to the man's voice.

"Go back home to your wife." The woman spoke to the man as if he were a child on the verge of a tantrum.

"It's been over half a year since I've fucked my wife. She never wants to do it."

Sung-han was on tenterhooks over whether the man and woman would cut the trip short to stay at a hotel. Stuff like that happened all the time. He needed to take at least one of them to Atsugi to meet his quota; otherwise, he would have to start over. He kept driving as he listened closely to the conversation in the backseat. The forcefulness of the man was being met with equal and opposite stubbornness from the woman.

"Driver, drop me off here, please," said the woman.

Sung-han stopped. The woman shook the man off and got out.

"Bitch! It's her fucking PMS," the man cursed as he sank into his seat. "Wake me up when you get to the Atsugi Interchange." He lay down.

Sung-han got on the highway and sped toward the Atsugi Interchange. As the taxi sped through the darkness, the shrieking wind and the rumbling from the

449

ground filled Sung-han's ears. He calculated the distance to the car in front of him as he passed it. He gripped the wheel so tight he could feel his palms moisten with sweat. Rigid with tension, Sung-han kept his eyes on the road.

After he dropped the man off, he calculated his earnings. He'd comfortably surpassed his quota, but he debated whether to quit for the day or go back to Shibutani or Shinjuku to keep working. He felt like his body was reaching its limit, though, and it would be dangerous to push himself. He headed toward the taxi garage.

The next day was his day off. He woke up in the late afternoon and sat in front of the television in a daze. Lately, it was getting harder to recover from his fatigue. He drank the beer his wife Setsuko brought for him and picked at the food on the low table. He wanted to take another nap before dinner. His two children hadn't come back home yet.

"Give me another beer," he called out.

"Another?" Setsuko was getting worried about how much her husband was drinking these days, but she handed him another can. She opened the evening issue of the *A— Times*. "Honey, isn't this about your father . . . ?"

she said.

Setsuko pointed to a corner of a page. The headline read, "Searching for Mother: The Story of Three North Korean Siblings." Sung-han saw a picture of two young women and a teenage boy.

Ten years ago, two sisters and a brother repatriated to the Democratic People's Republic of Korea, but they continue to search for their Japanese mother. Shortly after repatriation, their father became ill and passed away. They have longed for their mother ever since.

The three siblings live in Yomson Village in Riwon County, Hamgyong Province. They are Kim Yuko (23), Sadako (18), and Yong-il (15).

Recently, Yuko's husband Son Ryo-won told us in a letter that the mother's name is Toritani Sadako (60?). She was born in Kagoshima Prefecture and lived with her husband Kim Shunpei in Osaka's Higashinari Ward, Taisei Street Ni-chōme. In October 1973, Kim Shunpei repatriated to North Korea with three children, while Sadako remained in Japan with two older daughters: Yukiko (32) and Sunako (25). They supposedly live in Kyoto, but we have been unable to establish contact with them. When Yuko was twelve, Kim Shunpei brought her and her two younger siblings with him to North Korea.

After falling ill, he spent three years in the hospital before
passing away.

Currently, Yuko and Sadako work at a brick factory.
According to Mr. Won, Yuko is already a mother. Bereft
of their father and separated from their mother, the three
siblings' sadness is never-ending, and their wish to see
their mother and older sisters again only grows stronger.
Japan and North Korea do not have diplomatic relations,
and the three siblings are unable to visit Japan to look
for their mother. "The inability to travel between the two
countries brings us nothing but bitterness," they say.

"It *is* about your father, right?" said Setsuko, her eyes
round with surprise.

"No question." Sung-han stared down at the picture as
if to drink it in with his eyes. The two sisters resembled
Kim Shunpei, while Yong-il, with his thick eyebrows and
lips, resembled Sadako.

The three siblings were wearing short-sleeved shirts.
As far as Sung-han knew, Hamgyong Province was in
the northernmost part of North Korea and had two
mountain ranges, including one that extended down from
China called Paektu Mountain. The winters there were
extremely cold. Sung-han had expected Kim Shunpei to

live in Pyongyang since his donation had been so large, but instead he'd been placed in the far north. Sung-han felt angry for some reason.

"Who would've thought a newspaper would tell us where your father ended up?" Setsuko shook her head in amazement at the mystery of causality and retired to the kitchen.

Sung-han poured himself some more beer and stared absentmindedly at the television.

It was from Setsuko's siblings, who lived in Osaka, that Sung-han had first heard about Kim Shunpei's death. It wasn't clear when exactly he'd died. Sung-han's two elder cousins sent him a telegram as well. After meeting with them briefly in Osaka, he'd never heard from them again. They had died, apparently. Ko Nobuyoshi had died too. Everyone was leaving this world. The only thing that remained were hazy memories. Sung-han had two children that he could call his own. Even after his parents, siblings, and relatives left him, he didn't consider himself particularly forlorn.

But he was moved by some other emotion when he saw the picture in the newspaper. He had six relatives in North Korea. When Harumi's eldest son was a first-year

453

student in high school, he'd announced that he wanted to help build the foundations of his country and left for North Korea on the first boat. Apparently, he had a wife and three children there. And after Hanako committed suicide, her two children left for North Korea as well. They had repatriated at a young age, and Sung-han didn't know their whereabouts. None of them had been told that Kim Shunpei was in North Korea with them, even though Sung-han had discovered where the children were located through a Japanese newspaper. That was most peculiar. In any case, there would be no point in bringing together relatives in North Korea who wouldn't even recognize each other, especially since they'd been out of touch in Japan. His half-siblings in North Korea weren't putting up walls. It was Sung-han who was dragging a wall along with him, and that was his own problem to work through. The problems of Sung-han's generation had nothing to do with Sung-han's children, nor with his half-siblings.

Sung-han looked at the blurry photograph once more. The more he studied it, the more like Kim Shunpei those two young women looked. And Yong-il looked like Sadako. They were like Sung-han's own children, mixed with both Japanese and Korean blood. Harumi's children and Hanako's children were like that too, in a way. Sung-han couldn't see any rhyme or reason to it. As the days passed by, Sung-han got busy with work again, and he forgot about the newspaper article. Whenever he had a day off, he did the same thing as always: wake up in the early evening, drink beer in front of the television, nap another hour or two, eat dinner with his family, and drink more beer in front of the television. Then a letter arrived from the *A— Times*.

> *Our sincerest apologies for the abruptness of this letter.*
>
> *In our evening issue published on May 2, 1984, we printed an article about three siblings living in North Korea (a.k.a. the Democratic People's Republic of Korea). We don't know if you saw this article or not, but we've attached a copy here for your convenience. To summarize, these three siblings repatriated to North Korea by way of their father (Kim Shunpei). Three years later, the father passed away, and his young children had a terrible time of it, not being able to speak Korean. They were put up in orphanages and moved from place to place, and five years ago they ended up living in Hamgyong Province. The oldest daughter Yuko married a man named Won at the brick factory where they both*

worked, and they have children. The thing is, they miss
their mother in Japan terribly, and Mr. Won sent us a
letter asking for our help in finding her. However, we have
been thus far unable to locate Toritani Sadako, nor her
two daughters in Japan. In the process of searching for
her, we learned that Kim Shunpei's son resides here in
Tokyo as a taxi driver. We communicated this knowledge
to the siblings, who have expressed their wish to meet you.
Forgive our forwardness in reaching out, but if you wish
to visit them in North Korea, we will do everything in our
power to help.

Plenty of Sung-han's Zainichi compatriots had visited
North Korea to see their parents or siblings. News from
those visits trickled down to other Koreans in Japan.
Sung-han heard about people who went missing, or
political criminals who were thrown into jail. Whether
those reports were true or not was a different matter, but
it had become clear to Koreans in Japan that North Korea
wasn't the paradise they'd been told it was. That was to
say nothing of the unimaginable travails of being half-
Japanese in North Korea as his half-siblings were. A new
wave of conflicted feelings came over Sung-han after he
read the letter. He knew nothing would come of visiting

his half-siblings in North Korea. People had to live out their fates. It was Kim Shunpei's fate, too, to have gone to North Korea.

Sung-han put off replying to the *A— Times.* Going to North Korea cost money, and he wouldn't be able to go there empty-handed either. There was no way Sung-han could afford such a trip. But that was only part of the reason. What really depressed him were the conditions and effects that arose from his biological relationship with his father. Those conditions and effects were no longer supposed to have a hold over him, but they were like chains he could never break free from. If he wasn't himself, who was he? Was this irrefutable principle of cause and effect what people called love? He couldn't disavow the ties that bound parts of his being to someone else. Why hadn't he stayed and listened that day, ten years ago? Even if he wasn't going to remain in Osaka as everyone wanted, he could at least have stayed and listened for a while. Instead, Sung-han had turned away cruelly as Kim Shunpei called after him, *"Jane, jane . . ."* Wasn't that the kind of cruelty that Sung-han had hated about Kim Shunpei? Was it right of him to abandon Kim Shunpei in the last miserable moments of his miserable life? Was that his revenge? Sung-han drank and drank. He looked over at his sleeping children and thought back to those four children on the floor of Kim Shunpei's house, looking at him with rabbit-like eyes.

At three a.m. later that night, Sung-han cut his shift short and went along the Koshu Kaido road toward the taxi garage. At this time of night, most of the vehicles on the road were taxis. They sped toward the city center with abandon, their tires squealing on the pavement with each green light. Sung-han, though, went at a more leisurely pace. A large cargo truck passed by him. As Sung-han absentmindedly watched the truck gain distance from him, he heard a weak voice behind him saying "*Jane, jane* . . ." Sung-han spun his head around and saw a black, cloudy darkness expanding over the back seat. He turned back around and gripped the wheel as he took a deep breath. Keep working, he told himself. He stepped on the gas pedal.